CCBS **TXTBK**

CCBS Press

Cross Cultural Business Skills Minor

CCBS TXTBK

Reader for the elective course: CCBS minor

Hogeschool van Amsterdam
Amsterdam University of Applied Sciences

ISBN: 978 90 79646 28 9
NUR: 812

CCBS-Press

Third edition 2017
Editorial managers: Sander Schroevers, Aynur Doğan
Series editor: Sander Schroevers
Cover design: Erica Frank, Designer Gráfico, Vitória, Espírito Santo, Brazil
Cover graphic: © SH69T Studio
Inner design: Sander Schroevers, Jaguar Print
Text copyright: Fons Trompenaars, Peter Woolliams, Sander Schroevers, Aynur Doğan,
Riana Schreurders-Van den Bergh, Trompenaars Hampden-Turner, Tom Johnston, Ian Lewis,
Leonel Brug, Jaime Offermans and Roy Gerritsen.

A CIP catalogue record for this book is available from the British Library, the Library of Congress,
the German DNB/VLB and the Netherlands Deposit Collection of the royal library in The Hague.
CCBS books are exclusively available from the StudyStore campus bookshop at HvA Fraijlemaborg.

Table of Contents

1.Preface

The skies nowadays are full of airplanes carrying professionals, travelling for business abroad. They need to be able to communicate effectively in cross-cultural settings or build trust with culturally diverse partners. This book aims to prepare its readers for such practical business situations. Named TXTBK, it is a tailor-made publication for participants in the elective course Cross-Cultural Business Skills, offered at the Hogeschool van Amsterdam. TXTBK is divided in many chapters: serving as a semester syllabus, explaining *what* we work on *when,* and in *which way.* You will find separate chapters addressing the team *assignments* throughout the semester, while others explain the *individual assignment.* The last part of this book offers a section called Exams reader that presents a collection of reading chapters for both the Mid-term exam and the Final exam.

Learning goals
After having perused this book, you will be familiar with the key principles of cross-cultural communication, and be able to identify and analyse instances of international professional challenges. Considering the evolving role of cultural diversity within today's classroom or workplace, makes this appear like an exciting endeavour. Cultivating cross-cultural intelligence is a skill that can be learned...

I would like to thank my dear colleague Aynur Doğan, who contributed much to this textbook. And may I close here, by wishing you all a good read.

Sander Schroevers

2. About CCBS

CCBS is an acronym for 'Cross-Cultural Business Skills', an elective course ('minor') initiated by prof. Sander Schroevers in 2010, and taught together with communication and editing specialist Aynur Doğan at the Hogeschool van Amsterdam, Amsterdam University of applied sciences, the Netherlands. The course's rationale is a simple one; our economies have gotten so interconnected, that knowing about cultural differences has become a competitive advantage. CCBS aims to orient bachelor students and/or part-time professionals in the fundamentals of applied cross-cultural business skills, including the management model and methodology of amongst others prof. Fons Trompenaars. To arrive at a better cross-cultural awareness in this global marketplace, the participants perform the following activities, they:

I.   Research and write a book chapter on a chosen country.
II.   Conduct an online survey with a minimum of fifty professional respondents, from that particular country.
III.   Interview (and record) native professionals on a business skill.

And towards the semester ending they celebrate these results in a festive book presentation, fully respecting the maxim: 'work hard, play hard!'. As every semester their final research is published as an English management book, under the imprint 'CCBS-Press'. Further details can be obtained via minorccbs.com, which showcases the writings, interviews, and some selected lectures. We are glad to offer further information and digital flyers in some twenty-eight languages. Let's connect!

3. Eight assignments, plus SIS-codes

During this semester the following six assignments are intended for developing international competences. The division of the credit points is visualised in the infographic, and listed with their SIS-codes as an overview in the table below;

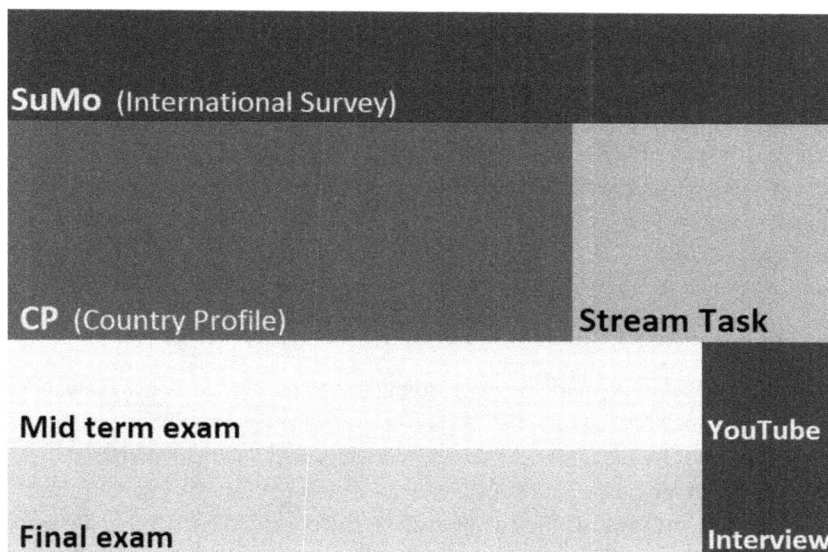

In SIS: programme parts descriptors	Credits	SIS-code
SuMo (International Survey)	6	6600INSU16
CP (Country Profile chapter)	8	6600COPR16
Mid-term exam	5	6600MTEX16
Stream task (Databases, Photoshop, Book review)	4	6600STA_16
IV & YT (Interview & YouTube)	2	6600INTV16
Final exam	5	6600FIEX16

4. Teams

At the semester start you will be asked to choose a specific country, together with several team members. We advise you to choose both the country and your team members well, as you will perform several research and writing tasks with this group during the entire semester.

Each team is responsible for the final quality and time management, and will be assessed as such. We suggest the team discusses the separate team roles during week one, for which we have selected an online team role test, see explanation in the following paragraph. During the project classes (or via Skype for part-timers) teams regularly will be invited for a team coaching session, during which feedback will be provided, and a general progress and quality check will be performed by one of the lecturers. Such coaching sessions are by appointment only, and mandatory for all team members. Yes, via Skype too...

The grading is by group mark, however some assessment forms also include a personal variable, for instance the CP (book chapter) assignment has a group mark, and an individual mark. Because of this we expect any team member(s) not happy with the participation level of a team member to hand in anonymous peer review forms towards the end of each semester term. The fact that we work with a group mark, also implies that each team members is benefitting from equally well written and researched assignments. Unfortunately, this also applies to the unwanted situation if one team member commits plagiarism.

Respecting part-time students
In case of mixed teams between fulltime and part-time students, we would like to point out, that in principle part-timers are not thought capable of calling or meeting during their office hours. But we trust that good team working agreements can be made around such situations. For all further details on the actual team assignments, we would like to refer you to the specific guideline chapters.

5. Dividing team roles

In this semester you will be part of a team together with a number of fellow students. Being part of a team, is something that you will most likely find yourself in, for the most part of your future professional career. Working in a team can be complex business since every individual has a unique personality with an own set of characteristics. Also, in most cases you will find that your own standards in terms of i.e. quality and motivation can differ from your team members.

Team role test
In order to speed up the process of getting to know your team members and increasing your chances of performing in a successful manner this semester, we suggest you to fill in a team roles test. This team roles test is based on the theory of *Meredith Belbin* (British researcher and management theorist) and the Big Five personality traits from Costa & McCrae in 1992, which emerged as a robust model for understanding the relationship between personality and various academic behaviours.

The goal with every member of your team, filling in this test is that you will get an overview of all the roles that are present within the team. In a perfect situation all of the nine defined team roles will be represented, but this will be most likely not be the case.

Please follow the hyperlink below to fill in the team role test (also in German, French, Spanish and Dutch), you will see your results as soon as you finish. After all the team members have filled in the test and the table, you will have a clear overview of the roles present or missing in your team.

Website: www.123test.com/team-roles-test

6. Class members info

In larger classes it is not always easy to remember someone's name, let alone someone's contact data. Nevertheless we expect that all class memebers work effectively together, already from week two onwards. We therefore have a so-called pdf-Facebook ('smoelenboek') and an Excel-file with all contact information, and a listing of team and stream choices. Our pdf-Facebook looks just like this example below and is called Photobook_SeasonYear.pdf;

Class-list
The Excel worksheet contains all possible necessary data, with a preference for people's **personal mail addresses (Gmail, Hotmail etc.)** as it easier to stay in contact afterwards. Of course only if you please so. It looks like this example;

7.OneDrive

Sander Schroevers

Introduction

Why an external tool? Well, because the CCBS elective course hosts a large amount of non-HvA students, so we needed to look for an easily accessible workflow solution. OneDrive allows us to give anyone access to working files in a few mouse clicks. All documents we do not (yet) want to put on our public website, can be found or stored here. There are a few basics we would like to inform you on before you start using this semester tool.

Mail invitation

Upon registration in lesson one of CCBS, you will receive an invitation e-mail to join our folder. Please follow these instructions, and do not delete this message as unwanted spam or so, because you need to access this online storage tool regularly for assignments.

YOU WILL NEED TO REGISTER !

Please realise that each team member will need to register ONCE for OneDrive. If you don't, you probably won't be able to upload your deliverables, or perhaps us lecturers cannot even see the deliverables you've uploaded. So please don't trouble trouble. As it doubles trouble, and troubles teachers too...

Mandatory folder structure

Clean up your folders folks! If not we will deduct spectacular credits....
Also, make separate folders in which you store your different drafts. Document names need to be according to TXTBK descriptions. It is impossible for the lecturers after a deadline to check your drafts when the folder is a huge mess... Why not make a mess-folder called *archive*. Help us, to help you!!!

8. Assessment guidance notes

To ensure parity of treatment for all students, the CCBS lecturers have adopted a common set of assessment criteria for the team assignments. The assessment tables can be found in each assignment paragraphs below. It will provide you background information on the marking strategy, and cover important areas such as details on the process and product requirements for each of the assignment deliverables, submission dates, grading criteria and expectations associated with specific assignments.

Feedback
We realise that grading and feedback are interconnected tools for helping students make progress. And feedback is a fundamental aspect of delivering high quality education. We therefore will provide constructive oral feedback during the team consult appointments. Beside we will provide digital feedback during the several draft stages of the CP and YT/SC deliverables. For CP we make use of the (mandatory) online OneDrive MS Word function: **Comments**.

For deliverables like the SuMo assignment, feedback is provided several times concerning the quantity and quality of the respondents.

A uniform assessment for the Stream tasks is not possible through generic criteria and expectations, due to the wide variety of distinct tasks.

Grades only will be entered towards the end of the entire semester. In case of urgent grading issues please discuss directly to your lecturers, not via the school's organisation, as they are busy enough as it is. Muchas gracias.

9. Free-riding policy

It sometimes happens that during a group assignment someone makes use of the efforts of the other group members while doing little in return. How you divide work within a group is your own freedom and responsibility.

During the lessons you can always request a complaint form, which can also be downloaded from our online depository (OneDrive). Please file such a form and hand it in to Sander or Aynur. We will always treat the form anonymously, but will need to address the matter with the student(s) in question of course. The choices are the following: (a) when there are valid reasons, we will need to find a solution, (b) without good reasons it depends on the amount done, and will result in agreeing to give some points to the working team members, and 'peeling' these off of the own result. When no work has been performed there will be an alternative assignment, in agreement with the relevant lecturer. We hope to create a fair environment this way during any CCBS semester. We trust on the experience of solving such matters in a good way, satisfying all parties involved. This should be a positive elective course in the end.

10.   Deadlines & the-angry-coach

Because we actually publish the work of teams as a book, you may understand that deadlines are pretty strict, due to editing, production and prepress activities. Let me therefore introduce you to Pops-the-angry-coach, a true New Yorker, who coaches our semester through softly spoken moments of inspirational reflection (recorded video and sound messages). So let's keep our CCBS quality coach cock-a-hoop (happy), by strictly following up on his due dates, as specified in the Lesson-Plan.

Team effort
Bear in mind please, that all team members are responsible for the team's final product, and will be graded jointly and simultaneously. Not happy with a team mate? Use the free-riding form on OneDrive. Sorry to sound all so official, but maybe better to be clear about things from the start.

Upload files, don't mail
A small reminder, you will hardly mail the deliverables, as OneDrive is the place to upload all materials. Except for the video-interview, which may ONLY be uploaded on our YouTube channel, as it simply will be too heavy in Mb, for the OneDrive class folders.

Okay, basta !

11. Alumni programme

At CCBS we strongly rely on information and contacts of people in other countries. For a great many assignments we would like you to develop cross-border contact and research skills. With that in mind, wouldn't it be great if people with such local knowledge and an exact comprehension of what CCBS entails could help out? We therefore would like to stay in contact with former students as well as contacts developed during the interviews etc. As a result we prefer to ask students for their 'real' mail address, as a school address will eventually disappear. Please inform the Alumni-Stream of your preferences, as it is of course voluntary.

What are the benefits?
Alumni cardholders also get complementary drinks at the book party,
Alumni get reserved seats at our symposia, and back-stage entrance,
Alumni get access to great pdf data on a log-in protected folder,
Alumni get a plastic alumni card and cross-cultural certificate,
Alumni get access to all CCBS publications as e-book,
Alumni can make use of the LinkedIn contact base, to find stagiaires,
Students can get help with local needs (survey, interviews, country related tips),
Students looking for work placements may post requests,
Students have an accessible save geographic listing with little need to explain,

CCBS ALUMNI CARD
校友 | CCBS ALUMNUSKAART | بطاقة خريجي

UNIQUE ONLINE DEPOSITORY
www.minorccbs.com => alumni
LOG-IN CODE: ccbstxtbk

BENEFIT ENTITLEMENTS: networking, reserved front row seating during symposia, exclusive downloads, free entrance & tokens at book-presentation, selected web lectures, all e-books, live class participation.

Document No:
V01ALMN-STREAM2014

LinkedIn: Cross Cultural Business Skills, Amsterdam

C C B S < < < < since 2010 < < < < < < < < WWW.MINORCCBS.COM< <
< < V01ALMN-STREAM2014 < < < < < < < < < < < < < < < < < < < <

12.   Semester Evaluation

Every 'minor' has a mandatory evaluation towards the end of the semester. Our quality assurance department even demands an 80% score for this, otherwise we will get a fail, and after two consecutive fails, the 'minor' is no more... So please make sure you file the online evaluation, in fact our manager has made it mandatory.

How does it work? It is a digital online survey, which you may access after a mailed hyperlink. This link will stay live just for a small amount of time. Therefore please don't wait, but finish it before the end of the last week, that's when we'll have the festive book presentation first at school, and afterwards in town.

Survey sample questions

The questions to expect are the following ones;

Minor programme
- The objectives of the minor are clear
- There is a good tie in between theory and practice
- The individual components of the minor complement each other well
- I am satisfied with the attention given to theoretical knowledge
- I am satisfied with the attention given to training of practical skills
- I am satisfied with the attention given to the professional field
- The lecturers coordinate properly
- I am satisfied with the lecturers way of teaching
- I am satisfied with the lecturers way giving feedback
- Please mention tips and tops regarding the SurveyMonkey project.
- Please mention tips and tops regarding the Country Profile project.
- Please share your experiences with this working method. "
- Tips & Tops regarding Minor programme

Information Provision
- The information provided in advance about this minor gave me a good picture of what to expect
- The minor came up to my expectations.

Testing and assessment
- I am satisfied with the testing of this minor
- I am satisfied with the number of tests for this minor
- The assessment criteria are clear
- The assessment criteria are correctly applied.

Level and workload
- What is your opinion of the level of difficulty of this minor?
- What is your opinion of the workload of this minor?
- I am satisfied with the number of hours spent on this minor
- Average number of hours per week spent on this minor:

Final mark
- All things considered, I award this minor the following overall mark: (1=very bad, 10=very good)

Part B - specific questions
- The best three lessons for me were:
- The least two lessons for me were:
- What topics did you miss in all lessons (day- and night)?
- Which countries did you miss in the lessons, and if mentioned, why?
- I award the guest lecture on Portugal the following mark:
- Would you like to invited for future CCBS symposia as alumnus?
- Would you like to invited for future CCBS parties as alumnus?
- Are you willing to give a testimonial for external CCBS communications? If so, please type this and add your name and job title and organisation or company.
- *End of questionnaire.*

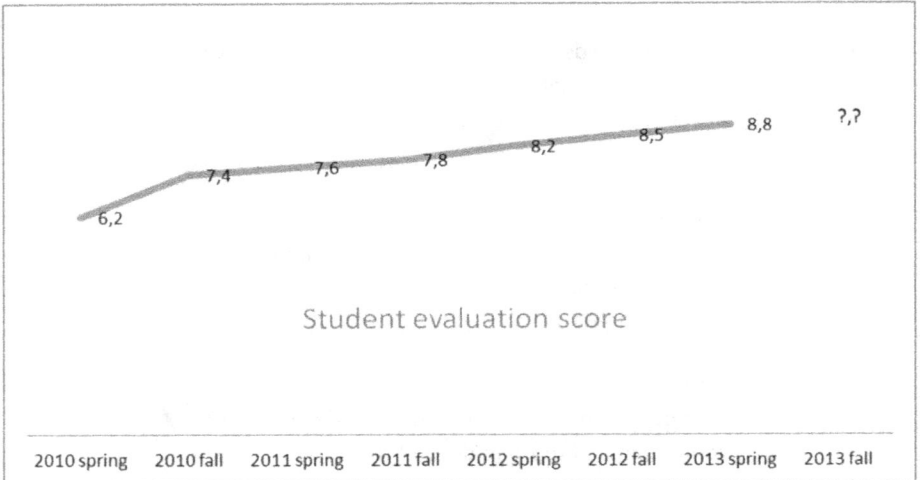

6,2   7,4   7,6   7,8   8,2   8,5   8,8   ?,?

Student evaluation score

2010 spring   2010 fall   2011 spring   2011 fall   2012 spring   2012 fall   2013 spring   2013 fall

Graph: the student satisfaction (scale: 1-10) development from 2010-2013

Going up!

Looking at the slow but steady upward trend of the student evaluation score, we now have set our goal to finally obtain a NINE-score. A good grade is also important for us lecturers, so should you feel we've earned it, don't hold back :-) Neither do we, when we really liked a stream or team task you performed. And please bear in mind that for every seven we receive, we will need three tens to top it... *So curious!*

13. Accreditation

In order to be open to students from other HvA departments, as well as schools from elsewhere in the country (Kies-Op-Maat) every 'minor' first needs to be accredited. This is a preceding analysis of our handed-in accreditation description on qualitative aspects of the educational module. This is performed by the exam board, and confirmed by the Dean. Besides this departmental check of the Faculty of Business and Economics, there also is a yearly overall 'Hogeschool van Amsterdam' quality assurance, performed at corporate level. The following stakeholders apply:

Responsible Programme manager:	Mrs. Hans Seubring-Vierveyzer
Responsible Co-ordinator:	Sander Schroevers
Board of examiners:	Commercial Economics, part-time, HvA
	Faculty of Business and Economics

We welcome:
This minor is meant for: HvA (Hogeschool van Amsterdam) full-time students, KOM (Kies-Op-Maat) full-time students, HvA part-time students, HvA-exchange students, self-registered (paying) students from foreign non-HvA partner institutes or private companies/organisations.

Entry requirements
There are no specific entry requirements for this minor. According to the study programme exam regulation, article 3.10 under 5: a student must have obtained her/his propaedeutics, with a minimum of forty (40) credits (EC's). Therefore the intake-level is equal to European Qualifications Framework (EQF) level 5, Associate Degree level. Furthermore the intake-level is equal to the specific CROHO-final level of the core-phase of a course. Notwithstanding the foregoing, students must obtain approval from their study programme's Examination Board in order to enrol in a minor. The Examination Board may decide to publish a list of minors in which students can enrol without the need for personal permission.

A minor consists of 30 credits and forms part of the post-foundation year phase. Students choose a minor based on their ambitions and its capacity to foster the final qualifications of their study programme. The minor must be an addition to other components of the student's course of study.

Results
The final result of the minor is the weighted average of the results of all the separate educational units. The tests described in the matrix above, are only passed when the result is 5.5 or higher. When assignments are carried out by duo's or groups, the result will be a group mark, for the participating individual students, (after a peer-assessment is filed by all team members).

Learning plan scheme
Below is an overview of the educational units of the minor, the followed teaching and testing method, the number of EC's and the number of
contact hours measured from a full-time perspective and per individual course programme part (i.e.: not per week). The total average number
of contact hours per week is 16 hrs. the work load around 38 hrs. per week

Programme item	Teaching method	Testing / assignment	EC	Hours
International Survey SIS: 6600INSU16	In-class teaching, team consults by appointment	International questionnaire, respondents evaluation	6	34
Country Profile SIS: 6600COPR16	In-class teaching, team consults by appointment	Written country analysis	8	41
Mid-term exam SIS: 6600MTEX16	Study: book/web-lectures	Written knowledge test	5	11
Stream task SIS: 6600STA_16	Coaching & guideline briefings	Peer-assessment, staff interview + assessment	4*	13
Interviews SIS: 6600INTV16	In-class teaching, team consults by appointment	Recorded native C-level feedback assignment	2	18
Final exam SIS: 6600FIEX16	Study: book/web-lectures	Written knowledge test	5	7

Dates and frequency of examinations and tests

Two opportunities to take the foundation year examinations and tests will be offered every academic year, with the first immediately following the conclusion of the unit of study concerned. Two opportunities to take the post-foundation year examinations and tests will be offered every academic year, with one of these immediately following the conclusion of the unit of study concerned.

Standardisation of assessments

Examination or test assessment results are expressed as one of the following: a grade on a scale of 1 to 10, with a maximum of one decimal point, in which grade 1 or 1.0 stands for 'very poor', grade 2 for 'poor', grade 3 for 'highly unsatisfactory/very unsatisfactory', grade 4 for 'unsatisfactory', grade 5 for 'slightly unsatisfactory/fair/weak', grade 6 for 'satisfactory', grade 7 for 'quite satisfactory', grade 8 for 'good', grade 9 for 'very good' and grade 10 for 'outstanding/excellent'.

For further details may we refer to the: 'Teaching and Examination Regulations (OER): minor relevant regulations'? Ask your study advisor for this document or obtain it yourself from the institute's intranet.

14. Educational recognition

The CCBS semester has had quite some recognition from within the educational field. Below is an overview of several interviews and presentations touching on innovative CCBS particulars as the different concept for studying foreign cultures, the concept of self-steering streams, and the fact that students self-publish books and videos. Furthermore the fact that student streams organise external symposia is worth stating.

- Session at EAIE conference Istanbul: 'Now students write books' *(see adjacent image),* with explanation of the Country Profile workflow.
- NVAO Good Practices Workshops, Leuven, Belgium: duo-presentation.
- CCBS course described in an Interview with Sander in Transfer Magazine, article by Annette Posthumus.
- Concept of external symposia got explained a.o. in an article in the Pan-European FORUM magazine, winter issue.
- Invited to explain CCBS innovations on Academic Day for colleagues of the International Business School.
- 'Around the world in 80 hours', workshop (HvA Onderwijsconferentie), on the concept of own knowledge production by students.
- Copenhagen conference of the European Association for International Education, session 8.05, on intercultural learning techniques.
- EAIE Dublin: session 10.17, Implementing cross-border learning.
- NUFFIC: in-class video recording for Study-In-Holland.

Poster for Istanbul conference session: 'Now students write books!'.

15. Media attention

At CCBS you will be working on external products or events. Things we can share with the world. This can be on our website in the form of an article or video production, but also via our pocketbooks, which are for sale at regular academic bookshops. Furthermore we regularly organise symposia or seminars on location, like for instance our Chamber of Commerce country series. Especially these attract the writing press. Until now we have had some sweet publications in the following media:

- RADIO4: a short mentioning of our Korea symposium.

- SPITS: front-page and article p.4 on a symposium we organised.

- FINACIEELE DAGBLAD: An article in the Dutch national financial newspaper on the CCBS Korea seminar (in Dutch).

- FunX: longer radio interview on 'Meer Marokko' symposium.

- FOLIA: CCBS 'Meer Marokko' symposium (in Dutch).

- FOLIAWEB: An Article about the Korea Seminar by Foliaweb (in Dutch).

- FOLIA: Emirates lesson visited anonymously by journalist (in Dutch).

- A newsletter by KITA on the CCBS Korea seminar (in Korean).

- FOLIA: Overprint from Folia Web on CCBS pocket book (in Dutch).

- HAVANA: An interview with Sander Schroevers (in Dutch).

- TRANSFER: A student interview in Transfer magazine on the self-publishing of management books (in Dutch).

16.   Writing a book

How many papers have you made so far during your studies, and what happened to all the work in the end? At this course we believe that our participants are capable of high quality work, provided that we can inspire them to do so. For the CP assignment the class researches and writes a cross-cultural management book together. The good news is that at the end of the semester you will have become a true writer. Your very own name is on the back-cover of the book, but also in library catalogues or for instance GooglePlay. May we advise you to add a heading 'Publications' to your CV ?

Photo: a previous edition for sale in a campus bookshop

Visibility
You will be happy to know, that all your team's hard work can be seen elsewhere. We send copies to all mayor libraries, in the Netherlands and abroad. Also will we make digital copies of the book partly available via the GoogleBooks network. Just type in your own name, and the book will appear quite high in the search results. Showing the title and ISBN details.

Selected CCBS student editions

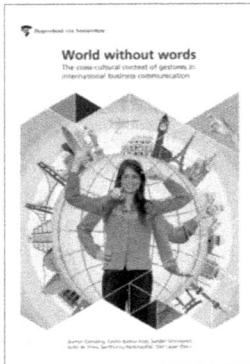

World without words
The cross-cultural context of gestures in international business
2012, HvA minor CCBS
ISBN 978-90-79646-11-1

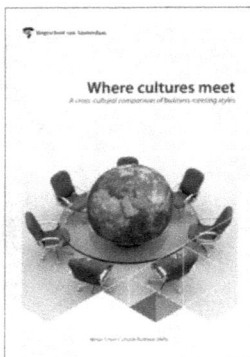

Where cultures meet
A cross-cultural comparison of business meeting styles
2013, HvA minor CCBS
ISBN 978-90-79646-17-3

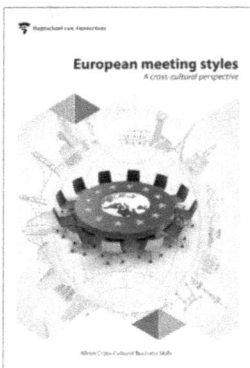

European meetings styles
A cross-cultural perspective
2012, HvA minor CCBS
ISBN 978-90-79646-14-2

17. Events

Ooopen lectures

The Ooopen lectures are a one-country theme event, where Sander presents together with CCBS expat students. CCBS exchange students are asked to present their country there. Normally we afterwards organise an (illegal) in-class bar, respecting the proverb: 'work-hard, play-hard!' To let such events go smoothly, an event-stream is taking care of organising and hosting such an event. Everyone interested is welcome to join the lesson here. The Ooopen lectures are however not meant for external professionals nor for press. But you'll love them anyway.

External symposium

Each semester we will also organise a large-scale event, in close cooperation with an Embassy or other representative body. Here we will invite external professionals, and journalists. The symposium will be a high-end event, and implies serious hosting, public relations and event-management.

Book party CCByeBye

In the last week, we proudly present our co-written management book. Here you are invited to bring along an invitee (partner, family). Every CCBS student will receive one complimentary copy of the book, and can buy extra copies at cost price, (larger quantities only when back-ordered beforehand).
And since this is the end of the semester, we will also take a moment to look back on what has been achieved, and say farewell to new friends from other countries or schools. Naturally we will celebrate the book launch with an (illegal) in-school drink. But after the books have been shared, those interested will together move to the city-centre to close the semester in style => school's cool!

18. Web lectures

Web lectures have been a much appreciated service from the very first CCBS semester. It helps before an exam, and indeed we ask some exam questions from them. And also in case of unexpected schedule changes, they might offer a good opportunity for an alternative lesson. You will be send a hyperlink in those unforeseen circumstances, or may refer to the **WatchList** on OneDrive.

What?

An integral lesson is recorded, not just as a video, but also offering its PowerPoint slides simultaneously. By simply clicking on the desired slide, that's where the video starts to talk. Play-back or pause whenever you feel like it, and watch not only from your computer, but also on your smart-phone or tablet, (allowing for Higher Education on a beach)... As it concerns streaming video's, downloading is difficult (and too heavy).

Where?

You can access a web lecture in the following ways:

- surf to:www.hva.nl/webcolleges
- click on a hyperlink from the **URL-watch list**, which we have uploaded on OneDrive.

Mind you, that when accessing from home you first need to log-in with your HvA-ID and password. In school there generally will be IP-address recognition.

Hogeschool van Amsterdam

HVA LOGIN

Typ je HvA-ID en wachtwoord.

HvA ID:

Wachtwoord:

Aanmelden

Voor de veiligheid moet je uitloggen en je browser sluiten wanneer je geen toegang meer nodig hebt tot afgeschermde applicaties.

19.   A5 Word template

by: CCBS lecturers

Because we are writing a book together, it is important that all chapters look alike. We therefore ask all teams to only upload texts in the A5 template document. Just download the template (Dutch: stramien) from OneDrive. Thank you for only offering chapters made with the correct A5-template on OneDrive. This A-5template is a zip file that includes a blank template with properly set margins, gutters, and MS Word styles. To show you how the work in it, we chose to copy text from the A5-template style guide, which provides formatting information for your team's chapter interior pages such as header and footer settings, proper use of MS Word styles, standardised page numbering, and correct placement of common front and back matter sections. Below you will see instructional texts providing you with helpful tips for creating a professionally formatted chapter. Please read the paragraphs below carefully.
The A5-template is available from CCBS-OneDrive folder:

- Log-in and go to: **Downloads** => **A5-template**
- Now download the template zip file.
- Unzip the file at your OWN computer.
- Safe it and please rename it under your team's name.
- Type directly in the appropriate sections, headers etc.
- Or copy texts into it, do this however WITHOUT any formatting (Paste special => Unformatted text).

Because working together on a book requires guidelines, or even strict rules if you like. Let's take a look what is important when using our *A5-template*.
The text you are reading right now, is the *body text*, and body text can have NO other lay-out changes than *italics*. In other words we may not <u>underline</u> words, or use other **fonts** or colours. Neither are interlinear changes, font size or anything else allowed.

Headers and styles

We work with several levels of headers (Dutch: kopteksten). The header is meant for the chapter title, the sub-headers are to be used within your chapter, and generally will be those specified by the Country Profile format. One level lower are the paragraph headers, these are just a bold version of the normal body text. Please ONLY work with so-called styles, so do NOT copy a style by trying to create the same lay-out features, but really change the style of a word or phrase. How? Simply by selecting the words and clicking on the style you would like to have. You can do this on the menu bar in Microsoft Word, that you can see below;

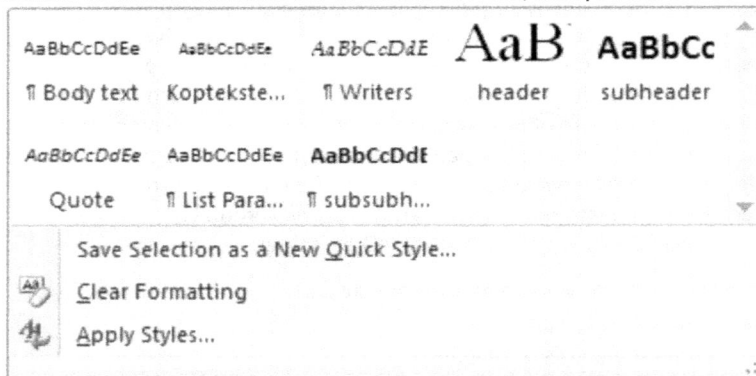

AaBbCcDdEe	AaBbCcDdEe	AaBbCcDdE	AaB	AaBbCc
¶ Body text	Koptekste...	¶ Writers	header	subheader
AaBbCcDdEe	AaBbCcDdEe	**AaBbCcDdE**		
Quote	¶ List Para...	¶ subsubh...		

Save Selection as a New Quick Style...

Clear Formatting

Apply Styles...

The actual template menu bar looks slightly different, but the same concept applies. To enlarge the amount of choices either scroll down or click on the icon at the lowest right side of the Styles menu box.

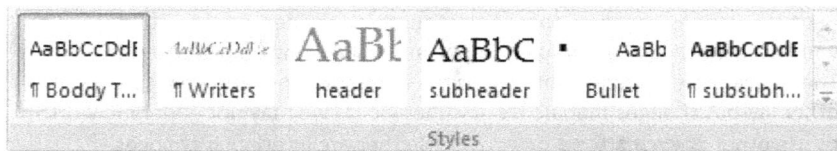

AaBbCcDdE	AaBbCcDdE	AaBl	AaBbC	▪	AaBb	AaBbCcDdE
¶ Boddy T...	¶ Writers	header	subheader	Bullet		¶ subsubh...

Styles

Copying texts into your chapter
If you copy a text, please do so with the menu choices: Paste => Paste special => Unformatted Unicode text. When copying texts from the HvA databases or from internet, only paste this as *flat text*, meaning without any hyperlinks or formatting.

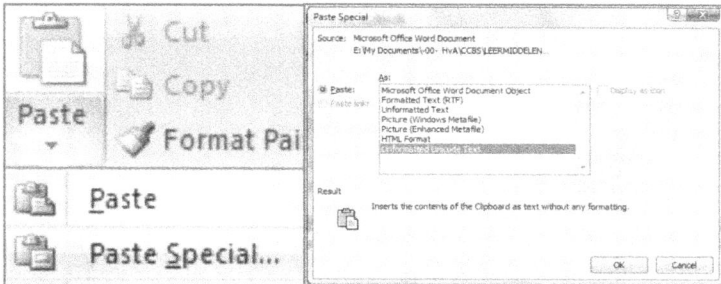

Choose: Paste Special => **Unformatted Unicode Text**.

Sentence case headers only (in MS Word)
All headers in your chapter MUST be edited in the 'Sentence case' mode, (Dutch: 'Zoals in een zin'). Please DO NOT use all caps or uppercase headers.

Right ☑ **Sentence case headers**

Wrong ☒ Capitalize Each Word Headers

Wrong ☒ UPPERCASE HEADERS

The image below shows you the preferred use within MS Word;

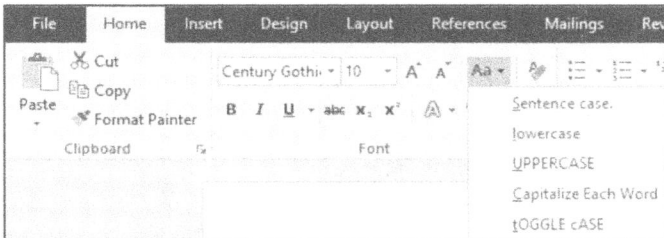

Only left-alignment, never justified or block (in MS Word)

We never use the so-called 'block' or 'justified' alignment for the book.
This refers to the appearance and orientation of the edges of the paragraph.
At CCBS you only can hand-in **left-aligned texts** (the most common alignment), meaning the left edge of the paragraph should be flush with the left margin. To do so, simply use the marked alignment button below;

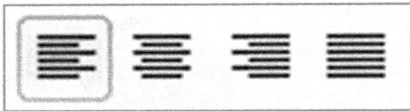

Using tables

In the template folder on OneDrive is a downloadable file, which you can use to produce a table in, and copy this to your A5-template. Please make sure you also apply the correct caption style (Dutch: onderschrift). Below you see an example of how we will format tables. Please use the table below as a basis for including tabular information in your chapter. Just copy-paste a table like the sample below in your own text, including the grey coloured caption line.

English	Portuguese
Personal information	Informações pessoais
Qualifications	Qualificações

Table: Translation of CV elements

Bullet points
We only use the following bullets in writing a chapter text in the A5-template;

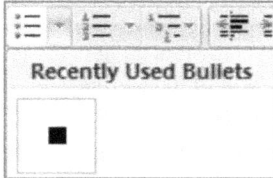

Therefore please ONLY use the quick style button called 'BULLETS', for making bulleted lists.

▪ Mudes   http://www.mudes.org.br/
▪ Catho   http://www.catho.com.br/

Localised quotation marks
This paragraph explains the sometimes unexpected results of working with a Windows version of another country. For example, when you are working on a computer with a German, Polish, Bulgarian, Czech, Estonian, Georgian, Icelandic, Russian, Slovak, Slovene or Ukrainian version of Windows and MS Office, please make sure that any quotation marks are used in the English way: **'xyz'** or **"xyz"**. Meaning both on top and opening with inside bound apostrophes, instead of the Bulgarian, Czech, Estonian, Georgian, Icelandic, Russian, Slovak, Slovene or Ukrainian: **‚xyz'** or **„xyz"**.When using a Latin language version of Windows we suddenly see angle quotation marks (*guillemets, angulares* or duck-foot quotes): **« xyz »**. The French add a space around the quote, where the Catalan, Polish, Portuguese, Russian, Spanish word processors use angle quotation marks without a space around the quote. In Finnish and Swedish we would see right quotes citation marks, and double right-pointing angular quotes, can also be used.: **"xyz"** or **»xyz»**. As you can see: a lot of fuss over a comma :-) but please take this into account when writing, it saves us so much time...
Just to make it sure, in your CP you are expected to use double quotation marks in the English way (**"xyz"**) for quotations (yep, what's in a name...).

Saving text on OneDrive
Please always save your work within the correct subfolder in your team's OneDrive folder. We have had considerable loss of time, working in the wrong versions of a chapter, due to the fact that they were saved in the wrong location.

So please follow the guidelines of your lecturer, during coaching sessions or correspondence, regarding document (version) names, file locations and due dates. This way we are sure to produce a great book!

Apply English typography rules
Since we are publishing an English book, we want to ask you to to use the spelling checker called 'English (United Kingdom)' and not 'English (United States)', or 'Engels (Verenigde Staten)'. Mind you that most computers standard have the United States setting, so please change this manually when writing your Country Profile.

Assessment
How well a team applies these rules set out above, is judged during the team product assessments, and even part of the final grade. It also seems fair, as not doing it, will result in a lot of extra work for others. So they should get the points we take away from teams that didn't follow the above explained. Thanks for your understanding and cooperation.

20.   PowerPoint template

Whenever you will be presenting something in class (e.g.: native presentations or particular stream items), we would like to ask you to prepare your slides in the CCBS PowerPoint template, which is available on OneDrive. Log-in and click on:
=> **Downloads => PowerPoint template**
And download 'Template slides for CCBS presentation.ppt' to work in.

Lay-out
Please use the following lay-out and typography elements:

- Font: Calibri (Body).
- Turquoise colour scheme.
- The bar texts in capitals.

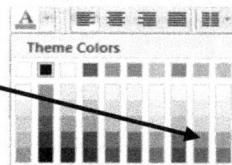

Signatures preferences
The logo's signatures we use, are the following:

21. Resources: HvA databases

drs. Aynur Doğan

Using HvA databases is a requirement within the CCBS minor to accomplish most assignments. As a third or fourth year student your research skill needs to be developed. Finding and transforming information from databases enhances your work output and its quality. Efficient desk research leads to more creative solutions. Experience clearly shows that students get a much higher grade for the assignments, when using the HvA databases in their research. But also they will prove as helpful, once you start writing your thesis. CCBS organises an instruction lecture, where you will be able to practice in class, simply because practice makes perfect!

What
Using HvA databases are multipurpose for the assignments: SurveyMonkey, County Profile, Interview, and even for quite some streams they will offer rich resources.

Where
From school or from home or elsewhere, you first will need to log in to desktop.hva.nl to get into the HvA databases. Once online go to the address: **bib.hva.nl** Once there, choose English (right top) and Databases. Now you will see databases in alphabetic order A-Z and some preselection check-boxes.

Hogeschool van Amsterdam

HVA LOGIN   SEARCH THE HVA LIBRARY

Typ je HvA-ID en wachtwoord.

HvA-ID:
                                   Databases A-Z   ▶ Journals A-Z
Wachtwoord:

Aanmelden

Tools

From the online HvA library home page you can view several instruction video's.

Coaching needed ?

During coaching classes (see lesson plan) you are more than welcome to ask tips and advice regarding the use of HvA databases. We are there to help you.
And at the HvA mediathèque's (libraries), the so-called *information specialists* have been trained professionally to really able to support you with this.
Ask for them at the library counter therefore, and they will come for you.

Search tips

1. Use "quote"-signs for 2 or more words: "leadership Italy"
2. Truncation means the use *-sign for relevant hits.
   Examples Ital* for Italy (verb) or Italian (adjective)
   or *cultur* meaning for intercultural or cultures.
3. For multiple letters in words use <?>
   For example: wom?n will get you both women and woman.
4. Sometimes you see Thesaurus link = control keywords/synonyms
   for Leadership: management, control, etc.
5. Boolean operators And-OR-Not: including or excluding other topics,
   "Leadership and Italy", or "Italy not Croatia".

Time consuming

Doing research, finding the perfect information simply takes time.
The research phase sometimes even costs more time than actually writing.
From experience: 40% for searching, 40% for writing and 20% for rewriting.
When you have bad luck four hours of searching will just provide you with half an A5 page of rewritten information. On the other hand sometimes luck strikes.
Also do not get overwhelmed by the amount information or discouraged by less.
Just continue, and probably the next day you will already find more relevant outcomes because of your trained skill by then. A great moment to do desk research are the in-between class moments, of which you will have a few when waiting for the CCBS evening class, depending on which TRACK you are in.

May we suggest that you save research outcomes as much as possible in your OneDrive team folder. In addition, it needs to be mentioned that for some countries you will have more hits in academic sources than others (e.g. there's more information on Germany than Peru). Nevertheless, each team still is expected to proof their searching results via HvA database engines during the coach moments, as well as in the team's OneDrive folder. **Please communicate openly with your lecturer when most of the sources are in fact coming from Flightpack and/or Globesmart** (these two brand names refer to country readers in your team's OneDrive folder), so that we can find an alternative strategy. If we find out during the grading, **it will namely result in an insufficient mark**.

Information selection steps

You are going to (speed)read a lot while searching. How do you efficiently select information you really can use? In other words, how do you find within a short time span useful sources. Effective teams make a clear division of research tasks between group members: segmentation of sources, thus preventing any overlap or loss of time. Use the following strategies, tips and tricks, when searching;

1. Let's see what we can do after typing in a combination of keywords in search field, like for example; [executive Brazil* or Brasil*].
2. When you get more than 100 hits show, you have to narrow the results by using better specified keywords/synonyms.
3. When you get less than 100 results, you can easily scroll down following these easy tips below.
4. Reading the main title: does it match your main research topic? No, go to the next. You can read faster because the searched keywords are automatically marked.
5. If yes, read the subtitle. Check again: is this what my topic is about? If No, scroll to the next result.
6. If yes, read the summary. Still okay, speed read the whole article, save it in your research folder (TEAM folder). If not really that useful, also not on a paragraph level, then it's a pity, sigh and scroll to the next result.

7. So you will have to read lots of text which you might not use for your assignment. Think that this is also the ability to enhance your knowledge, or simply: welcome to the world of science...

Other languages?

Sometimes it is well worth to check if databases offer content in the language of your chosen country. It could also be a perfect way to find respondents.

Conclusion

So let's conclude before we will discuss the databases you are expected to use this semester. We want each team to not only find relevant scientific information, but also to always quote the source. This enhances the credibility of our final products: the pocketbook publication, and our website articles. Therefore you are expected to always use the APA-reference style button. Also when you copy/paste small fragments. Also when you write parts in your own words, also when you export, or save a whole pfd in your team folder on OneDrive. Your lecturer by the way will check this. During the coaching sessions, but also online. Now let's see what the HvA databases have in store for us;

Loging in from home?

At Wibauthouse (WBH) the computers are connected to the network, and therefore have IP-address recognition. Researching from home, means that you will need to identify, to prove you are in fact a HvA-user of the database. You will see this screen appear after clicking on the database of your choice. Simply enter your HvA-username and password.

Hogeschool van Amsterdam

BIBLIOTHEEK
INLOGGEN DATABANKEN

JE GEBRUIKT EEN COMPUTER BUITEN HET HVA-NETWERK

Voor toegang tot de databanken van de Bibliotheek, log je in met je HvA-gebruikersnaam en wachtwoord

HVA-gebruikersnaam

wachtwoord

Inloggen

Book 24/7

This database offers more than 10 thousand academic books free of charge. The books can be found on: (advanced) search above: enter the keyword(s). On the right hand side of the page, you can also navigate directly to the cross-cultural bookshelf, by selecting the theme: **International business**. You can scroll book chapters, select texts and just copy paste in to a Word document. However always (read: ALWAYS) mention the source. How?

Citation

Book 24/7offers the possibility to cite sources. After having selected an item, you will notice the *citation* link right after the @ sign. They here offer a few reference styles, now select the APA-style. Then copy/paste the whole description into your document under the bibliography, collect this also in a separate folder (team folder OneDrive). For more details about the in-text citation please check our "How to cite sources" section. Where we give examples how to integrate the source into your text, in different manners.

Potential use of database

Finding sources for writing the Country Profiles (book chapters);
Interview for YouTube/SoundCloud invitations (names of scholars);

Science Direct **ScienceDirect**

This Elsevier search engine includes business oriented academic journals, periodicals, trade publications. It really offers you great academic research, but it will take you time, like any academic I suppose. Some of the magazines resemble even our CCBS course learning goals.

After typing in your search keywords (or click on 'advanced search') you are able to select on the left side of the page: under limit your results: Full pfd. Further, select the desired publication types, you may also limit the publication years. This database also offers the APA-style when selected, any sort of copy/pasting is allowed. To be successful in this database, you need to be very specific with your keywords. Tip: type in several spellings of a word, when co-existing, for example like this: "Leadership Brasil or Brazil". Full pfd-files are available after a query search. Please save the selected results in your specific folder on OneDrive. This way we can follow your progress, and give you higher grades.

Citation
This database also offers the APA-style citations when you select a source. The button to "export citations" can be found in the middle top.

Business Source Premier **◢ EBSCO**_host_

Business Source Premier is amongst the most used business research database, providing full text for more than 2,300 journals, in all disciplines of business, including management.

ProQuest

This database includes business oriented academic journals, periodicals, trade publications. For instance the renowned magazine **Cross Cultural Management** is full-text available with a one year delay. ProQuest also offers you great academic research, and it again will take you time. Time invested however will be rewarded in your grade, if you are able to find relevant academic research, and refer to it in your Country Profile chapter.

Emerald Insight

Although this database only has few fully accessible documents (indicated by a green square), they do offer some series and journals of relevance. Like the **leadership series**. If an article is really necessary, you are entitled to ask at the HvA library for it, otherwise Sander will try again.

IEEE digital library

This more ICT oriented database, nevertheless has a few possible sources for our research, check it, the more serious sources in your CP, the higher your research grade naturally.

Springer Link

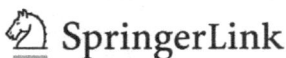

Is effective to search in, it also offers some relevant journals and books, however; often it needs to be paid for. If it is really a vital chapter or paper, please do ask our librarians what options exist to obtain a copy.

LexisNexis Academic

This search engines is pretty large for practical reasons. You can read newspapers in several languages. LexisNexis also is a source for **finding company employees** worldwide.

How to search

Under the company search, you can **Create an executive list.**
Under **Geographic Information** select the country of your team's research.

Often the results will be endless, sometimes more than nine thousand.
First, the LexisNexis search shows only three results. Click on the button "View all companies". This will show lots of information on each company, including the names of executives, CEO's , people in management positions, company information, addresses, e-mail (mostly general), telephone numbers, even financial data is normally available.

We have a separate instruction file called: '*How to collect email addresses from LexisNexis.pdf*' available on OneDrive in the folder path:
"01_Guidelines" => "SuMo" => SurveyMonkeyTools.
This explains precisely how you can transport up to 8000 hits into an Excel sheet. Some teams obtained much faster results by just typing: [executive + country name], as this gives you more direct email-addresses or other contact data. The same goes for terms like 'CEO' etc.

Step by step:

1. Select under "International companies": "find a company".
2. Then choose the desired country.
3. Select the second row above: "Create a company list", select which country, click on further.
4. Select what information you want: email, website, names etc.
5. Transport to Excel file.
6. Upload the file to your team's OneDrive folder.

Attention

You will get company names, names of executives, e-mails which are general company mails: info@blabla.com. We have noticed in past semesters that shooting out 800 invitations at once by one single e-mail, the results remain minimal. Most cultures in the world are relationships-oriented.

We would recommend that you make a polite phone call (or Skype) to a selected employee (name&position), and explain your goal. Personal e-mails are much more effective, as is asking people to help you out, or asking people to forward your request, like a snowball-effect, to colleagues in that company or country.

Potential use of database

Find company members, managers as potential respondent-natives for your country to participate in the SuMo project; they are by the way also handy for the interview & YouTube assignments, scheduled later this semester.

Journals A-Z

Beside searching in databases A-Z, on the front page of bib.hva.nl, you could click on this listing: on alphabetical order by selecting your field. Look up for example Cross Cultural Management, or the International Journal for Cross Cultural management, then choose your topic to specify.

22.   Resources: web links

We've gathered links and resources on the internet what we consider valuable resources for information on cross-cultural business communication and the CCBS research assignments.

Traffic light indicators

During this semester a special sources stream will cooperate with the CCBS lecturers in supplying us with an up-to-date hyperlink list. This will be available in a link-list pdf from our OneDrive depository. The file will be updated regularly. This file indicates three possible levels of appreciation for each source: GREEN; perfect to quote in your writing assignments, YELLOW; very possible to use, however we prefer not to see in-text references too often, throughout your work. RED: simply not acceptable as a mentionable source in any of the CCBS assignment deliverables.

> **WARNING:** mind you that listing any **RED SOURCES** in your bibliography or in-text citations will result in an insufficient mark. Cite safely and read our tip sheet below for unsurpassable towering-high CP-grades!

We certainly allow to read such sources, but citing them will only harm the image of our final products. In our assessment of your materials we will refer to the sources listings. The better sources, the higher score.

Internet address	Short description	quote?
www.executiveplanet.com	Multilingual webpage on business do's and don'ts in over 40 counties.	**yellow**
www.kwintessential.co.uk	USEFUL SOURCE BUT DON'T CITE. Commercial translation, globalis- ation, and localisation agency, with a high focus on cultural awareness in their services or trainings. Etiquette tips on seventy countries. Not bad, but please refrain from mentioning them in your writings.	**red**

www.wikipedia.org	A good starting point sometimes for perfectly fine information, but not useable as mentionable source in any of your writings. Do check out the other language entries too, when searching. Perhaps use an online translation service to do so.	red
http://ccm.sagepub.com	International Journal of Cross Cultural Management. Provides latest research on cross cultural management issues.	green
www.census.gov	US webpage offering demographical data per country. Also prognoses about the future can be obtained here.	yellow
www.cia.gov/library	World fact book, this information is less objective as to expect from the CIA, but offers very accurate statistical country data.	red
www.economist.com	This is a commercial webpage but shows interesting business news facts. Type country name in the search field.	green
http://culturevalues.wordpress.com/	Comparing Hofstede values per country	yellow
http://news.bbc.co.uk/2/hi/country_profiles	History, culture and economics per country	green
www.culturescope.nl	In Dutch, on European Union member states	yellow
www.doingbusiness.org	World bank country reports	green
www.export.gov/index.asp	Country specific trade and legal info	yellow
www.geohive.com	Statistics on countries	red
www.worldbusinessculture.com	Simple do's and dont's	yellow
www.intercultures.ca	USEFUL SOURCE MAY CITE. Canadian governmental site with rich sources. Use their input as a starting point to further do desk research elsewhere, or in books and academic journals.	green
http://www.rvo.nl/onderwerpen/internationaal-ondernemen/landenoverzicht	In Dutch, trade orientated country profiles. Country specialists could also be intermediaries to local respondents perhaps?	green

www.culturalsavvy.com	webpage on business do's and don'ts a few counties.	**yellow**
www.culturebriefings.com	webpage on business do's and don'ts for 16 counties. Briefings are for sale.	**yellow**
http://culturecrossing.net/	Open wiki with a respectable amount of countries. The information posted in our individual country guides is submitted by people who are either natives or residents (or former residents) of the featured countries. Maybe a good spot to ask for help too?	**green**
www.alloexpat.com	Expat forum, with many many countries. Seems like an excellent spot to find respondents, real live information etc.	**yellow**
www.goinglobal.com	Claims to advise on CV, resume for work abroad. Also informs on worldwide employment trends and industry outlooks	**yellow**
www.expat.hsbc.com	Resources include country guides, and an expat experience report. Offering services all around the site naturally, but try it out.	**yellow**
www.cyborlink.com/besite *or:* www.international-business-careers.com	Site provides information regarding aspects of living and working abroad. Looks old, but good link lists per country nevertheless.	**red**

Discovered great sources yourself?

New websites appear (or disappear) at the speed of light. Should you stumble across a valuable resource for our research, than please report this to Aynur. If judged of high value by the lecturers, you even might qualify for a half bonus point on one of your grades at choice (with a maximum of 4 ECTS). But please NO teacher-spamming in this regard :-)

23. Citing sources

This section describes how you should cite your sources of information in your written assignments. Anytime you include information that you have found somewhere else, you will need to acknowledge the source of that information. We want you to use the **_author-date reference style_** of the American Psychological Association (APA), which is the most widely used citation system in the social sciences. Please use the APA style of citation for both your text and your bibliography. Specific examples of this system can be found below.

WHY do I need to cite my sources?
If you include information from other sources without acknowledging them, you will essentially be presenting someone else's work as your own. That is called plagiarism, which is basically intellectual theft. If reported to the exam commission, plagiarism could lead to disciplinary action. You can avoid that situation by carefully citing your sources. In the process, you will make yourself more credible as an author. You will also make it easier for your readers to find the information you are citing.

WHEN do I need to cite my sources?
You need to cite your sources anytime you use specific information from them, in your own text. There are different ways to include that information:
- **Quoting** - reproducing someone's exact words (word-for-word).
- **Paraphrasing -** rephrasing or reformulating someone else's ideas or explanation of some topic in your own words.
- **Summarising -** summing up or briefly stating the main points of someone else's content (ideas, theories, etc.) in your own words.
- **Copying -** reproducing* tables, data and figures in your own text.

* Note: _copyright laws require prior permission from the author or copyright owner to reproduce copyrighted material like photographs or graphics/charts._

Sorry but **DON'T use the MS Word Reference functionality** in our BOOK... It really causes problems for the printer, and often isn't right too.

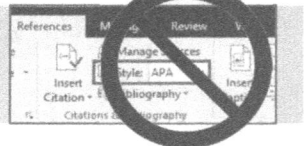

Sample bibliography

Abderrahman, H., Najoua, F., Shouhail, R. (2015) Employee perception of Diversity in Morocco: empirical insights. *Journal of Global Responsibility*, 6(1), pp. 4-18.

Abdullah, A. (2013). Telephone interview. 25 February.

Adekola, A., & Sergi, B.S. (2016). *Global Business Management: A Cross-Cultural Perspective*. Routledge.

Advameg. (2010). *Culture of Azerbaijan*. Retrieved from everyculture.com/A-Bo/Azerbaijan.html on 1 April 2017.

Aioanei, I. (2006), Leadership in Romania. *Journal of Organizational Change Management*, 19(6), pp. 705-712. Retrieved from http://www.emeraldinsight.com/doi/pdfplus/10.1108 on 10 March 2017.

Akudowitsch, V. (2013). *Der Abwesenheitscode: Versuch, Weißrussland zu verstehen*. Suhrkamp Verlag: Berlin.

Almelo, A.M. (2005). *Transformational Leadership Influences On Employee Trust And Satisfaction In A Suriname Context The Case Of Ckc Bem*. Dissertation. Maastricht School Of Management.

Alvesson, M. (2002). *Understanding organisational culture*. London: SAGE publications.

Analoui, F. (1999). Eight parameters of managerial effectiveness: A study of senior managers in Ghana. *The Journal of Management Development*, 18(4), pp. 362-389.

Barton, D., & Ye, M. (2013). Developing China's business leaders: A conversation with Yingyi Qian. *Mckinsey Quarterly*, (3), pp. 120-125.

Baudelot, C., & Establet, R. (2009*). L'élitisme Républicain: L'école Française À L'épreuve Des Comparaisons Internationales*. Paris: Seuil.

Bendt, H. (2017). *Humprey Bendt: "We hebben dienende leiders nodig in de politiek"*. Suriname Herald. Retrieved from http://www.srherald.com/suriname/2017/aytur7588/ on 5 April 2017.

Bendt, H. (2017). Personal interview. 24 February.

Things to keep in mind

- Whether directly quoted, paraphrased or summarised, all your sources should be acknowledged with the **surname of the author(s), and the year** of publication. When quoting something directly, you will also need to list the page number(s), or paragraph number(s) in the case of a website, to indicate where the specific phrase or sentence(s) can be found in the source. See the chart below for examples.

- A quotation is a string of words (anywhere from one or two key words up to several complete sentences) reproduced *exactly* as someone said or wrote them. It is always important to double and triple check your version to make sure it is exactly correct. If you are aware of a language or spelling error in the quote, you can insert [sic] in block parentheses to indicate that you are aware of the mistake and that you were not the one who copied it incorrectly. You can substitute a word in a quote for the sake of clarity (such as using a noun instead of a pronoun) by placing the changed word in block parentheses.

- Quotations should always be presented within quotation marks, e.g.: "The crux of intercultural adaptation is the ability to have an alternative cultural experience" (Bennett, 2005, p.25). (Note how the reference to the source in this example is placed in parentheses *after* the closing quotation mark but also how the final full stop comes *after* the reference. The reference in parentheses is considered to be part of the sentence!)

- If the quoted material itself contains a quote, you will need to use a different variety of quotation marks for the quote-within-a-quote. If you use double quotation marks for the main quote, you will need to mark the quote within the quote with single quotation marks. For example:
  As Schroevers (2014) notes, "intercultural communication itself calls for a constant and careful use of the 'listening-and-learning ladder'" (p. 312). (Note how the final quotation marks pile up in this case.)
- If you want to discuss an author's view about something or use information from a particular source but you prefer not to quote it word-for-word, you can paraphrase the material instead, reformulating it in your own words. Be careful not to repeat too many of the same words, but also be careful that the words you choose do not change the meaning of the original!

Two places to acknowledge your sources

You will need to mention your sources both in the text itself and in a bibliography following the text. **In-text citation** is necessary every time you introduce a new piece of information or a new thought from a particular author in your text. You might refer to the same source several different times in the same text, but you will need to acknowledge that source each time. At the end of your text, you will need to provide a complete and comprehensive listing of all the sources you have used, arranged alphabetically according to the last name of the (first) author of each source. The author names and publication dates that you have mentioned throughout your text will refer to the titles mentioned in this '**bibliography**'. The table below gives you an overview of guidelines on how to do this:

Tip !

Use the **'Citation' button** in HvA databases, like for instance Books 24x7, that will give a pop-up with the APA referencing (when that radio button is selected).
-
Ask a good team to help you out, Aynur can give you a tip on whom to ask too.

Sources	In-text citation	Bibliography example
Book: one author	Trompenaars (2011) describes cross-cultural awareness as a "prerequisite for innovation" in contemporary business contexts (p. 46).	Trompenaars, A. (2011). *Adding Values: The Cultural Side of Innovation*. Rotterdam: Transnational Management Associates.
Book: two or three co-authors	Schroevers, Doğan and Schreuders (2014) discuss this idea in relation to meeting styles (p.45).	Schroevers, S., Doğan, A., & Schreuders, R. (2014). *Euromeetings: How Cultures Confer*. Amsterdam: Stichting minor CCBS.
More than one source	Several studies (Doğan, 2011; Schroevers & Doğan, 2012; Holden et al, 2011) have mentioned how...	
A chapter in a Book		Frankhuizen, J., Koning, de, B., Sabatini, S. & Schepper, de, B. (2014). Argentina. In: S. Schroevers & A. Dogan (eds). *World-wide Workforce II. An intercultural benchmark of global recruiting practices* (pp. 95-110). Amsterdam: CCBS-press and the Hogeschool van Amsterdam.
e-Book	As mentioned in GoingGlobal (2017), most organisations in Algeria focus on the long term.	GoingGlobal (2017). Retrieved from http://www.goinglobal.com/guide-article-detail/?guide_id=75&guide_article_id=1158 between 20 January till 9 March 2017.
Full text book or magazine from an electronic database (HvA)	...(Mole, 2003).	Mole, John. (2003). *Mind Your Manners: Managing Business Cultures in the New Global Europe, third edition*. [Books24x7 version] Retrieved from http://rps.hva.nl:2307/toc.aspx?bookid=4929 on 27 October 2013.
Image on the web (date of publication)	This country is known by its diverse culture. (Manray, 2009).	Manray, S. (2009, October 2). Maps [image]. *Just Culture*. Retrieved from: www.flickr.com/article.aspx?ID=9692 on December 2014.

Sources	In-text citation	Bibliography example
Full article from internet [author available]	...(Dogan, 2006).	Dogan, A. (2006). *MonkeySurvey: About Asking Europeans*. Retrieved from www.wgsn-edu.com/edu/10759 on 3 October 2012.
No date [note that "n.d." stands for "no date".]	...(Jobsite, n.d).	Jobsite.(n.d.). *How to write a CV that works.* Retrieved from Jobsite http://www.jobsite.co.uk/worklife/write-a-cv-that-works-10159/ on 5 November 2014.
Website of an organisation (date of Retrieval)	...(Geert Hofstede, n.d).	Geert Hofstede. (n.d). Retrieved from www.dimensions.com on 27 January 2015.
Television and radio programmes (date of publication)	As Schroevers (2014) mentions in a television interview...	Schroevers, S. (2014). TV interview on *Wereldveroveraars*, BNR television, 21 April.
Podcasts (date of publication)	As Pikkebroek (2014) contends, interculteralists are apt to be...	Pikkebroek, T. (2014, February 15). *RAM*, Podcast radio programme, VPRO radio. Retrieved from www.vpro.nl/ ram/10627490 on 15 June 2014.
Chapter in book by editor(s)	...(Klojo, 2006).	Klojo, A. (2006). Intercultural Theory. In: J. Brand, ed. *The Power of Europe: On Management and Organisation* (pp. 95-110). Amsterdam: Press3asy.
Thesis	...(Schroefbeest, 2013).	Schroefbeest, S. (2013). *International Publication Strategy of CCBS*. Thesis. Catholic University of Nijmegen.
Image in a book	...(Smith, 2016, p. 69).	Smith, S. (2016). *The Art of e-Books*. New York: Schriiver & Sons.
E-mail, lecture or INTERVIEW (telephone, Skype, WhatsApp)	...(Ource, 27 November 2015).	Ource, S. (2017). Telephone interview. 27 November.
Film, video, DVD	...(Scott, 1998).	Scott, T. (Director). (1998). *Enemy of the state* [DVD]. United States: Miramax Films.
CCBS Survey (ongoing online SuMo project)	...(CCBS Survey, 2017).	CCBS Survey. (2017). *Worldwide Recruitment Survey*. In SurveyMonkey online: Amsterdam University of Applied Sciences

Note that if you cite the same source more than once, the way you refer to it in the text may change, depending of the number and type of authors:

Type of citation	1st instance in text	Subsequent citations in text	1st parenthetical instance in text	Subsequent parenthetical citations in text
One source, single author	Mackey (2010)	Mackey (2010)	(Mackey, 2010)	(Mackey, 2010)
One source, two authors	Mackey and Fletcher (2009)	Mackey and Fletcher (2009)	(Mackey & Fletcher, 2009)	(Mackey & Fletcher, 2009)
One source, three authors or more	Baker, Ainsworth and Sprague (2011)	Baker et al. (2011)	(Baker, Ainsworth & Sprague, 2011)	(Baker et al., 2011)
Groups as authors (easily identifiable by means of abbreviation)	Organisation for Economic Co-operation and Development (OECD, 2014)	OECD (2014)	(Organisation for Economic Co-operation and Development [OECD], 2014)	(OECD, 2014)
Groups as authors (no abbreviation)	Swarthmore College (2008)	Swarthmore College (2008)	(Swarthmore College, 2008)	(Swarthmore College, 2008)

Bibliography versus Reference list

Although APA calls for a Reference list, for our project we use a Bibliography.

A reference list includes only, the sources you cited in your Country Profile.

A Bibliography lists all sources you read, also if you do not cite them.

Enough sources in Bibliography?

Mind you that we require a minimum of ten (10) different sources.
Of which three (3) minimally ought to be from academic databases.

Tips for referencing

Below you will find a few possible phrases for use in the pocket book, preceded by some general tips on how to cite in-text and how to cite in the bibliography.

The year (2014) after the authors' names refers to the title mentioned under the same surnames in the bibliography. Mention only the surnames in the text (and note that the names mentioned here merely serve as examples!)

When the full title of the book is mentioned in the introductory phrase (e.g. the first two below), it is NOT necessary to add the year of publication.

Note that the main title is ALWAYS separated from the subtitle by means of a colon (:), NEVER by a comma...

Note that the titles that appear in the list of sentences below are given in italics.

Only the direct quotes themselves should be between "quotation marks". Indirect quotes (= paraphrased material) is never given between "quotation marks".

Where there are "quotation marks" around the [...] in the sample phrases on the next page, the text is considered to be a direct quote from the earlier publication. Where there are no "quotation marks" around the [...], whatever is added there is considered to be an indirect (= paraphrased) quote.

The verbs used to introduce the direct or indirect quotes are important in that regard as well. Verbs like state, claim, put it and say ordinarily call for a direct quote. Verbs like consider, show, see it ordinarily call for an indirect quote. Note that the verbs introducing the cited material in the following phrases are in the present tense.

Sample phrases

In the country profile *Venezuela: [...]*, Mačiulytė and Szabo show how [...]

As Von der Gathen and Armborst state in *Germany: a Great Country*, "[...]" (p.4).

According to Vazquez Zermeño and RuzBenelli (2014), "[...]" (p.34).

Vaschenko and Sanz Martinez (2012) consider this [...]

As Chaudry and Syed (2012) see it, [...].

As Hamidović and Mekić (2013) put it in their study of Colombia: "[...]" (p.22).

Rodrigues Gantois and GanéoChuba (2014) claim that [...].

Klarenbeek, Acquoij and Koppelman (2014) note that [...].

Gjorgjieski, Boulahrouz and Smith (2012) argue that [...].

[...], as Hessels and Weghorst (2012) also mention.

[...], which Schuijt, Versloot and Waij (2012) refer to as "[...]" (p.9).

- - - - -

Note: Direct sources for books and journals should always offer exact page numbering.

Signal phrases

A phrase, clause or sentence that introduces a quotation, paraphrase or summary is called a signal phrase. As a writer you will need to employ signal phrases to make the distinction between your own ideas and those of others. The verb in a signal phrases can be either in the present or the past tense. By using the present tense you will be emphasising a closer connection with your own position (e.g. in terms of time but also shared views, interpretations, etc.); the past tense may indicate more of a distance between the work you are referencing and your own position. Mention the year of the publication you are referencing between parentheses. Here are some sample phrases (see above):

- Albert and Heijn (2016) argue...
- As Aynur (2016) notes, ...
- Sandertje (2007) concluded...
- Moreover, Doğan (2015) added...
- According to Schroefbeest (2016),

Opt for more interesting vocabulary

Acknowledge	Endorse
Add	Grant
Admit	Illustrate
Argue	Imply
Assert	Insist
Believe	Note
Claim	Observe
Comment	Offer
Compare	Point out
Confirm	Reason
Contend	Report
Declare	Respond
Deny	Suggest
Disclose	Testify
Dispute	Think
Emphasize	Write

24.   Style Guide

The CCBS Style Guide will help you write your Country Profile effectively by providing advice on guides to style, examples of common word forms at CCBS, and helpful grammar and language tips.

Abbreviations, Contractions and Acronyms
- Abbreviation: deleting letters from the end of a word (ante meridiem becomes am)
- Contractions: deleting letters from the middle of a word (mister becomes Mr.)
- Acronyms: formed from the beginning letters of words (Portable Document Format becomes PDF)
- Do not use full stops after any abbreviations, contractions or acronyms and close up space between letters to avoid space wastage use (7pm not 7 pm)
- When using an acronym that may be unfamiliar to your readers, write it in full the first time it is mentioned, with the acronym following in brackets; thereafter, use the acronym alone.
- Ampersands (&) should only be used if they are part of official titles or names. Otherwise, write 'and'.
- Use spaces to separate out people´s initials (A L Smith)
- When discussing large numbers in text, it is fine to use k/m/bn as shorter ways of spelling out 1,000/1,000,000/1,000,000,000 (or writing out 'one thousand'/'one million'/'one billion'), just ensure you keep to one style, and keep that style consistent throughout your chapter.
- If you are using Latin abbreviations such as eg, etc and ie, make sure you know what they mean and when to use them. Do not use full stops after them and do not italicise them

Capitalisation
Do not use capital letters unless they are completely required for example, the first word in a sentence, the pronoun 'I', the first letter of a proper noun (specific name), the first letter of months, days, and holidays (but not seasons), the first letter of nationalities, religions, races of people, and languages, the first letter in a person's title, geographic areas: cities, states, countries, mountains, oceans, rivers, historical periods and the first letter of each major word in the title of a book, movie or article.

Oh, and thank you for NEVER EVER putting CP headers as well as sub headers in Uppercase (all caps), or 'Capitalize Each Word'.

Numbers

- Spell out whole-number words for one to ten; use figures for numbers above ten.
- Use a mixture of a figure and a word for very large round numbers (such as multiple millions/billions etc), or abbreviate it to 'm', 'bn' etc. For example, the company sold 2 million cars.
- If there are a lot of figures in a paragraph or text, some above ten and some below, use figures throughout to allow easy comparison for the reader
- Spell out words for 'first', 'second' and so on up to and including 'tenth'; use numbers and 'st'/ 'nd'/ 'rd'/ 'th' for larger numbers
- Always use figures and symbols for percentages, measurements and currency.
- Use either the 12- or 24-hour clock – not both. The 12-hour clock uses a full stop between the hours and minutes; the 24-hour clock uses a colon and omits am/pm
- If using the 12-hour clock, do not use additional '.00' for times on the hour, and close up space between the number and the 'am' or 'pm'.
- Always put the date before the month
- Do not use 'th' etc with dates – just the number and month – and never precede the number with 'the' for example, Easter this year is on 27 April.

Names and titles

- Use capital letters for prefixing names and not for job titles or descriptions, eg 'vice chancellor' NOT 'Vice Chancellor'.
- Use a person's title, forename and surname when they are first mentioned, on other occasions, either use surname only, or title and surname, and also be consistent with this.
- It might be important to note that it can be helpful for readers to clarify the sex of the person if their name is unfamiliar or unusual.

Highlighting/emphasising text

Bold

- Use bold lettering cautiously and only for emphasis on those parts of the text which you wish to stand out. This could be a name, a date, or another key piece of information.
- Any punctuation, which follows bold text, should not be bold. The exception is if the whole sentence is highlighted in bold.

Italic

- Italics are used to highlight or flag part of a text, so it stands out from what is around it. For instance book titles, journals, films etc should all be flagged with italics if they are published work.
- If reference is being made to a short story, song, article etc within another publication simply use quotation marks.
- Use of italics are also relevant when foreign words are embedded in the text, this includes species and genera names in Latin.

Underlining

- Avoid underlining anything for emphasis; generally an underlined word suggests a hyperlink.

Words spelt differently in American English

Do not use the US spelling unless you are quoting an American speaker or taking it from an American text (in which case the original should be kept).

Some British/American Examples

British/American	Example
-our/-or	Colour/Color
-ise/-ize	Organise/Organize
-yse/-yze	Analyse/Analyze
-re/-er	Centre/Center
-lling/-ling	Travelling/Traveling
-lled/-led	Travelled/Traveled
-ller/-ler	Traveller/Traveler

Dunglish

Avoid Dunglish expressions

- Not: This paragraph goes about leadership in Germany.
- But: This paragraph is about leadership in Germany / This paragraph outlines leadership in Germany.
- Not: That is how it looks like.
- But: That is how it looks / That is what it looks like.
- Not: Did you spoke to Mr Schroevers?
- But: Did you speak Mr Schroevers? / Have you spoken to Mr Schroevers?
- Not: It is said as well that the Dutch are very direct.
- But: It is also said that the Dutch are very direct.

Emphasis

To emphasize a word in English, italicize it. So, never use a grave or acute accent. (In English, these are used to indicate acoustics or articulation).

Numbers

Remember that English usage of full stops and commas in numbers is the opposite to Dutch.

- One thousand = 1,000 (not 1.000)
- One euro and 50 cents = €1.50 (not €1,50)
- Forty-five Euros = €45 or €45.00 (not €45,-)

Plurals

Do not apply Dutch rules of forming plurals with apostrophes to English words.

- Babies (not baby's)
- CEOs (not CEO's)

Abbreviations

English writers do not use abbreviations in texts as like the Dutch do. Do not invent your own abbreviations. Here are a few examples:

- e.a. = and others
- o.a. = among others
- d.w.z. = i.e.

Possessives

Possessives in English are indicated with apostrophes.

- Jort's Toyota
- Mr Schroevers's Jaguar
- My mother's house
- My parents' house (apostrophe after the s because there is more than one parent)

Sentence emphasis

Unlike in Dutch, in well-written English sentences the emphasis is placed at the end of a sentence. What this means is that less important (or known) information is placed at the beginning of the sentence and the most important part of the message (or new information) is placed at the end.

- Not: Working with people is what attracts me most in this position.
- But: What attracts me most in this position is working with people.

Punctuation

General rules

Use as little punctuation as necessary while retaining the meaning of the sentence. When using stops (. ? ! : ;) you must always insert a single space. Punctuation is always closed up to the preceding word exceptions to this rule are ellipses and dashes.

Apostrophes

Apostrophes indicate a missing letter or letters in an elision (where two or more words are run together), eg it's (it is), aren't (are not), I'll (I will).

They are also used for the possessive eg Switzerland's culture. To form the possessive of a plural noun, usually you will add the apostrophe after the terminal s: the bees' knees (that is, the many knees of several bees).

The most common exceptions to this rule are the plural forms of men, women and children: men's, women's and children's. To form the possessive of a singular noun, add 's: the bee's knees (that is, one bee has many knees). When a noun ends with an s and the final syllable is pronounced, the possessive s is added, eg Dr Huw Jones's research.

Commas

A comma is generally used where you would naturally pause if you were to read the text out. If the comma is being used to separate a part of the sentence you must insert a comma at the beginning and end of the section in question. Commas can be used to help the reader negotiate a complex sentence. However, they are not to be used to connect a succession of linking sentences. If a sentence has multiple clauses a comma must be used followed by an 'and'.

Brackets

() – round brackets are used the majority of the time, even when brackets are with in brackets.
[] – Square brackets are used when making an insert of your own in a quote this is to indicate that they are your words and not the speakers.
The full stop only appears within the brackets if the sentence is entirely in parenthesis.

Colons and semi-colons

Use a colon before a list, a summary or a quote and to complete a statement of fact. A semi-colon is used to tie two separate sentences that are closely linked and to separate points in a list that follows a colon and already contains commas.

Dashes

Shorter en-dashes are used for dates are used for dates (2013-2016). The longer en-dashes are used for terms of equal weight (the Swiss—French culture)

Double quotation marks

Every time you use a direct quote you must use double quotation marks. The only time you do not use them is when there is a quote within a quote, in this instance you only use single quote marks within double quotations.

Hyphens

Hyphens are used when words with prefixes such as pre, re, co appear alongside the same vowel (pre-emptive, re-evaluate, co-operative) but not when the vowels are different reactive, deactivate). They are also used to bind two word adjectives in order to make the sense: (18th-century business).

Common mistakes in previous CPs

Below is a listing of frequently corrected items in previous Country Profiles. Thanks for avoiding the mistakes below, and following the instructions from this paragraph;

- We often see manuscript in the final draft, that contain TWO SPACES behind each other, often made on a MAC. Please hand in work that uses just one space when needed. Great!!!
- Avoid using "/" (*slash*). Use "and" or "or" instead. For example, he/she is going to catch up to/join the group, should be: he or she is going to catch up to and join the group.
- Always add page numbers from books or magazines with quotes. If it is only one page you add the letter 'p.' (so with a period). In case your quote is on more pages you write a double P (for example: pp. 95-96). For more examples please refer to the chapter showing in-text citations.
- If you are unsure whether a page number is necessary, it is best to include it, as the editor will be able to judge whether or not to remove it.
- Use double quotation marks, "like these", throughout and only use single quotation marks, 'like these', for a quote within a quote.
- Punctuation is placed outside the quotation marks, unless the punctuation mark is part of the quote (as in a quoted question):
  "There is so much to do here".
  "Is there a lot one can do here?"
- Italicise all quotes (this means diagonal or sloping typeface, *italics*), as mentioned in A5 template guidelines.
- Always italicise the names of all magazines, as well as book titles.
- Take care to remain gender neutral. Using nouns such as 'the applicant', 'the employee' or 'the manager' is best if you are unsure how to remain gender neutral. Please avoid using he or she frequently.
- Do not use the Oxford or serial comma. The following is:
  Incorrect: Take along a CV, application form, and certificates.
  Correct: Take along a CV, application form and certificates.
- Do not use contractions unless they are part of quotes. In academic writing you need to use formal English, which means you cannot use contractions such as "can't",
  "isn't" or "they're". But write out as "cannot", "is not" or "they are".

- Add a, b, c to citations if there is more than one with the same author and date. For example:

  Boland, R. (2014a). *Hong Kong Business Card - Hong Kong Business Card Etiquette. About Travel.* Retrieved from http://gohongkong.about.com/od/a/HKNameCards.htm on 22 October 2014.

  Boland, R. (2014b). *Hong Kong Job-Hunting and Employment Advice. About Travel.* Retrieved from http://gohongkong.about.com/od/a/jobs_in_HK.htm on 22 October 2014.

- Foreign words, such as *monsieur* and *amigos*, should be italicised each time.
- Website names should be given without the domain name. Thus, the ".com" etc. at the end of the name should be omitted. In the case of websites the year that the website was updated should be provided in the citation.
- Going Global is a good source for general information, but it should only be used once or twice. It is better to use local versions – specific to the country that you are researching. For example, if you are researching recruitment in Spain, it is best to use a source on recruitment that has been written and published in Spain and specifically for the recruitment purposes in Spain.
- Table captions should be numbered consistently in all CP's.
  The titles of the tables should also be the same. For example, all should use "Linguistic conventions" and not change it to suit the specific country (Finnish linguistic conventions'). Use the same template format (size, italic, etc.) as indicated in the A-5 template for all CP's.
  Do not move or resize the table.
- Use only single quotation marks, '...', for quotes, dialects or slang, technical words that are not clear from context and understatements. However try to use single quotation marks as little as possible.
- Remember to use a full stop after an ellipsis: "One needs the application to make an immediate impression on the reader...".
- Do not use contractions unless they are part of quotes. In academic writing you need to use formal English, which means you cannot use contractions such as "can't", "isn't" or "they're".
- Newspaper, website and book titles must be in italics in running texts.
- Check each entry on Bibliography for grammar mistakes, especially punctuation mistakes. Note that some website names appear in lower case letters at the top of the site page. However, if you go to the bottom of the home page, you will see the copyright information along with the site's official name. This should show you if it should begin with capital letters. Also, double check the spelling of the titles and names.

- Avoid using numbers repetitively. For example, if you have sets of numbers in successive sentences, you should write the number as words in the second sentence for ease of reading.
- Use round numbers, such as 60% rather than 59,3%.
  Do not include decimals.
- Use numbers only when they are significant to the reader. For example, if there are more than twenty official languages in a country, it is not necessary to give the percentages for all twenty. Just give the percentages for the two or three most widely spoken of the twenty.
- If a sentence begins with a number, write it out as words. Not: 90 percent of the population understands English. But: Ninety percent of the population understands English.
- All numbers below ten should be written as words.
- Zoom in - screen size should be extra bigger- when checking the bibliography on italics, dots, comma's etc. before your send out to the final editor.
- Always place the date you retrieved the information after the web link:
  Hines, T., &M. Bruce, (2014). *Fashion Marketing*. Retrieved from
  http://www.saigontre.com/FDFiles/Margaret_Bruce.pdf#page=132 on 3 November 2014.
- Results of Survey must be written as one block. So, structure the information and quotes by subject. For example, place all the information and quotes pertaining to language in one paragraph and all pertaining to the interview in the next, and so on.
- It is also important to refer back to the theory you have discussed, if his is clear from the information provided in the survey. For example: "These findings are in line with theory from Trompenaars, discussed earlier, regarding power distance in India...".
- Add in 'in conclusion' when you give the last suggestions from the survey.
- In Bibliography-section: - 'Available' should be replaced by 'Retrieved from' - The second line of a reference must begin after one TAB, see format in A5 instruction template.
  - No white spaces in between references in Bibliography
  - The date should be written as: DAY/MONTH/YEAR example:
  27 November 2017 (there should be no comma before the year).
- When quoting, the introductory line is followed by either a colon or a comma, and the quote itself starts with a capital letter: Another respondent recommends: "*Minimum knowledge of one of the local languages is often required. As an HR professional, I often see people applying without proper preparation, this is also vital however*".

- Avoid overusing the same transitions, such as 'next' or 'however', 'and' etc. Here's a list of the possible words you can use to show the relation between two sentences:
  a)   To summarize or conclude: therefore, in other words, hence, in short, accordingly
  b)   To show time: after, before, during, next, finally, meanwhile, immediately, subsequently
  c)   To show place or direction: above, below, nearby, close, far, left, right
  d)   To indicate logical relationships: therefore, consequently, as a result, thus, since, because
  e)   To show addition: and, also, in addition, furthermore, another, besides, moreover
  f)   To demonstrate concession: of course, naturally, granted that, certainly, to be sure
  g)   To indicate importance: more important, less important, most of all
  h)   To give examples: for example, for instance, specifically
  i)   To compare: also, likewise, similarly, same as
  j)   To contrast: however, on the other hand, yet, although, even though, different from, unlike, nonetheless, nevertheless
- Use pronouns consistently. In other words, if you discuss one person, the pronoun should not be plural:
  a)   Incorrect: The applicant must be sure that their work experience is indicated.
  b)   Correct: The applicant must be sure that one's work experience is indicated.
- Avoid starting with the same word/ alliteration, overuse of the country name and repetition. For example, if two successive words start with the same letter: Nowadays, Norway... You should rephrase it to prevent confusion: Nowadays, this country...
- When discussing the survey results, if there is an indication of the respondent's profession, you should substitute 'respondent' with 'professional', 'recruiter', 'participant' etc. to avoid repetition.
- Do not use pronouns if they do not clearly relate to a specific person or noun. For example: "They do not like open confrontation". In this sentence, who is 'they'? Rather replace it with the specific noun: "Koreans do not like open confrontation", without overuse the word Korean(s) in 2-3 sentences or text block.
- Edit your quotes for grammar and spelling errors and to make the sentences flow more smoothly. Note that each changes should be indicated in block parentheses:
  Incorrect: One respondent states, "They do not want to read past the first page".
  Correct: One respondent states, "[the recruiters] Do not want to read past the first page".

Useful writing tools

Interesting tools from within the HvA databases include:
- **Van Dale** dictionaries NL-GB and GB-NL
- **RefWorks** bibliography software

Online reference may be found on:
- **www.bibme.org**
  for bibliography entries (alternative: www.easybib.com).
- **www.m-w.com**
  Merriam-Webster's online dictionary and thesaurus (synonyms).

Style guides
A style guide is a reference guide clarifying some of the most common errors in English grammar, punctuation and usage.
- http://ec.europa.eu/translation/english/guidelines/documents/styleguide_english_dgt_en.pdf

Localised MS Word versions
Please always adjust your computer's spelling checker to UK English.
Also please bear in mind that if you are typing on for instance a German or French versions of MS Word, you are importing local style conventions that aren't used in English. And although there exist many distinctions, let me give two examples:
- The extra spaces in French official writing (before punctuation marks).
- The different German, Polish quotation marks (turned contrastively).

English Language support WBH Inloopspreekuur

Every Thursday between 10:00-11:30 at WBH at the Centre for Market Insights WBH-06C24, there are free consultation hours where you can go without an appointment. They may help you with your text.

Academic writing check by CCBS

What we do, as lecturers, is that we give you feedback on content, lay-out and academic writing skills. Our final editor from Pretoria, South Africa therefore mainly checks the consistency of your citations and bibliography.

Grammarly - free checking plug-in

This free service is meant for writing mistake-free on the web or as an add-in for Word (download). It goes beyond the basic spell check and grammar check built into the word processor, as Grammarly can identify correctly spelled words that are used in the wrong context. Grammarly scans your texts for common and complex grammatical mistakes, and Grammarly catches over ten times more critical grammar and spelling errors than Microsoft Word.
www.**grammarly**.com

Hire a freelance editor at Fiverr.com

In recent semesters several teams hired actually quite good and cheap final editing support via the website www.fiverr.com. For a few Dollars they managed to hand-in rather perfect chapters. Click on '**Writing & Translation**' and then '**Proofreading & Editing**'. Just choose one you feel confident about, and take up contact to check delivery speed etc. Just make sure the work is done in UK English (instead of US). Most CP's tend to be around 2000-3000 words.
Why not share any good experiences on Facebook, it's *our* book in the end.

erbook2016
Level 1 Seller
I will proofread and edit 1000 words and check for
★ 5.0 (15)
STARTING AT €4.25

Rewrite your content
In native English
Edited to perfection

jmillington
Level 2 Seller
I will rewrite your content in native english
★ 5.0 (10)   FEATURED
STARTING AT €12.69

I am a professional writer with years of experience in writing, editing and publishing.

juliableck
Level 2 Seller
I will proficiently proofread and edit 1500 words in 24 hours
★ 5.0 (24)
STARTING AT €4.23

25. Ephorus - text check

It is each country team's task to check that none of the material produced is in violation of any copyrights. You will check the texts by uploading them into Ephorus. This service will check to see if any of the text has been copied from other sources. Ephorus has an almost scary accuracy in showing which part of phrases were copied from websites, databases, e-books, previous papers of students or other digital sources. You should use Ephorus at the end of the writing period, when during the coaching sessions your texts have been discussed from an editorial point of view. Calculate the time you will need for using Ephorus and make sure to upload your CP on time. You can only turn in one final draft, and only as one single file, no portions per student so to say. Below are the steps how to upload files:

1. Once your team has obtained a **'GO'** from Aynur or Sander,

2. Go to **http://student.ephorus.com**,

3. On top enter the CODE: **s.schroevers@hva.nl**.

4. Type **your name** and **other information** please.
    (can I ask you to write your team **CP's COUNTRY NAME**
    instead of STUDENT No. please, that's easier for us).

5. Upload the document you want to hand in.
    (please only upload a COMPLETE CP-file,
    so no parts of a CP, just one team document).

6. Check the box **'Agree'** ('Akkoord').

7. And click on **Send** ('Verstuur').

The upload pages look like the images below:

Inlevercode		Code	
Student nr.		Student no.	
Voornaam		First name	
Tussenvoegsel		Prefix	
Achternaam		Surname	
Email		E-mail	
Opmerkingen		Comment	
Document		Document	Browse...

Deze tekst wordt gecontroleerd op overee
documenten en wordt opgenomen in de d
☐ akkoord

This text will be checked against other texts for similarities and will
be saved in a database.
☐ agree

[Verstuur] [Send]

Processing your document(s)

After a while, the lecturer will receive a report showing the percentage of text found to have been copied. If you do not hear from us, you are through basically. Based on the colours used, we can easily see how much has been copied without authorization. The result below is obviously rather dramatic (97%)...

TIPS:

For English language users we recommend the website: www.plagiarism.org

Sander has written a booklet on plagiarism in Dutch (*Citaat en plagiaat*),

Please watch Aynur's web lecture on Copyrights.

26.   Authorship contract

Besides making sure we do not plagiarise by citing our sources carefully, and by checking all texts we produce, we also need to make sure your own authorship rights are taken care off. For that reason we have drawn up a professional author contract (*auteursovereenkomst*). It clearly states that you have the intellectual ownership, and allow us to use it in a book publication and on the website. Besides that, the contract also covers the school's back, when later on appears that someone did plagiarise, but just didn't get caught at the time of printing. During the kick-start event we ask all involved students and lecturers to sign this contract. The text (both in English and Dutch version) is copied here below;

Author contract

The parties to this agreement: the authors and the lecturer of the elective Cross-Cultural Business Skills course (hereinafter referred to as CCBS), under the part-time department of commercial economics at the Hogeschool van Amsterdam, agree to publish a paperback edition of a nonfiction book with the working title:

B☺☺K.

1.   Author's grant
Authors grant the exclusive rights to print, publish, distribute and sell their texts to the lecturer of the elective Cross-Cultural Business Skills course (CCBS).
These rights encompass the following;
a)   The name of every author will be mentioned in conformity with the in-class division of tasks and responsibilities.
b)   The exclusive right to publish the work(s), in whole or in part, throughout the world, in book form or in digital format, including, but not limited to: online databases, open or closed networks and telephone data publishing.
c)   CCBS is allowed to revise the work(s), in whole or in part, for the benefit of renewing dated information and/or adapting to technological needs for publishing or distributing the work(s). Also the revisers will procure the right to have their respective names mentioned.
d)   CCBS is granted the right to allow third parties any of the above-mentioned rights, both in the Netherlands as abroad.

2. Warranties and indemnities

Every author represents and warrants that she/he is the sole author(s) or holds sole rights to the work, that the work is original, and that no one has reserved the rights granted in this agreement. The authors also represent, to the best of his/her knowledge, that the work does not contain any libellous material, and is not in violation of any rights of privacy or any other rights of third persons. The warranty encompasses as well:
a)   Any borrowing of texts, images, graphics and/or tables of others.
b)   Use may only allowed after prior permission in writing (e-mail).
c)   Use of external material is only allowed as a quotation, provided that correct citing is made in the running text or bibliography.
d)   The author also warrants CCBS in the case that use of external material may not have been indicated by the Ephorus plagiarism scan, but knowledge of such is nevertheless present.

3. Net receipts

Since this publication is issued by an institute of higher education, the retail price will approximate the actual manufacturing cost(s), only to be increased by direct costs for sales of the books. Possible gross sums received by or credited to CCBS from sales of the books, will be balanced with all direct and indirect project costs. In the (unlikely) case that any net results remain, these will be exclusively diverted for future book presentations, or other book or database related activities.

4. Author's copies

CCBS agrees to provide the author with one (1) complimentary copy of the original edition of the publication. In addition there will be a possibility to download an e-Book version (pdf file) of the publication.

5. Amendments/miscellaneous

If there is a disagreement between the parties arising out of this agreement, it will be resolved in good faith. This agreement shall be deemed executed under the jurisdiction of the Amsterdam court, the laws of the Netherlands shall be the applicable law of this agreement. This Agreement reflects the entire understanding between the parties and it may not be changed except in writing signed by all parties.

Auteursovereenkomst

De ondergetekenden hierna te noemen auteurs, en de docent van de minor Cross-Cultural Business Skills, zijnde onderdeel van de deeltijdopleiding Commerciële Economie, aan de Hogeschool van Amsterdam hierna te noemen de samensteller, zijn het volgende overeengekomen ter zake van een publicatie (voorlopig) te betitelen met:

B☺EK,

hierna te noemen het werk,

1. Overdracht

Iedere auteur draagt het recht tot het openbaar maken en verveelvoudigen van het werk over aan de samensteller (docent van het vak CCBS). Dit recht omvat:

a) Dat de naam van iedere auteur zal worden vermeld, op een wijze conform de in de klas overeengekomen taakverdeling.

b) De uitsluitende bevoegdheid om (een deel van) het werk te exploiteren in boekvorm, alsmede via een online databank, in een gesloten of open netwerk, en op ieder ander in aanmerking komende wijze, telefonische data-ontsluiting daaronder inbegrepen.

c) De bevoegdheid om (een deel van) het werk te doen herzien en/of te vertalen en/of te bewerken ten behoeve van alle voorkomende informatie- en/of communicatie middelen en het herziene, vertaalde en/of bewerkt werk. Tevens hebben de respectievelijke bewerkers van de inhoud hierbij recht op eigen aanvullende naamsvermelding.

d) Het recht om een of meer van de hiervoor omschreven bevoegdheden geheel of gedeeltelijk aan derden toe te staan, zowel in Nederland als daarbuiten.

2. Vrijwaring

Iedere auteur staat er voor in, dat het werk geen inbreuk maakt op rechten van derden en dat zij/hij bevoegd is tot deze overdracht. De vrijwaring omvat mede:

a) Iedere overname van teksten, beelden, grafieken en/of tabellen van andere makers.

b) Plaatsing kan slechts plaatsvinden na voorafgaande schriftelijke (incl. e-mail) toestemming.

c) Overname is toegestaan binnen de grenzen van wat als citaat geldt, mits onder juiste bronvermelding in de lopende tekst en/of literatuuropgave.
d) De auteur vrijwaart de samensteller ook voor de gevallen dat een tekst niet door de Ephorus plagiaatscan is herkend als zijnde overgenomen, maar er wel wetenschap is van overname.

3. Exploitatie

Aangezien het werk vanuit een educatieve instelling wordt verspreid, is de verkoopprijs voor losse exemplaren in boekvorm bepaald op basis van de productieprijs, slechts vermeerderd met de desbetreffende boekhandelskosten. Eventuele inkomsten uit het project worden in eerste instantie met projectkosten verrekend, in het (onwaarschijnlijke) geval dat de inkomsten de kosten overtreffen, worden de gelden uitsluitend aangewend voor toekomstige boekpresentaties, of andere boek- en databankgerelateerde activiteiten.

4. Auteursexemplaren

Iedere auteur ontvangt van de opleiding bij verschijnen van het werk één (1) gedrukt exemplaar. Daarnaast bestaat de mogelijkheid om het werk als e-book (PDF bestandstype) te downloaden.

5. Aanvullingen/wijzigingen/geschillen

In gevallen waarin deze overeenkomst niet voorziet of indien wijzigingen noodzakelijk zijn, wordt ter zake overleg gepleegd tussen de auteur en de opleiding. De tot stand gekomen aanvullingen of wijzigingen zullen worden vastgelegd in een schriftelijke aanvulling op deze overeenkomst die door betrokken partijen zal worden ondertekend. Op deze overeenkomst is Nederlands recht van toepassing. Geschillen voortvloeiend uit deze overeenkomst of uit daarop gebaseerde overeenkomsten zullen zo mogelijk in onderling overleg tot een oplossing worden gebracht. Indien geen oplossing kan worden bereikt zullen deze worden onderworpen aan het oordeel van de bevoegde rechter te Amsterdam.

27.   Online survey tool

Soon after the start of the CCBS semester, teams will start collecting contact data of professionals from their chosen country and try to invite respondents at the right level to file the online survey your lecturers have created beforehand.

What?

We have opted for a paid plan of the online service Survey Monkey (www.surveymonkey.com), which offers many professional tools and functions, and ways to export and analyse the ranking or multiple choice the answers as summary results. Furthermore we can obtain the text bits from the open ended questions easily.

Where?

It is actually pretty simple, all you need to do is to make sure potential respondents get a hyperlink, and remind those who haven't reacted to your request. Happy surveying!

28.   SurveyMonkey (SuMo)

drs. Aynur Doğan

The SurveyMonkey assignment is an obliged part of the semester Cross-Cultural Business Skills. We use the method of a quantitative online research. Our questionnaire mainly contains questions on leadership styles across the globe. Each sample target has to include at least 50 professional natives. This applies to each of this semester's country teams. This assignment therefore means collecting enough respondents. Try to search and persuade those potential natives to participate in this international research. Your learning outcome for this assignment is, to develop an ability to trace and contact professionals across borders.

The text below explains you the assignment, the tools, and the survey results itself. The SurveyMonkey assignment accounts for six (6) ECTS. This quantitative research assignment is meant for all joining the CCBS minor (i.e.: part-time, fulltime and exchange students).

Team effort
The SurveyMonkey assignment is carried out by the same people that work on Country Profile assignments. You will receive a (weighted) group grade.

Where ?
The Survey can be found via a hyperlink, once our final questionnaire is online. The lecturers will announce when it is open for filing, and send you the link.

Some past teams decided to translate their survey version, as they expected to increase the amount of respondents. It is true that in some cultures people prefer to read their own language. Experience shows us that successful teams always start as early as possible with this assignment. Due to technical issues, we will however use the translation only in the invitation mail, and not the system.

When ?
The kick-off of the assignment is scheduled at the beginning of the course.
For exact dates just look at the **Lesson Plan** which is handed out in class and available as a pdf from OneDrive and Facebook.
You will be contacted by for data or for a coaching appointment.
Of course you could also ask for coaching yourself.

Assignment introduction
So as a team you perform several assignments this semester, all around the country you chose in week one. In addition to writing a Country Profile (qualitative desk research), an in-depth interview with a local professional as well as academic (mp3 or video), you also will use **A QUANTITATIVE RESEARCH METHOD**: AN INTERNATIONAL (ONLINE) SURVEY. Now the main idea is that each team will try to come up with a number of potential respondents. You can do this via social media, search engines or via certain HvA databases, and naturally the best; via your own personal contacts or network. We believe that you will truly learn to cross boarders, if you both search and have to persuade professionals in another country to participate in our research. It allows you to practice your business acquisition/sales skills.

Here is how it goes: in the first place you will need to enter your list of potential respondents in an Excel sheet and show that to the lecturer. Most important data are: (sur)names, f/m, email addresses and/or phone numbers. Experience has taught us that in order for you to have at least 50 valid respondents per team in the end, you will need to approach a great many more people, a list of 400 people is common, as the average online respondents' rate is only about 10-15%.

It is important not to feel discouraged when progress is not remarkable. And let's be honest: how much do you like these questionnaires yourself? The trick is to encourage and persuade them without being annoying. Tell them they are helping education, and a better understanding between professionals in this globalising world. Explain that each participant to the survey will receive a complimentary copy of the analysed data in return. Don't give up after the first NO, but send 2 days later a friendly short reminder letter or announcement.

Use some of the standard correspondence lines we offer on OneDrive. Please be polite and careful in your communication. You might remember Sander's lesson indicating that Dutch are amongst the most direct cultures in the world. Meaning that people elsewhere could get offended, whilst you don't even know it. Bear in mind that we would like to ask respondents also in the future for other research. Than we want to emphasise the importance of getting an early start as a team for this assignment. The CCBS Minor has set up an account on Survey Monkey specifically for this assignment. The lectures have composed one single questionnaire for all country-teams. All you have to do is send out the hyperlink and a request. The only deliverable we ask you, is to contact enough local professionals in your team's country of choice. It's quite normal to have a minimum of 400 potential respondents in your Excel list, some teams had thousands even...

Finally, we will only export the outcomes from the SurveyMonkey database of those countries, where the team obtained answers with a minimum of 50 respondents. We need to limit at fifty, simply because otherwise the data isn't valid from a scientific point of view. The more involved respondents also answer the OPEN QUESTIONS we post in the survey. We select the most interesting ones, and compare these against existing literature (OneDrive) or academic research in the journals (HvA databases). You are urged to use the answers to open questions in your chapter (CP-assignment).

Uploading to OneDrive
During this course you will need to file potential respondents in an Excel file. The lecturers will want to look at your candidates before you start sending out invitations. Because we want to have equal professional respondents in all countries, in order to have a valid research method. Besides uploading data lists we of course also allow a print-screen of posts on Linkedin-groups.

Thank you for **uploading** your **RENAMED copy** of the **Excel file** in the **'SuMo_SurveyMonkey'** subfolder, within your country team folder.

Questionnaire

From the start of week two the CCBS lecturers will show you the survey questions online. Some of the questions only ask for a *single answer* (multiple choice), some questions allow for *multiple answers*, and other questions are *open*. We normally will work with a point-scale, where respondents can choose between different scores in an answer. Of course we would never use any private respondent information. But we do however allow respondents to enter their e-mail addresses, so we can mail them the report, or otherwise a download link to the report. Besides teams are able to send the (template) thank you letter to those respondents who filled in the questionnaire completely. As After Sales each team will be sending a final thank you letter to their respondents, indicating where they can download an e-book version of our book as well.

Mandatory connecting the SuMo with the CP

Whether you have finished your assignment, (meaning 50 or more people filled the questionnaire) or not , you will need to use both the outcomes or open answers as direct quotes supporting or highlighting a statement in your Country Profile (CP-assignment) for the book. This is of significant importance when your country's survey outcomes support or contradict your (desk research) findings in literature. Also remember to add this to your bibliography in the correct way. The teams will be mailed a so-called 'shared link' from SurveyMonkey via which you can see all the results. This may only be used by participants of the present semester, and isn't for public use in other words.

Hunter Domain Search

Consider using *Hunter* to find mail addresses (paid service however).
Hunter Domain Search makes it easy to find email addresses associated with a single domain name (ex. domain.com). To find a domain simply insert or copy and paste the domain name into the input box located in the dashboard.

Exporting LinkedIn contacts

You can export all your LinkedIn contacts to a .cvs file and import this file into Excel following these easy steps: (1) Go to your LinkedIn homepage and click on the tab 'Connections', (2) Click to 'Settings' symbol in the top right corner of the page, (3) Click 'Export Linkedin Connections' in the right column on the page, (4) Choose 'Microsoft Outlook (.CSV file)' and click 'Export' and save the file. (5) Open your saved .cvs file in Excel. (6) Go to 'Data' in the tab section and click 'Text to columns', (7) Choose 'Seperated', click next, choose 'Comma', click next, choose 'complete', (8) Clean up the empty columns and you're ready! When exporting your LinkedIn contacts, LinkedIn only gives you First & Last Name, Email Address, Company and Job title. Further info online at: https://www.linkedin.com/help/linkedin/answer/50191?lang=en

Tips from previous semesters

- Some teams simply chose to pay for a temporary premium package on LinkedIn, which saved them lots of time, they claimed.
- Certain cultures tend to respond differently. E.g.: Korea or China hardly use Facebook but have own social media.
- Secondly people respond less to e-mails in quite a number of countries. So you will need to find alternative successful strategies. This seriously influences your team's grade.
- Some teams got amazing results, by becoming member of LinkedIn business groups, and then asking for help in the local language.
- People reacted well to the promise of sending a pdf-version of the final book.
- We had a huge problem when a team put all the recipients in the CC-field of an e-mail. Threatening complaints to the HvA board of directors etc. etc. Please take PRIVACY of recipients most serious...
- And simply join the SuMo project classes in the first semester weeks. Aynur will explain you the right techniques to success.
- One CCBS team made an attractive group/forum on international leadership in the UK, and after that simply contacted the people one by one. They had a huge success with this strategy.
- A CCBS team for the Dominican Republic also managed to ask quite a few people for both SuMo and the interviews via approaching people directly in Spanish on LinkedIn.

Finding respondents

- Do not underestimate your own network. With a few questions you usually will find connections. In previous semester most respondents were from your own contacts.
- **Social media (LinkedIn)** is probably the best tool for finding potential (native) respondents. Either by searching or asking within a specific group. It is amazing what this can achieve with some attention. Please search for large groups to post the announcement we are writing a book and need therefore participants for the survey. Sometimes you have to apply for this group by sending a motivation letter and wait few days for acceptance. More than 10,000 members. Previous teams speeded up in one week from 0 till 50 filled in questionnaire.
- Even if you do not know people, you can always ask. I have seen a colleague in action in the waiting room of an airport: amazing...
- Experience has shown us that personally addressed mails work best, not Dear Ms/Mr, without names. You may want to try the functionality called 'mail-merge' ('samenvoegen' in Dutch, 'Seriendruck' in German etc.), in which you can connect an Excel file with a mail programme.
- Some HvA databases allow you to search and export personal data. Like for instance **Euromonitor** or **LexisNexis academic** > International company > choose region (country), click on ONLY headquarters if too many hits. This allow you to search for companies, including names and contact data of individual company members). There is an instruction for LexisNexis in the OneDrive subfolder [06-Tips&Tools] how you could transport data to Excel.
- A good method in LexisNexis is to search for keywords like: *executive* or *CEO* and just the *country name*. This will allow you quick overviews of leaders.
- Mind you sending invitations to info@addresses is not very effective. An example: we had a team in a previous semester that made a list of over 600 (...), and only 2 responded. Besides they had quite some work responding to secretaries that were not amused to be in the invitation list, and required to be removed from it.

- Once you know the format of an organisation's e-mail address, you can easily construct the mail addresses of the management, as their names are often on the corporate website, or for instance in the HvA databases.
- Look for member listings on trade or other country specific platforms or organisations.
- Ask people or organisations if you can use their network, especially bilateral organisations often have member listings on their website. **Bilateral chambers of commerce**, or trade clubs.
- Often you could to ask to forward our invitation to people within an organisation or even the same company. This is a fast way of obtaining the quorum. Be careful however that your Excel contains enough variety, this as otherwise our research can easily be criticised.
- There is also a template letter to ask for help with finding other potential respondents. [see: OneDrive].
- A bit naughty, but pretty effective trick is to hack LinkedIn. In Google type in your team's country and some other query elements. For example: **"site:linkedin.com Spain CEO gmail.com"** (repeat also with other query elements like: hotmail.com etc.). Please make sure you are discrete in your communications, because you now basically have access to a lot of information, without someone's permission.
- Previous semester lists. For some teams we may have an list from previous semester. Please use the contacts of others carefully. Some have requested they won't appreciate if you contact them again.
- We have noticed in previous semesters that getting the questionnaire questions translated by an international exchange students at the HvA, or anyone else you know, especially for those countries where English is less commonly spoken, results in a boost in the amount of respondents. This was the case with country teams for Brazil, Taiwan, Argentina and Korean. Teams sent the translated version to potential respondents in a separate word-document to assist them while filling in, or directly in the e-mail body text.

Proof of respondent data

On OneDrive is an example for collecting names, e-mails, etc. of your potential respondents. It's even possible that those contacts will give you additional names of other potential respondents. In order to obtain enough real respondents around the deadline, the excel sheet should contain something like 300 persons, is our experience. Obtaining enough respondents isn't that easy. Stay polite, but persistent, is the message!

If you do not work with LinkedIn or Facebook, than we ask you to at least write down information in an Excel file for the bold elements below; the tracking of activities *(in italics)* is mandatory. You can just tick whether you have sent an invitation letter, sent a reminder or thank-you letter. You could mail-merge this Excel list in Outlook or otherwise in Word file and copy paste to the mails (more work), so you could send personalised messages.

> **Surname**
> **Name**
> Phone/Skype
> **Female/Male**
> **Company**
> **Website**
> 1 personal 2 LinkedIn/Facebook 3. Search Engines
> Country of origin
> **Country of current residence**
> *Invitation Sent*
> *Reminder*
> *Thank you letter*

How many do we have?
We understand that you want to know a few times how many respondents of your country have already filed the questionnaire, so please check the shared link (SurveyMonkey) we will send you. Clicking this will show all results so far. Aynur will mention it in classes and mail this around for part-time teams too.

What if we don't have enough?

Those teams that really try, of course will see this reflected in their grade. Please realise that this assignment stands for a good ninety (90) work hours per person... So officially around 250 hours per team is the norm. We will calculate your team efforts in a fair way, based on past experiences. We know that certain countries tend to be less responsive than others.

Template letters

Sample texts for the invitation letter and the reminder letter can be found on OneDrive.

> => **Guidelines**
> => **SuMo**

You should find the invitation, reminder and thank you letters (or e-mails) in the SurveyMonkeyTools folder. You have to edit them a bit, for example change the text in to your own country details, etc. The thank you letter can be sent when the book is completed. You may wish to attach the eBook version of our joined CCBS research.

TIP: you could also use these letter for social media as an announcement to find potential respondents. **Of course for social media you'll need to make a SHORTER VERSION, and for some countries ask to get it TRANSLATED in the local language.** There is also a letter to ask for help for finding other potential respondents. And do not hesitate to send the reminder letters 2-3 days later because the deadline always seems to be sooner than you expect.

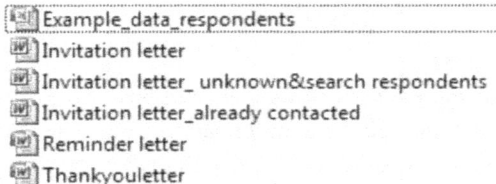

- Example_data_respondents
- Invitation letter
- Invitation letter_ unknown&search respondents
- Invitation letter_already contacted
- Reminder letter
- Thankyouletter

Assessment of the International Survey (SuMo)

Product (4 EC)
The criteria below are used for assessing the quality of group work.

Criterion:	
Professional practice requirements	**Score**
Amount of potential respondents in Excel during mid-check:	
Amount of respondents at moment of final assessment:	
Results on integrity check of IP-addresses:	
The information in Excel follows the prescribed format.	1 2 3 4 5
The type of respondents meets the desired professional level.	1 2 3 4 5
The Excel reflects desk research, using several alternative sources.	1 2 3 4 5
Use of own networks, or creative ways of obtaining respondents.	1 2 3 4 5
ADDITIONAL GRADING CRITERIA	
Bonus: translated questionnaire. *Bonus:* found new source useful for other teams as well.	

Process (2 EC)
The criteria below are used for assessing the process of group work.

Criterion:	Evaluation specifications:
Coaching attendance and attitude.	
Time management desk research.	
Responsiveness to lecturer's feedback in emails or coaching appointments.	
Uploaded Excel on OneDrive correctly.	
Produced and uploaded an up-to-date-list of contacts for future use on OneDrive.	
Motivation and efforts of team members.	
Pro-activeness in contacting of potential respondents or alternative possibilities.	

Weighted grade:

29.   How to see answers in SuMo

Below is an overview on how to access the SuMo database, and read (or copy) individual answers per respondent;

Link to the results

Aynur will generate a result hyperlink, that leads you to the closed-off content of our online survey. She will mail the link, as well as place it on the CCBS Facebook group discussion. A link will look somewhat like this (fake sample):

https://nl.surveymonkey.net/results/SM-338KG5WX/

Seeing individual respondents

After you have copied the URL, you will see the setting below;

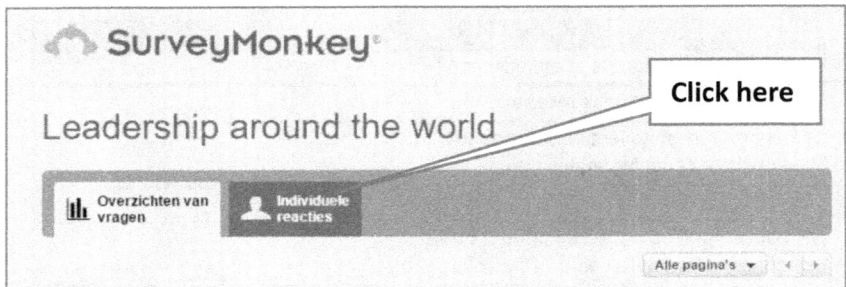

Now please click on the second tab: 'Individual Reactions'. After you have clicked the second tab, you'll get to the situation on the image on the adjacent page;

By clicking on the left pointed little arrow next to the respondent nr. bar;

You may navigate to earlier respondents. Mind you, since SuMo is an ongoing academic research, we compile ALL responses in one database. This means your respondent can only be in a certain range. Aynur will mail and post AFTER WHICH NUMBER YOU CAN START therefore. This way you can check exactly which respondent comes from which country, and has what position, and if you are lucky they left you their e-mail address, so you could ask for follow questions, or even request a recorded interview with them. You now also can use answers to open questions in your CP, and quote these anonymously, e.g.: "like a Georgian manager in the telecom sector puts it: … xyz…", or when a name is mentioned by adding the person's name.

30.   Analysing SuMo results

You have spent hours on tracing potential respondents on Facebook and LinkedIn, you must have mailed hundreds of professionals, and probably have been on the phone pushing them time after time. For this assignment you are now going to see how you can make (meaningful) use of the collected data. Because integrating the SuMo results in your CP is an obliged part of the Cross-Cultural Business Skills semester.

Where to get it from?
Sander or Aynur have send you an Excel (and an updated version on Facebook) plus a pdf with the individual answers of all (validated) respondents. Per separate person the pdf will look like this;

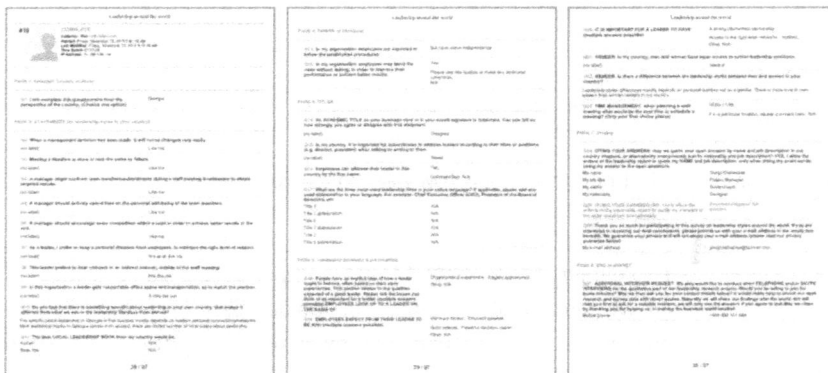

You now will need to use this document to find relevant examples, quotes, citations that support your CP text, and integrate this as a direct quote in the relevant paragraph(s). We count the amount of quotes when grading your CP, just so you know. Don't have enough answers to the open questions? Simply refer to material from your interviews, otherwise call some people directly to obtain the missing knowledge.

As you can see, people quite often are willing enough to write down their phone numbers. The one below gave his cell phone number, and now kind of expects our contact by mail first, but when in a hurry, just call politely.

Q27. **ADDITIONAL INTERVIEW REQUEST**: We also would like to conduct short TELEPHONE and/or SKYPE INTERVIEWS for the qualitative part of our leadership research project. Would you be willing to join for some minutes? May we then ask you for your contact details below? It would really help to enrich our desk research and survey data with direct quotes. Naturally we will share our findings with the world. -We will mail you first to ask for a suitable moment, we will only use the answers if you agree to that.May we close by thanking you for helping us, in making the business world smaller!

Mobile phone   +995 599 101 886

All we ask, is to consider the good name of our school, and therefore behave politely, professionally in a way you would like to be addressed yourselves.

Integrating open answers into your CP's

This feature really makes our book look stronger, as we are offering new self-made knowledge to the world. The fact that you have found respondents who are recognisable by their family name as native citizens, and are mentioned by job title as well, makes our research quite reliable to the readership. There are two ways you may make use of this (mandatory) technique: by name or quoting anonymously.

Option I: quoting by name
Some people allow us to have their name mentioned.
Let's look at the sample below;

Q24. **CITING YOUR ANSWERS**: may we quote your open answers by name and job description in our country chapters, or alternatively anonymously just by nationality and job description?-YES, I allow the writers of the leadership report to quote my NAME and job description, only when citing my exact words, using my answer to the open questions.

My name	Giorgi Chkheidze
My job title	Project Manager
My sector	Government
My nationality	Georgian

Here you can just copy the name from the PDF into the A5 template in MS Word. Please double-check the spelling, as there is nothing worse than misspelling someone's personal name. You could make use of an open answer in your CP by stating something like this: … As Giorgi Chkheidze a governmental project manager puts it: "Success mostly depends on a leaders personal connections and networks"…

Option II: quoting anonymously
Some people prefer to NOT have their name mentioned. Nevertheless, what they file in question 25, allows us to still quote them directly. Let's look at the sample below;

Q25: **CITING YOUR ANSWERS:-NO; I only allow the writers of the leadership report to quote my answers to the open questions anonymously.**

My job title	Coordinator
My sector	Vocational Education
My nationality	Georgian

You could make use of an open answer in your CP by stating something like this: … In the words of a Georgian vocational training coordinator: "Success mostly depends on a leaders personal connections and networks"…

How to get to the detailed results ?

Aynur has generated a so-called 'RESULT HYPERLINK', that leads you to the closed-off content of our online survey. She will mail the link, as well as place it on the CCBS Facebook group discussion. Normally such a link looks somewhat like this (fake link):

https://nl.surveymonkey.net/results/SM-338KG8WX/

Should you prefer the EXCEL FILE, to make your own calculations, she has uploaded the latest version on OneDrive. But for now let's take a look at what we expect you to produce for your CP first;

Click on the result-hyperlink, and scroll down until you reach the question you are researching about. Yes, you will need to scroll quite a bit, as we have many countries for each question… The next image shows you a small part of an answer.

When a management decision has been made, it will not be changed very easily.

Beantwoord: 1.242   Overgeslagen: 5

(geen label)							
	Very much like me	Like me	Somewhat like me	A little like me	Not like me	Not at all like me	Totaal
Q1: Argentina	0,00% 0	12,00% 3	40,00% 10	20,00% 5	12,00% 3	16,00% 4	2,01% 25
Q1: France	0,00% 0	44,44% 8	5,56% 1	16,67% 3	33,33% 6	0,00% 0	1,45% 18
Q1: Georgia	12,82% 5	35,90% 14	23,08% 9	17,95% 7	10,26% 4	0,00% 0	3,14% 39
Q1: Germany	12,31% 8	55,38% 36	13,85% 9	4,62% 3	12,31% 8	1,54% 1	5,23% 65
Q1: Greece	18,60% 8	37,21% 16	20,93% 9	6,98% 3	16,28% 7	0,00% 0	3,46% 43

Imagine that in this case you study Germany. We can clearly see that the answer score for this topic is extremely on the left side of the table columns. Obviously in this case the average German idea (70% in most left cells namely) on this topic has a somewhat distinct preference. How will you use this in your paragraph now? It depends a bit on the total amount of answers.

With 50 respondents or more, you may use %
But between 25-50 only use unspecified terms!

As we can see in the table above, Germany has a total of 65 qualified answers (we strive for a validated data set, therefore Aynur deletes all incomplete or fault answers). If the amount is above fifty, you will be allowed to use EXACT PERCENTAGES in your text. If between thirty and fifty answers, you need to remain more neutral in your description, by using more GENERAL or UNSPECIFIED TERMS. This will be discussed with you anyway during the coaching team session(s).

Some phrasal idiom suggestions

The listing below is an attempt to provide you with some basic statistical vocabulary review. Otherwise try to look for a survey research report, and copy and modify useful phrases.

- The statistics of our leadership survey show that the number of ...
- The data would seem to suggest that...
- From the figures it is apparent that...
- Several noteworthy results were...
- As can be seen from our leadership survey, ...
- This finding is consistent with X's contention that...
- This finding reinforces GLOBE's assertion that...
- Consistent with Hofstede's findings, ...is positively related to...
- When one looks at the statistics, one can see that...
- Taking into account the statistical data, we can surmise that...
- The implications of this research are manifold.
- The current study has practical implications as well. First, ...is intuitively appealing and is easily understood by leadership analysts.

Some independent synonyms

Try to write with variation. Don't use the same word over and over again in your text. If you need more specific vocabulary, why not use the VANDALE DATABASE at bib.hva.nl? Especially the Oxford OTE (the Oxford Thesaurus of English) is a magnificent source for finding just the right word. Below you can see what they offer for the lemma Majority:

- the greater number, by a two-to-one majority, larger part/number, greater part/number, major part, best/better part, main part, most, more than half; bulk, mass, weight, (main) body, preponderance, predominance, generality, lion's share.
- quantity, number, total, aggregate, sum, quota, group, size, mass, weight, volume, bulk, load, proportion, portion, part.
- the full amount, the grand total, the total, the aggregate.

Reader-friendly figures please

Even if it says 47,7%, it is easier to write **'almost half'** or **'about fifty percent'**. Make things readable, as our book is not about mathematics.

Which results are interesting to write about?

The once that show a significant difference. So in case the percentages are evenly divided over the different columns, or all are in the neutral middle area, just scroll on to a more useful question. Instead look for questions where there is majority for the left or right side of the tables spectrum. Another option is to compare or equate a country's score with countries with a rather different score. This is visible via the 'RESULT HYPERLINK'.

Quoting the SuMo questionnaire

Obviously you will need to quote the Survey Monkey as a source several times. But it is a bit like with salt, food tastes disgustfully nauseating when you put in too much, when just right it tastes so good. Well, it is the same with SuMo in-text references. Not more than 2-3 per page. Below are samples of how to correctly quote and mention SuMo.

IN-TEXT REFERENCING: txt txt (CCBS Survey, 2016) txt txt.

BIBLIOGRAPHY EXAMPLE: CCBS Survey. (2015). *Worldwide Leadership Survey*. In SurveyMonkey online: Amsterdam University of Applied Sciences.

We ask you to also indicate in **BLUE MARKER** the used SuMo quotes in your CP drafts, so we can see this during the coaching sessions.

SAMPLE previous semester:
Survey results and what local respondents say

A survey has been filled in by more than hundred Swedish managers who shared their professional knowledge and experience on leadership in Sweden (CCBS Survey, 2016). The most important results of this survey can be summarised as follows: Firstly, relative to leadership, 75% of the professionals answered that it is wise for a manager to actively spend time on the wellbeing of employees. Secondly, the Swedish professionals considered that the most typical Swedish leadership terms that are unknown by foreign countries are consensus, flat organisation and avoiding confrontation. One professional encapsulated these terms as follow: *"No eagerness for added responsibility. No eagerness for decision-making. Lack of sense of urgency. Many meetings to reach consensus. Lack of clarity due to indirect communication, avoiding confrontation"* (CCBS Survey, 2016).

Thirdly, most of the Swedish professionals answered that subordinates never have to address their leaders by their position or title when talking to them. These comments support the theory of Hofstede that Sweden is a low-power distance country. Lastly, in respect to the question if employees may bend the rules in order to improve their performance or achieve better results, the answers were the same. Although Trompenaars stated in his 7 dimensions model that Sweden is a universalism country, so rules are rules, the answers were a bit contradictory. Employees can bend the rules up to a certain level. Some professionals explained: "*It is okay to bend rules if it is in the best interest of the company and customers without compromising on external promises, ethics and laws*". (CCBS Survey, 2016).

SurveyMonkey

About CCBS global fact tank
CCBS global fact tank is an ongoing academic research project, of the Amsterdam University of applied sciences, that informs on cross-cultural business topics. CCBS is an acronym for Cross-Cultural Business Skills. Every six months CCBS surveys C-level executives around the world. Its key focus is covered under the following five areas of activity: management, meetings, leadership, recruitment and business presentations. Since its first international poll in 2012, the CCBS global fact tank has conducted interviews in 72 trade nations.

SuMo Analysis paragraph assessment

Product

The criteria below are used for assessing the quality of group work.

Criterion:	
STATISTICAL CONTENT	
The team obtained 50 qualified/validated respondents (or more), the team obtained a lower amount but showed evidence of working hard.	
If not enough SuMo open-answers were available, the team looked for alternatives elsewhere (e.g.: via direct interviews, phone calls to respondents, Social Media, Internet blogs, magazines etc.	
Team made 4-5 STATISTICAL ANALYSES or conclusions based on SuMo data set(s) inside their paragraph 'What local respondents say'.	
Team used 3-4 RELEVANT QUOTES of answers to open SuMo questions inside their paragraph 'What local respondents say'.	
Writer(s) correctly used challenging STATISTICAL VOCABULARY.	
CONTENT	
The level of practical information is adequate for professional use.	
The writing style meets professional publication qualifications.	
The APA citation requirements for the CCBS survey have been met.	
ADDITIONAL CRITERIA	
Bonus for adding professional (business) INFOGRAPHIC	
Bonus for connecting analyses results to a theoretical meaningful theory, or other conclusions on books of scholars.	

Process

The criteria below are used for assessing the process of group work.

Criterion:	Evaluation specifications:
Coaching attendance and attitude	
Responsiveness to feedback	
Uploaded on OneDrive correctly	
Time management	

31. Country Profile (CP)

Sander Schroevers, Aynur Doğan, Tom Johnston

This guideline describes the type of content we expect to find in the country profile that you need to write along with the other members of your team. If approved it will become part of the pocketbook. Please read the whole (long) chapter carefully. With this assignment, you will research various aspects relating to management and leadership in the country your team has chosen and then process what you have learned into an informative profile of that country. The intended readership is professional people. Your country profile should include the following sections:

1. **Title & Introduction**
   Title and list of authors
   Introduction
2. **A xys-ish* leadership profile**
3. **How the XYZ characterise outstanding leaders?**
4. **Power distance in XYZ**
5. **Survey results and what local respondents say**
6. **Local leadership literature analysis**
   In-country leadership specialist
   In-country leadership bestseller
7. **How to achieve leadership empathy?**
8. **Methods of feedback**
9. **Bibliography**

Each of these parts is described individually in more detail below.
That information should be presented in a flowing narrative; a text that simply lists separate facts is not enough! Present your information in well-structured paragraphs with clear topic sentences. Use as much as possible words in the

native language to give the reader the 'flavour' of the culture. Be sure to make explicit for your readers any connections that you see between the bits of information. If different team members will be write different sections, make sure no information gets repeated and that the text reads as if it had been written by one person. Make your country profile a cohesive, flowing and reader-friendly text!

We expect all teams to have their 'first draft', a raw self-written version of the CP research topics, uploaded on the team OneDrive folder by the indicated deadline of the semester. There will be a second draft that allows us to check whether you will have incorporated the YouTube/SoundCloud findings as well as the SuMo analysis in a uniform way. After that there is a quick feedback moment, after which the lecturers decide which chapters get a GO to move to the next stage: the final draft. Those draft chapters that do not make the impression to be able to catch up with the desired final outcome will here be drawn out of the project, and receive a 5,8 team grade. Teams can try to upgrade this by performing an alternative assignment. Before this Go/No-go selection all teams must upload their final draft texts on plagiarism in the Ephorus database, if needed we will supply you with feedback (corrections, suggestions, etc.). In your 'final draft' (due date: see LessonPlan) you will need to have incorporated and/or responded to any feedback (corrections, suggestions, etc.) that you receive on your earlier draft. Your grade for this assignment will be based on the final draft of your country profile, as well as the process and coaching sessions behaviour. Approved texts will eventually be published in the CCBS pocket book, as well as in an eBook version on GooglePlay.

Deliverables always on OneDrive
Each team is asked to produce a document in the CCBS A5 Word template. You will need store this on OneDrive, inside your own team folder.

Log-in and click on:
=>   TEAMS => Your team's country =>   CP__CountryProfile

Working on your CP **in OneDrive**

Dear people, we expect you to work **exclusively** in Word online on OneDrive.
This allows us, as well as your team members to place comments, visible to us all.
We therefore strongly advise you to read the comments made by the lecturers.
If you are finishing a draft, and uploading a new draft, you must always delete
the comments that have been fixed or repaired.

Comments functionality
The picture below shows how it looks like to use the comments functionality
(Dutch: *Opmerkingen*) of MS Word on OneDrive.

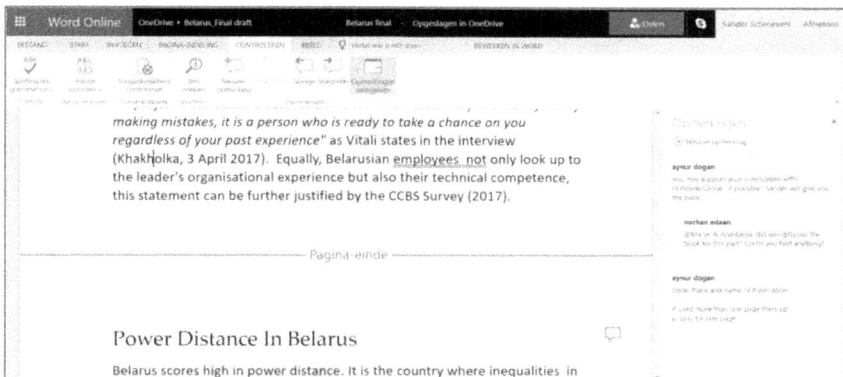

To navigate between comments: simply click on the balloon, to surf to the
comment, or click on the comment to go to the relevant section in your CP.

Thanks for using the original Microsoft software (as available for free on
OneDrive), as we always get some tricky layout problems with Open Source
versions.

Description of each CP section

Title & introduction

Title and list of authors

Add the names of each member of your team just below title of your text. Please decide among yourselves whose name will be mentioned first, second, and so forth. Please also double-check the spelling of all names. First and family names originally written in a different script (e.g. Russian, Farsi, Hindi, Chinese etc.) are used besides Latinised name versions in the final book, so please have them checked and provide these at an early stage. Mind you that also Croatian, Vietnamese, Polish names amongst others, have so-called diacritical marks.

Introduction

Length: about a THIRD of an A5 page

Apply the 'funnel' model to introduce the country you have chosen. Briefly present relevant and interesting cultural, linguistic, statistic, geographical, timeless information about the country and its (business) culture in order to provide a context for the subsequent discussion of the style of leadership that is typical of that country. Try not to come up with usual boring phrases, as it puts readers off already at the start of your chapter.

TIP: Write this part *AFTER* you have done your research for the rest of the profile and *AFTER* you have written the first draft of the profile so that you will know exactly what you will be introducing!

A XYS-ish* leadership profile

*XYZ-ISH= your country name, for instance: Swedish

Length: about ONE-AND-A-HALF full A5 page

Try to get at least 2-3 direct quotes from the SuMo open answers.

And another 2-3 direct quotes from your interviews. You make the knowledge!

NATIVE AUTHORS: please include a minimum of 2 (TWO) different in-country authors and use them as sources via in-text referencing.

Write a paragraph which identifies the attitudes and behaviour associated with leadership in the country of your team's choice. Take the pdf on OneDrive of the *FlightPack* series as starting point. Especially its paragraph called 'Leadership Styles'. Also read the pdf file called [XYZ Managing Employees.pdf] of a series called *GlobeSmart,* particularly the paragraph called 'XYZ: Effective Leadership Styles'. Both pdf-files (if available) have already been uploaded in your team's folder on OneDrive. After starting with these two sources, you are expected to enrich this with examples derived from alternative literature, GLOBE, direct quotes (SuMo), quotes from the internet (in-text mentioning the person stating it, according to APA referencing style), descriptions from other country materials, or even better, examples provided to you by people you interviewed. Besides country specific books to be found on Books24x7, the books mentioned below are mandatory sources for this CP paragraph. Mind you, teams that make use to heavily of the *FlightPack* as a source, risk receiving substantially lower grades. They are there just to help you getting started, not something to copy from.

Book John Mole (for European countries only)
Sign in to https://bib.hva.nl/ and click English (if you prefer) and then databases. Now select Books24x7, and in the new window log-in once more.
(Mind you: I experienced log-in errors which didn't show in the Dutch interface…)
Search for the author 'John Mole'. You need his book: 'Mind Your Manners: Managing Business Cultures in the New Global Europe', Third Edition.
Select the country your team is researching, now try to gather useful building blocks for your CP and see if the book perhaps offers a paragraph on leadership. You are expected to find a minimum of five to ten useful elements and intertwine these in your chapter text, and also to refer to Moles' book in your bibliography.

Book Richard D. Lewis
Sign in to https://bib.hva.nl/ and click English (if you prefer) and then databases. Now select Books24x7, and in the new window log-in once more.

(Mind you: I experienced log-in errors which didn't show in the Dutch interface…)
Search for the author 'Richard Lewis'. You need two of his books:

a) 'When **Cultures** Collide: Leading Across Cultures', 3rd Edition,
b) 'When **Teams** Collide: Managing the International Team Successfully', 2012 Edition, only for the countries: Sweden, France, Germany, Italy and Britain,
c) 'Fish Can't See Water: How National Culture Can Make or Break Your Corporate Strategy'.

Research in all three books on the country your team is researching, and try to gather useful building blocks for your CP and see if these books perhaps offers a paragraph on leadership for your team's country. You are expected to find a minimum of FIFTEEN useful elements and intertwine these in your chapter texts, and also to refer to Lewis' books with in-text citations and in your bibliography. We prefer you to find alternative books, ideally from academic journals or local in-country literature. Too many Google results however will result in a lower grade. We give higher grades if you were able to cite from localised and/or

How the XYZ (e.g. French) characterise outstanding leaders?

Length: about a HALF to ONE full A5 page
Search online for the GLOBE project scores of the country you are researching. The GLOBE study states that leadership efficiency is contextual, and depends on societal and organisational norms, values and beliefs, that may differ from country to country. In your paragraph try to describe what people's expectations are of leaders, using the 21 leadership scales GLOBE identified, and also categorise your team's country using the six leadership styles GLOBE introduced. Should your chosen country not be among the 67 GLOBE nations, sometimes the same research has been conducted by individual academics. Google Scholar might help there. If no data is available, try to find relevant information in other sources, in order to describe how the country characterises leadership in general. We will try to borrow the (huge) GLOBE bible, of 1300 pages, which teams may copy their country of study from => more info in class.

Power distance in XYZ

Length: about a HALF to ONE A5 page

Write a small paragraph and try to elaborate on how values in the workplace are influenced by culture, using the Hofstede dimensions. For instance, both Power Distance and Individualism affect the type of leadership most likely to be effective in a country. Match the country's dimension scores with examples taken from your text written in the section: 'A xys-ish* leadership profile'.

Survey results and what local respondents say

Length: about ONE full A5 page
Include a minimum of 4-6 statistical results from the SuMo survey multiple choice or closed question items, and 4-6 mixed quotes from the interviewees and/or SuMo open answers.
You need to elaborate on the results of the SuMo assignment in this paragraph. During the project classes as well as on OneDrive we will supply you with the SuMo Analysis GUIDELINE. Your deliverable will be discussed during coaching sessions, or via e-mail consults, after reading your uploads. We also ask you to specifically read through the answers to the survey's open questions, and use these where relevant as quotes in your texts. Quotes may also be used elsewhere in your chapter text. Make sure you cite these properly, according to APA-referencing style rules. We need to cite professionals, sharing their experiences, and opinions. Please be aware that CP's not containing any relevant SuMo findings will not be assessed for a grade, until this paragraph is convincing. In case there aren't any reliable answers to open questions from your SuMo assignment, make in that case direct interviews, or find quotes on social media, blogs or in articles by journalists (the HvA database 'Lexis Nexis' offers some ten thousand newspapers and magazines for instance).

Local leadership literature analysis

For this paragraph you most probably will need to contact local scholars directly and ask them for information, instead of just using a search-engine. Just like in the interview assignments that is exactly the skill / learning goal we would like you to develop: approaching people abroad with a professional question, and obtaining valid results. Please also use the academic databases on the HvA library website called: *ProQuest business collection* and do a search for academic articles exploring leadership in country XYZ or comparative research comparing leadership or managerial styles in different countries. Try to use the theories you read in the literature analysis with the practical stories and findings from the SUMO/Globe studies etc. to ground your practical tips in research.

ProQuest

In-country leadership specialist

Length: about a HALF to ONE A5 page

This is the SoundCloud assignment, transcribed into a paragraph. Ask around what the best local scholar on leadership is, and find data on the exact title of this academic researcher, the university, and summarise the relevant leadership research somewhat. Besides good-old Google, consider using the academic HvA databases, where often a so-called 'corresponding author' is mentioned with her/his direct mail address. Questions you could for example ask are:

- Are there aspects particular to country XYZ that make leadership somewhat different than the well-known leadership ideas of North American authors?
- Could you please mention two leadership role models from your country?
- What are the two most known book titles on leadership, written by authors from your own country?
- Are you aware of any interesting academic research on leadership specifically in your country XYZ, and might we have a copy of that? So we could refer to it in our chapter on your country?

▪ Would you grant us permission to mention your name in our book chapter? Naturally we will send you a first-draft for approval, and secondly will be happy to send you the e-book (once edited and finalised), before we will publish it.

In-country leadership bestseller

Length: about a HALF A5 page

Successful teams in previous semesters just googled the best academic bookshops in the capital, and called them simply to ask titles. Try however to ask more bookshops, as it is more reliable. Ask what the best **local** book on leadership is, and get bibliographical data like: author(s), title, subtitle, ISBN, publisher, year of publication etc. It needs to be someone FROM that country, we are not interested in translated books in other words. Local, local, local !!! The book specifically needs to be written by a native author from the country you research, or otherwise needs to cover leadership particularly in the country your team researches. Meaning that translated leadership books aren't valid for this section. We do not want local football players by the way (yes, one team suggested that in the past…). Please try to obtain a good enough quality image of the book cover, and upload that together with your final draft on OneDrive. TIP: for 25 countries the second GLOBE publication also offers in-country leadership literature analysis. Find out if your research country is mentioned in it, and summarise its findings.

How to achieve leadership empathy?

Length: about a HALF A5 page
How a leader may achieve feelings of empathy (appreciation) all depends on cultural background. Search in the database Books24x7 the book 'When Cultures Collide: Leading Across Cultures', 3rd Edition, by Richard Lewis and look if the books describes your team's country, and if it offers a paragraph: 'How to Empathize with XYZ' and elaborate on elements that relate to leadership.
The excellence team is asked to compare these findings and synthesize the comparison results into an interesting paragraph for the introductory chapter.

Methods of feedback

Describe the style leaders in the country XYZ use to provide feedback to their employees. Do this primarily on the basis of the paragraph called 'Feedback & Coaching' in the pdf file of a series called *FlightPack*. And on the basis of the pdf file called [XYZ Managing Employees.pdf] of a series called *GlobeSmart*, using the paragraph called 'Giving Feedback & Evaluating Employees'. Both pdf-files (if available) have already been uploaded in your team's folder on OneDrive. Besides using these two sources as starting materials (so no direct copy-paste, but just inspiration...), because you are expected to find OTHER supporting information from alternative first hand sources, such as interviews, open answers to the survey or personal expressions in social media, or simply good books or academic articles.

The excellence team is asked to compare these findings and synthesize the comparison results into an interesting paragraph for the introductory chapter.

Bibliography

Length: ONE-HALF to TWO A5 pages (depending on the number of sources)
On the last page or two, add a list of all the sources you have used in writing your country profile. Mention at least 10 different sources, with a minimum of 5 books (books24x7 and/or library) or academic articles (bib.hva.nl). Only mentioning of web links will not be accepted. For a sufficient grade be sure to list the various sources according to APA guidelines, and as described in CCBS TXTBK or as explained during the relevant lessons. Thank you for using the right font size, as well as placing a tab on the second line of a bibliography entry, within our A5 template.

Handing in work

Handing in work, while putting your lecturers in a state of euphoria...
Please make and upload your work in a sub folder on OneDrive within your team's [CP__CountryProfile] called [First draft]. Also please save only ONE single file in this folder, which is called: CountryName_FirstDraft. 'CountryName' here

refers to the country of your team choice, plus the draft version in the filename, please always add that. All other files **must be in an 'Archive folder'**. *Merci !*

Sources on OneDrive

As for your research, the following basic sources are a good place to start. Nevertheless you are only allowed to use these as background readings to get ideas from. We strongly advise you to find alternative sources elsewhere. Making only use of these sources, to summarise and paraphrase into your chapter, will mean we give a less high grade or sometimes even will lead to having rewrite parts of your chapter during the revision rounds.

- **FlightPack** (On OneDrive, or ask for pdf's relevant to your country; see especially: 'Leadership Styles', 'Decision-Making', 'Feedback & Coaching', 'Sharing Information', 'Forms of Address', 'Working with the XYZ's', 'Working Together',).

- **GlobeSmart** (On OneDrive; see especially: 'Managing Employees', 'Managing Outsourcing and Joint Projects', 'Improving Teamwork'.

So just find other sources

While all these sources are certainly useful, they are by no means the only good sources for information. Citing a variety of other (new) relevant sources will increase the value of your profile and could certainly raise your grade.

Country profiles that rely too heavily on the OneDrive sources like the FlightPacks, are less likely to receive higher grades.

And if a particular book on your country of choice is (really) unavailable at the (HvA) library, CCBS may be able to buy it if you provide the details. You will need to check this with Sander.

Be sure to keep track of every source you have taken information from, whether you have paraphrased it (reformulated it in your own words) or quoted directly from it. Double-check any passages you have quoted to make sure you have not misquoted or misspelled anything. You'll need minimum of 10 sources you have retrieved information from.

We recommend making use of the **citation link** in books from the BOOKS 24/7 databases. Just click on the small underlined _Citation_ link, like in the example here:

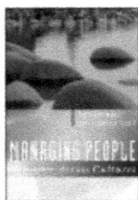

Managing People Across Cultures

by Fons Trompenaars and Charles Hampden-Turner

Capstone Publishing © 2004 (382 pages) _Citation_

ISBN:9781841124728

This book challenges Human Resource Management knowledge management and innovation by asking key

A window like below will pop-up, in this; please click in the APA radio button, and then simply copy the text under _'Citation for this title'_ and paste it in your bibliography page. Just delete the (c) sign before the year.

Citation for this title:

Trompenaars, Fons & Hampden-Turner, Charles. (© 2004). _Managing people across cultures._ [Books24x7 version] Available from http://rps.hva.nl:2307/toc.aspx?bookid=9163.

C Chicago C MLA • APA

Export to RefWorks

Even after your country profile is finished, you may also need to add relevant new information that you learn from the SurveyMonkey assignment. Once your team has finalised that assignment with your respondents, you might find that their responses about how leadership is carried out in their county will offer you new and useful insights. Discuss this with a staff member during your subsequent coaching appointments and then decide whether or not to incorporate it into your team's country profile. You could add the new information either as a direct quote (stating the name of your respondent, if they agree to that) or as statistical data from your survey. The same can be said about the Interview Assignment. In case you are able to use a direct quote from the interview, you considerably improve the level of our book as a whole, as we offer new information to the body of knowledge.

Suggested books

Sander owns lots of country specific books, which you may copy pages from with his copy card. Furthermore the **Books24x7 database** offers quite some country monographs. And why not check with the HvA **library**, we can obtain books from all over the country within two weeks. Below are some books we recommend:

- Trompenaars, Fons & Hampden-Turner, Charles. (1997). Chapter 6: *'Feelings and Relationships' in Riding the Waves of Culture: Understanding Cultural Diversity in Business* (2nd edition). < Available from Books24x7 >

- Mole, John. (2003). *Mind Your Manners: Managing Business Cultures in the New Global Europe* (3rd edition). < Available from Books24x7 >

- Lewis, Richard D. (2006). *When Cultures Collide: Leading across Cultures* (3rd edition). < Available from Books24x7 >

Assessment of the Country Profile (CP)

Product (5 EC)

The criteria below are used for assessing the quality of group work.

Criterion:	
Professional practice requirements	Score
The level of practical information is adequate for professional use.	
Focuses effectively on the specific country and/or business skill.	
The product follows the prescribed format (template, layout, size, use of headers, captions, bibliography, picture credits).	
The writing style meets professional publication qualifications.	
The product reflects knowledge of the most important conventions of written English in terms of structuring and presenting information.	
The product reflects sound desk research, in a semi-scientific way.	
The text has sufficient references to the team's YouTube interview.	
The text has sufficient quotes from the team's SoundCloud interview.	
CP has required nr. of references to SuMo open questions answers.	
The text has sufficient references to the suggested and other books.	
The text has sufficient references to academic journal sources.	
The APA citation requirements have been met.	
ADDITIONAL GRADING CRITERIA	
CP fails to pass the first Go/No-go round (grade: 5,8) CP fails to pass the external editorial board/publication (6,0-7,4)	

Process (3 EC)

The criteria below are used for assessing the process of group work.

Criterion:	Evaluation specifications:
Coaching attendance and attitude.	
Responsiveness to editorial feedback.	
Text checked by **native English speaker**.	
Correct folder and file-name on **OneDrive**.	
Uploaded on **Ephorus** after 'GO' - Aynur.	
Time management.	

32.   the Interviews

One of this minor's expected study programme parts (6600INTV16) consists of making TWO interviews; one video-interview and one audio-interview. Below is an overview of some first preparations team members already can make *before* any team coaching sessions;

- Prepare one computer with the necessary software, and do some test runs both in recording good quality sound files, as well as in editing the key message from the interview. This encompasses erasing the voice asking questions for instance.
- Or alternatively: get a phone call recording app, that allows you to make high-quality sound-files directly from a cell phone.
- Consider potential interviewees, via serious desk research.
- The SoundCloud (mp3) interviewee needs to come from the academic world, and have leadership as a specialism, from the chosen country.
- The YouTube interviewee (mp4) needs to be a cross-cultural consultant or trainer, from the team choice country.
- Start reading on the topic in your team's OneDrive country reference folder. Where the lecturers have uploaded country pdf readers for you. From that try to formulate useful and relevant questions.
- In previous semesters we noticed some teams forgot they were working in different time zones, as well as culturally bound day schedules. For instance, in some countries people start really early at the office, in others a siesta is respected, or people drink some wine for lunch, after which an interview can be just a bit too funny.
- Don't wait around after sending a first mail. Take ownership of the result as a team, and behave proactively, also to secure your minor grades.
- Know what you want, and more importantly **what your CP (still) needs**. Avoid fluff as much as possible, therefore pace the conversation.
- Don't be afraid to directly ask which quotes you still need.
- Also ask if they may know useful books, pdfs or other source material. And maybe they have some relations that are willing to file your SuMo as well?
- When someone takes time out of their day, you need to be sure you're reciprocating the favour. In other words, don't waste their time.
- Make sure you afterwards send them the pdf copy of the book.

Interviewing tips

Interviewing is at the very heart of journalism, so our best tip would be: 'Craft your questions people!'. To make you succeed in this critical skill we have selected some quick tips here below;

- Think about what you want your audio/video clip to sound like and what you need from an interview to get it closer to that end-result.
- Prepare your interviewee. Tell them what they need to know, well before you conduct the interview. A good way to do this is through a pre-interview. This is a perfect opportunity to debrief your guest on the interview flow, ask about hard stops, and double check name pronunciations, but also to check whether this person is a good interviewee of course.
- Do your research and read about your prospective interviewee or even see what relevant leadership information she/he is sharing.
- Make questions encouraging subjects to talk for longer blocks of time.
- As your interviewee is answering your question, be thinking about what you'll ask next and why. In other words: have your question list right in front of you, and be flexible in asking them at a fitting moment.
- Focus on the chosen CCBS skill, and try to get anecdotes, feelings, examples or own experiences around that particular topic.
- Try to develop a flow of questions that seems natural and conversational.
- The best questions are open-ended, and begin with 'How?' 'What?' 'Where?' 'When?' 'Why?' Closed-ended questions allow subject to only say 'yes' or 'no' and kind of stop the interview there. But one like: 'What does it mean that...?', 'How come?' asks to explain, rather than agree or disagree.
- As the Chinese say: silence is gold... Learn to wait, as most cultures hate silence and will rush to fill it. Ask your question, let them give you the rehearsed and generic answer, then sit there quietly and see what comes next. You'd be amazed how this yields powerful results.
- When starting the interview, turn off all noise makers (also on your computer or smartphone) and don't wear chinking jewellery when making your recording.
- You can be perfectly honest and say, 'Listen, I really need a quote from you encapsulating your experience on this issue'. People are helpful.
- If you or the interviewee made a mistake, you can always edit (a copy) of the mp3/mp4 afterwards. May we wish you G☺☺D LUCK ?

Transcript of the interviews

We expect you to provide us with a transcript of your interviews, by uploading it on OneDrive in your team folder, for both the YouTube and the SoundCloud assignment.
But nowadays it isn't necessary anymore to spend hours of typing to do this.
Why not consider using a '**Speech-to-Text**' app to do so? We have uploaded on OneDrive the file: [manual-on-transcription.pdf] for further reference.

After trying many of the options, we found a good transcriber is **Google Docs with speech to text option**. It works well, and is free. You can use it manually or through https://support.google.com/docs/answer/4492226?hl=en
Mind you that this feature is only available in Chrome browsers.

Secondly you can upload your file to **YouTube** and click the box that generates a transcription. This is completely free. Just be sure to mark your file as "private" if you're just uploading to get the transcription. Nevertheless there always is a level of uncertainty on the accuracy side.

Or try option number three: www.**audiotranskription**.de/english/f4.htm
which is available freely for Mac and Windows.

33. YouTube assignment

The YouTube assignment is an obliged part of the semester Cross-Cultural Business Skills, and accounts for a total of one (1) credit, which stands for 28 hours (per person). In your Country Profile chapter incorporate enough useful and relevant quotes of the video (you can also use the unedited materials by the way). For this YouTube assignment we will ask you to take up real contact with **relevant native cross-cultural consultants and/or trainers**, coming from your team's country of choice. We do so, because we believe that you learn so much better by doing. Reading a chapter is fine for your knowledge, but what about your skills development? For that reason we want you to practice:
(a) finding the right people, (b) taking up contact and (c) getting results after persuading. From my own experience I can say that the moment you cross (cultural) borders this can be a challenge. So a perfect learning situation.
For those who want to go the extra mile, we may borrow the AUAS DMCI-school's professional television equipment to interview people on location, but a simple Skype or video-call recordings is also fine to obtain results.

What?
Let's make some television, besides writing a book! These days anyone with a laptop or smartphone can record an interview with ease. For this assignment you are asked to locate and interview a cross-cultural trainer or consultant from your chosen country on this semester's research topic: leadership. We want to know what typically sets leaders in country XYZ apart from other cultures. Are there specific leadership styles or traits. Do they know of a good local writer?

Who?
Try finding such professionals via LinkedIn, specialised Facebook groups, or international cross-cultural member organisations (like SIETAR for instance: http://www.sietarusa.org/links, or http://www.worldwork.biz => consultants, but there are so many more associations or individual specialists). When inviting people, make clear we are asking their opinion to be quoted both in a book on global leadership studies, as well as an online video. Eventually it's fine to mention you are a student, but no need to make that the starting point.

When?
Around week 4 of the CCBS semester, teams will start interviewing professionals from the chosen country, in order to obtain direct quotes for the CP.

Potential interviewees
Before you start recording we would like to know who you will be interviewing. Please upload your interviewee list in Excel in the folder 4__Interview => YouTube subfolder on OneDrive and request a 'GO' from one of the CCBS lecturers. Please save this with the document name: YourTeam_interviewees.xls. In this initial stage, we also would like you to prepare your team's e-mail request which refers to the consent-form text as well.
If another language than English is used, please add YouTube subtitles (bonus).

How? Screen recording
For this assignment you will need to produce a quality video, with good sound (!) and image. It all starts with a decently working app or software, and some test-recordings beforehand (within your team). There are many screen recording applications available, either as a desktop application or a smart device app. In the paragraph below are some suggestions, but of course things change fast in the digital world. Should you be able to share better tips/tricks/tools with all class mates? Post this on Facebook and possibly qualify for (individual) bonus points, when agreed upon by the lecturer(s).

Checks before publishing the video
Make sure you mention the correct name, titles, function and organisation of your interviewee. Furthermore always double-check if they agree before publishing the video on CCBS' YouTube channel. The lecturers will keep the video private until an interviewee has agreed (preferably by mail) upon publication in the public domain.

When uploading your video on the CCBS YouTube channel, sometimes the system may ask for verification. If so: click on the first option and type: s.schroevers@hva.nl. Also the system may be occupied by another team.

Video interview tips

You are taking interviews from local cross-cultural trainers or consultants. Choose whether you will record a computer Skype session, or if you prefer to get the best quality from a smartphone video call. Based on that choice opt for software or an app to record the interview session. We have a curated list of the options in the next paragraph, but maybe you know of a better tool already.

Always practice first
Check in a test run if the sound is good, if there's no mark on the video, and the video quality is acceptable for post editing the file. Practice first how to use it and only then call your interviewee! Here are some tips for the interview:
1. Send the questions to the interviewee in advance.
2. Prepare yourself – dress properly, know your topic and your interviewee.
3. Have a pre-interview to make person feel more comfortable with the questions and to check quality of the recording.
4. Have someone making notes during the interview.
5. Take care of the copyrights.
6. **Filming tips**:
   a. Avoid external sounds – try to find a silent room and ask your interviewee do the same. Also both of you should use earphones with the microphone (avoid echo).
   b. Have the interviewee repeat your question each time.
   c. Be silent during the answer (do not show agreement with "yes", "okay", "right" and sounds like "ugh", "yeah") – your voice should not be heard.
   d. Think about the lightning – no direct light to the camera (no filming in front of a window). During the pre-interview find a suitable place with the interviewee.
   e. Change shots every 10 seconds, by using a different angle or 'lapshot'.
   f. Mind unnecessary things on the background – no bags, mobile phones, etc.
   g. Try to make the video more dynamic by inserting 'lapshots'. These are shots of the surroundings, or topics the interviewee mentions. You can afterwards edit these into the file, while keeping the original voice-over.
   h. Ask the interviewee for a final comment.
   i. Keep on recording when the interview is "over".
   j. At the end explain once more how you are going to use the footage and explain where it will be possible to look.
   k. Do after-sales; send a thank-you note after the interview and the link to the video after it is edited, approved and published.

Tools & Tech

There are plenty of screen capture and editing options out there, but below is a curated list of the options we recommend at CCBS;

Computer **screen capture**

- CamStudio - *free*
- Apowsersoft (PC) - *free, 100% online*
- Windows Movie Maker (PC) - *free*
- Camtasia (PC, cheaper via Surfspot*) - *paid*
- Screenflow-Softonic (MAC) - *paid*

Computer **editing**

- www.youtube.com/editor - *free, 100% online*
  Trim your clips to custom lengths. Add music to your video from a library of approved tracks. Customize clips with special tools and effects.
  Tutorial on: http://www.wikihow.com/Edit-Videos-for-YouTube
- Windows Movie Maker (PC) - *free*
- iMovie (MAC-users) - *free*
- Adobe PremièrePro (PC/Mac, cheaper via Surfspot*) - *paid*
- Camtasia (PC, cheaper via Surfspot*) - *paid*
- Avid Media Composer (30-day trial) - *paid*

Phone **editing**

- **Android**: VidTrim. Klipmix, AndroVid, VideoShow
- **iPhone**: iMovie, Directr, Majesto, SquareadyV

* Surfspot

Go to: www.surfspot.nl Here click on the option shown beside;
Choose a school: Hogeschool van Amsterdam
And now use your usual HvA log-in.
Once in, you can buy software at reduced prices.

Handing in video's never OneDrive

Please NEVER upload your video's on OneDrive, as we might overload in a day.
If you want the lecturers to have a preview first, please use: **Wispeo**
Wispeo offers a simple and free way to send large files up to 3GB to and from
any internet connected smart device. You may send the full resolution files, and
Wispeo converts your heavy video to lighter formats so the CCBS staff can see
your video right when we get it - no downloading required, unless we want to of
course. Mind you that send files will be expiring.

Upload videos to YouTube from computer

Only after you have received a GO from Aynur for your EDITED VIDEO then
please upload your work on CCBS's YouTube channel. Below is explained
how to do that.

1. **Sign into** the CCBS YouTube account,
   username: **minorccbs@gmail.com**, password: **hesheshes**
2. Click on **Upload** at the top of the page.
3. Before uploading the video chose the video privacy setting: **Unlisted**.
4. Select the video you'd like to upload from your computer.
5. Click **Publish** to finish uploading a public video to YouTube.
   As we set the video privacy setting to Unlisted, just click Done
   to finish the upload or click Share to privately share your video.

Upload videos to YouTube from Android/iOS.

Use the YouTube Android app to upload videos by recording a new video or
selecting an existing one:

1. Sign in to your YouTube account and your desired channel.
2. Tap the **camera** ⬤ from your home screen or account tab.
3. Select the video to upload. Use the gallery to select your video.
4. Apply optional enhancements to your video.
5. Adjust your video's title, description, and video privacy setting: **Unlisted**.
6. Tap ➤ to upload.

CCBS Identity

Your mp4 video and mp3 audio file will only be assessed with a grade, if they are professionally edited and ready for external publishing. For this we need a few things done first;

I.   Always start with a **Leader** (video mp4 animation, or mp3 sound logo).
II. On videos we add a small (CCBS logo) **Digital on-screen graphic** overlay in a corner of the screen. Choose the logo filled with the relevant country flag of your team choice (OneDrive).
III. Finish with **Closing credits** (video text slide or mp3 sound bite)

Use templates from OneDrive
For your convenience we have uploaded these files on OneDrive in the 3__Downloads section > SoundCloud + YouTube > Visual Identity
Here you will find the necessary movie and audio files to copy directly into your own multimedia production. Good luck!

Leader animation video
Simply copy the CCBS video file at the beginning of your interview, when editing.

Digital on-screen graphic
Use the country specific CCBS-logo for that please. We have logo's filled with the country flag of selected countries. Please use the one matching with your choice. They are to be copied from the OneDrive subfolder: > On-screen Graphics

Closing credits
We have uploaded an editable Photoshop file, in which you can make the closing credits of your video easily. You could save that as a JPG and include that in your video timeline, to finalise your video production. The paragraph on the next pages explains which options your team has for the so-called 'outro'.

Allowed for closing credits

This section provides information on what categories may be used in Closing Credits. The underlined credit lines cannot be used for Skype interviews, but only for live camera interviews on location. Choose from the following credits only;

- Interviewee:
- Interviewees (in order of appearance):
- Produced by:
- Directed and edited by:
- Devised by: *(Dutch: 'naar een idee van')*
- <u>Camera Operator:</u>
- <u>Sound Supervisor:</u>
- Production Design:
- <u>Floor Manager:</u>
- Digital assembly:
- <u>Post Production Co-ordinator:</u>
- Visual Effects:
- Question Setter:
- Resources Coordinator:
- <u>Filmed in part at:</u>
- CCBS wishes to thank:

Order of credits

The aim should be to run the credits in a logical sequence starting, where appropriate, with the names of interviewees or contributors and ending with the name of the person responsible for the production.

Multiple roles

No individual should normally be named in a credit list more than once. Where someone has fulfilled more than one credit-worthy function he/she may be credited for both (if more than 2 functions they must choose just 2 which most reflected their contribution) in a single credit line, provided the roles are significantly different from each other e.g. "Written and Produced by"

Mandatory closing elements

Please use the following texts and visual elements after the credits:

Mp3 audio closing elements

We offer a readymade **closing-audio-file** to be copied at the end of your edited audio file. You may also finish the mp3 with self-recording the following text:

Copyrighted material CCBS. We thank you for listening to our cross-cultural business skills series, and welcome you on our website: www.minorccbs.com

34. SoundCloud assignment

The SoundCloud assignment is an obliged part of the semester Cross-Cultural Business Skills, and accounts for a total of one (1) credit, which stands for 28 hours (per person). In your Country Profile chapter incorporate enough useful and relevant quotes of the audio file (you can also use the unedited materials by the way). Beware to use the correct APA citation technique when citing your interviewee. For this SoundCloud assignment we will ask you to take up real contact with **relevant native scholars or academics**, coming from your team's country of choice.

who is a scholar or academic?

The person you are looking for, is someone who teaches leadership at a university, and/or someone who wrote an academic paper on leadership in a peer reviewed academic journal (=> check bib.hva.nl). Check at a university from the country team choice, see who teaches leadership, and call or mail.

What?

Let's make some radio too! These days anyone with a laptop or smartphone can record and edit a radio interview with ease. For this assignment you are asked to locate and interview a scholar or academic from your chosen country on this semester's research topic: leadership. We want to know what typically sets leaders in country XYZ apart from other cultures. Are there specific leadership styles or traits. Can they share good local research on the topic etc.

How long?

That all depends on the quality of the interview. If it is really great and offering new knowledge, we will be the last to stop you. But in general we want the final edited audio production not to be longer than 2-4 minutes. The raw recording can be as long as you want. Unlike the video assignment here both raw and final version can be uploaded on OneDrive in your team's SoundCloud subfolder.

When?
Around week 4 of the CCBS semester, teams will start preparing interviewing professionals from the team's chosen country, in order to obtain direct quotes for the CP.

Potential interviewees
Before you start recording we would like to know who you will be interviewing. Please upload your interviewee list in Excel in the folder 4__Interview => SoundCloud subfolder on OneDrive and request a 'GO' from one of the CCBS lecturers. Please save it under the document name: YourTeam_interviewees.xls. In this initial stage, we also would like you to prepare your team's e-mail request which refers to the consent-form text as well. Please inform the interviewee that the recording may be used for educational purposes. And ask permission if small fragments may be used in either PowerPoint or (eventually) on our course website: www.minorccbs.com, when ready (...)

Recording/editing software

There are several phone-call recording apps available for your smartphone. Mind you that you still will need to edit the recorded file. Check beforehand if the file formats work therefore. We can recommend you the following audio editing software for finalising the SoundCloud interview. They can be used both for recording VoIP computer or Skype calls, as well as for the post production audio editing afterwards. Below are three software programs we can recommend.

Audacity
Audacity is a free, easy-to-use audio editor and recorder for Windows and Mac. This open source program, allows you to remove background noises, gives detailed zoom-ins for "ugh" removal and increasing speaking volume etc. Combine Audacity with a subject tutorial from YouTube and you will produce audio interviews like a pro. Go to: http://www.**audacityteam.org**/download/

Total Recorder
We have uploaded a licensed version plus a TXTBK version tutorial pdf on
OneDrive, in the folder 3__Downloads => RecorderSoftware.

www.ringr.com
The app RINGR allows you to record a conversation with anyone, anywhere in
the world, and have it sound like you're in the same room. It's available for both
mobile and desktop devices. 30-day trial, no credit card required.

Enabling Stereo Mix (PC) to record sounds
On newer versions of Windows, Stereo Mix is generally disabled by default.
To fix this, go down to the audio icon in your system tray, right-click it, and go to
"Recording Devices" to open up the proper settings pane. In the pane, right-click
on a blank area, and make sure both "View Disabled Devices" and "View
Disconnected Devices" options are checked. You should see a "Stereo Mix"
option appear. Right-click on "Stereo Mix" and click "Enable" to be able to
use it. This should work well for when you want to capture a Skype
interview, or record audio from streaming sources.

Non-English recording?
In case of a non-English recording, we ask you to **use YouTube instead** of
SoundCloud, so you can add subtitles over some background images (free of
copyrights). Also select a matching relevant national flag CCBS logo from the
OneDrive folder. Please refer to the YouTube assignment on how to upload.

Mp3 allowed on OneDrive

Audio interviews (unlike video's) are allowed to be uploaded on OneDrive.
If you want the lecturers to listen to them beforehand, simply store your edited
and finalised mp3 interview in your team's SoundCloud folder and make sure we
can find it by calling your **subfolder** FINAL MP3. The **filename** should start with
the country name in English the word LEADERSHIP and a very short specification.

Processing mp3 recordings

We want you to edit the raw material into a final audio file that meets
professional radio standards. Therefore please perform the following steps;

- Select the worthwhile parts, explaining the research topic for that
  particular country.
- Also select funny or strong remarks, that make the interview fun to
  listen to.
- Now start composing a new sound file in your editing software or app.
- Always start with the CCBS sound jingle, available from OneDrive.
- Usually adding a soft music loop in the background, makes the
  interview sounds more professional and attractive, we noticed.
  We have uploaded a tune on OneDrive. Avoid music copyright
  infringements, as YouTube automatically deletes such files…
- Close the mp3 file with the copyright notice at the end.
- Save your final version on OneDrive in your team folder.

Generally the lecturers will upload your work on CCBS' SoundCloud channel after
double checking copyrights and interviewee consent. The log-in details are the
usual ones, username: minorccbs@gmail.com, password: hesheshes

Interview assessment criteria (each 1 EC)

Product

The criteria below are used for assessing the quality of group work.

Criterion:	
INTERVIEWEES	
Excel file with potential interviewees, in team folder OneDrive	
Quality of potential interviewees	
Word document with interview questions in team folder OneDrive	
Interview questions relate to prescribed cross-cultural skill	
Interviewee (A) is an academic specialised in prescribed skill from or related to the country of choice.	
Interviewee (B) is a professional cross-cultural consultant or trainer from or related to the country of choice.	
Recording tests made BEFORE conducting final interview	
MULTIMEDIA FILE	
End product meets requirements of professional interview assignment	
COMPLETE **AUDIO/VIDEO** FILE has a max. of 2-4 min. after editing	
Overall usefulness of uploaded material (a) content, (b) quality	
Team edited CCBS jingle/logo bumper and copyright notices into file	
Interviewee allowed use on (a) website, (b) in lessons, (c) book quotes	
Useful photograph and BIO of interviewee available and agreed upon?	
ADDITIONAL CRITERIA	
Full bonus for interviewing VIP, or high ranked well known professional	
Half bonus for conducting the interview in a non-English language, and making English subtitles on YouTube (both YouTube, as SoundCloud)	

Process

The criteria below are used for assessing the process of group work.

Criterion:	Evaluation specifications:
Coaching attendance, feedback responsiveness, time management	
Followed guidelines on sharing audio mp3 (OneDrive) and video mp4 (Wispeo), and uploading on YouTube/ SoundCloud channels of CCBS	
Hyperlink (YouTube/ SoundCloud) supplied to CCBS staff on time	

Audio/video recording consent form

When you make audio or video recordings, please note that participants must consent to: (1) Participate in the research, and (2) to the Audio or video recording procedures. Download and mail the sample letter from our OneDrive; [Recording consent form.pdf]

See which text parts you want to use in your correspondence with potential interviewees. Most of the time they will not make any point of it. Nevertheless, we ask you to send this along with your confirmation, or when asking for permission. Simply because it covers our back, both the lecturers as the university, and when trouble calls you'll be glad you attached it...

35. Stream task

Besides several team assignments, for accreditation purposes we also need to schedule sufficiently individual assignments. That is the reason why you are asked to perform the stream task on your own. We also hope that your exams are categorised as individually :-). During lesson-1 you will therefore be asked to choose an individual specific semester task, in a field you are good at (or interested to be good at). In class you will receive a handout describing the tasks you can choose from, and you will be asked to file that in the online form in class during week one. Streams 1-3 are open. The streams A-D are only accessible after a selection procedure for which application talks are scheduled at the semester beginning, BEFORE the evening lesson. Interested in one of these management tasks? Simply indicate this on the form handed-out in lesson 1, and write your motivation on the flip side. In case too many people apply for the same positions, the CCBS evening lecturer will allot the activities.

The stream tasks concern the following open or closed options;

1	**Global database** (Research-Excel)	*Research Higher Education institutes around the globe, international media outlets*	Open streams
2	**Photoshop** stream	*Create multiple flags pictures in Photoshop using CCBS mock-up templates*	
3	**Book review** stream	*For those students who would like to go one step further, and dive deeper into cross-cultural literature. Here you will choose a book on a country, and summarise this. Quite a nice assignment for the truly motivated CCBS students*	
A	Event-managers	*The event-managers organise all CCBS public events: Dutch-culture, Ooopen lectures, Book party, CCByeBye.*	Application
B	Acquisition	*Trying to invite foreign students to join CCBS semesters.*	
C	PR/Free Publicity	*Trying to internationally get published on CCBS research.*	
D	Facebook promo	*Promote CCBS events, books and the semester on Social Media, including non-Facebook media like: VK, Weibo, as well as posting summaries in non-English languages.*	

36. Global database stream ①

This stream is normally chosen by the majority of the class. Its function is twofold: (a) experience researching in another country and/or language, (b) create datasets that are highly useful for the further development of this course. We would love to have a larger amount of exchange students, as this allows us to make better use of the in-class diversity in such a large group. The acquisition stream will therefore inform foreign universities and invite students to study at HvA. They will use the contact data collected via the first assignment. Secondly CCBS creates new own knowledge, through our book research and international survey analysis. We would like to share our findings with the world, and therefore have an active press policy, in which the PR stream offers articles to business magazines and newspapers worldwide. For this they need the contact data of media and journalists interested in the type of research we conduct at CCBS. The main idea is that students get interviewed themselves, and obtain valuable experience in dealing with the press. But now let's look at the details of this elective and individual assignment;

Deliverable ONE: 20 (new) addressees of HEi's

Hand-in the requested research data, by filing the first TAB (HEi/green) of the by mail provided Excel document **[_template.xls]**. You are expected to find 20 new unique detailed addressees in your Excel file. To pass and receive credit, you must have successfully fulfilled the HEi (Higher Education institute) research requirement by completing this elective assignment. We ask you to search online for contact date of international offices of universities. Check the website and copy the name and mail address and direct phone number of their *internationalisation officer*. Copy the found information in the Excel file containing.

We ask you to research the following elements;

- First choose your country from the pull-down
- University's name
- Name of person
- Position of person
- Direct mail address
- Phone number
- Website of HEi

To pass and receive credit for your course, you must have fulfilled this Higher Education institutes research. We assess your work on the detailed information, and if not too many cells are left empty. Mind you that the third (yellow) tab, provides an overview what is already available for the chosen country. You may either enrich the existing data, or find new unique contacts. These are to be entered in the green tab (on the left bottom of the Excel file).

Deliverable TWO: 10 (new) addressees of newspaper or business media

Hand-in the requested research data, by filing the second TAB (Media/red) of the provided Excel document **[_template.xls]**. We expect to find 10 unique addressees in your Excel file. We ask you to search online for contact date of editors of regular or trade media. Check the website and copy the name and mail address and direct phone number of their editor. Copy the found information in the attached Excel file containing. We ask you to research the following elements;

- First choose your country from the pull-down
- Secondly define the type of media using the choices from the pull-down
- Type the magazine, newspaper or media's name
- If it uses a sub-title add this in column D please
- Direct mail address of the editors (so never from the subscriptions, or advertisement departments)
- Direct phone number of the editors
- Website of the media

- Try to find out the name of the publisher/organisation issuing this medium
- Copy the address or at least the city here
- If mention of any social media is made, copy this here please.

To pass and receive credit for your course, you must have fulfilled also this media research. We assess your work on the detailed information, and if not too many cells are left empty.

Learning to obtain data in another language
Although it may look hard initially, it is still very well possible to trace valuable information across borders. Prepare keywords that you are looking for and translate these for example. For certain countries try to use services like **Google Translate**, to be able to read the website's information.

Double information doesn't count, updating old info does count
Only hand-in NEW contact data. You may not hand-in the same data as has been send to you, unless you were able to update certain address or name details from the yellow tab. These count as one date entry.

Finding complete listings
Sometimes listings of this type are freely available from the net. You are welcome to use these, do send a copy of the original in that case. But it still needs to be handed in using the original Excel file. Bonus points apply for handing in larger listings of course.

Using the template Excel file

As mentioned above, there are TWO different tabs that need to be filed. At the bottom left side of the Excel you can see a green coloured tab for HEi's and a red coloured tab for MEDIA. Just click on either to file your research data. The third (yellow) tab is the one containing existing data of YOUR COUNTRY, and purely for reference. In case you discovered in your double checking a set of contact data needs to be updated (different name, mail address, phone number etc.) than you must copy this into the red or green tab, and it counts as one data entry.

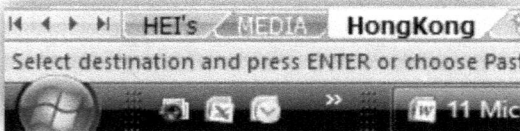

For certain cells please use the pull-down menu to choose the most matching value. Only use these values, and do not type any values manually please.

country	media	name
land	medium	naam
Denmark	Financial newspaper	Aktionaeen
Denmark	Easy newspaper	Arhus Stiftstidende
Denmark	Business magazine	Ase nyt for selfst aendige
Belgium	Newspaper	L'Echo
Ireland	Newsmagazine	siness plus
	Easy newspaper	
	Newsmagazine	
	Business magazine	
	Blog	
	Radio	
	Television	
	Independent journalist	
	Press agency	

Handing in lower quality?

All data entries must be copied into the file, empty cells results in a lower grade. All handed-in materials need to be personally double checked, as random quality checks take place after handing-in. Documents not meeting the criteria stated above will not be accepted, and the student will receive an 'incomplete' for his or her course grade. Also be assured if you hand-in GOOD quality work, we are not afraid to give you a (very) high quality score. Many thanks in advance, and do let me know when you have **real** problems with finding data.

What are the assessment criteria?

It is quite simple, you are asked to deliver 25 addressees, within a certain timeframe. The quality of your research is your grade in the end. If you are able to provide top information, you will receive a top grade. The criteria below are used for assessing the quality of your work;

Criterion:	
Professional practice requirements	**Score**
The level of **applied information** is adequate for professional use.	
The data focuses effectively on HEi and Media sources.	
The data is indeed new, and checked against 3rd tab entries.	
The data provided is complete (filing all boxes) or else compensated.	
The product reflects good **research**.	
Talent points: bonus issued for quality improvements.	
Responsiveness to lecturer's feedback.	
Time management., handed-in correctly.	
subtotal:	

37. Photoshop stream ❷

If you like visual work and have experience in Photoshop you may also opt for the second choice for the stream assignment. To finalise this 4 credits task at CCBS you will be asked to copy country flags as a so-called smart-object and to save these as JPG files of about 100 Kb (as long as the pixels keep on looking fine at least). The flags we ask for are mentioned below this briefing.
Handing in: please just send Sander the final JPG's (or PNG's) via WeTransfer. No need to return the (usually heavy) Photoshop file therefore.

Checklist
You will receive a download link to obtain the file via WeTransfer.
Open the file after saving it on your disk.
After clicking on the smart-object a second tab (or file in fact) opens.
It is here that you need to copy the country flag.
Once you save this, and return to the first tab,
you now see the flag inside the right perceptive and lightning.
Now please save the file as a JPG and not too heavy, or a PNG (depending on briefing by Sander). You need to use a standard filename, like for example:
e.g. [AUS_Wood_Flag.jpg] for the Australian flag on a wooden texture.

Only name files starting with the official country abbreviations.
You can obtain these from:
https://en.wikipedia.org/wiki/List_of_international_vehicle_registration_codes

NO BACKGROUNDS nor SHADOWS
Check beforehand with Sander if you need to uncheck the background and/or shadows in the file before saving the individual flag pictures.

Generic briefing for all Photoshop files

Below is an explanation for most files, please work according to logical analogy.

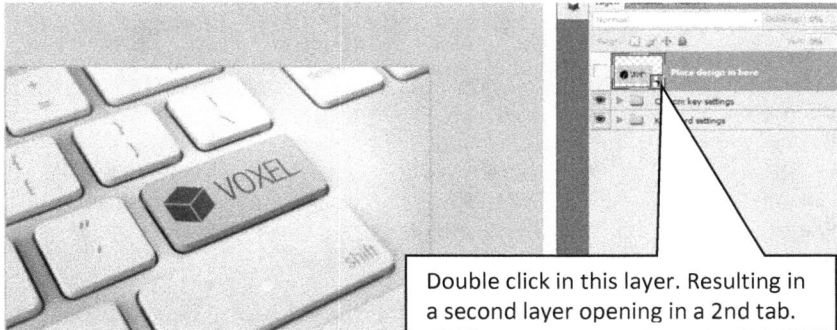

Double click in this layer. Resulting in a second layer opening in a 2nd tab.

Now copy the country flags needed.
Please copy the country flags always from Wikipedia:
https://en.wikipedia.org/wiki/Gallery_of_sovereign_state_flags
First click on a flag, to obtain a larger version and copy the Large version into the Photoshop second tab/file.
Copy the flag into the smart-object layer.
Draw the flag so that it fits the layer properly,
by clicking on the highest button in the left margin;
Sometimes it is best to first hit: **Control + T** to be able to scale the flag.

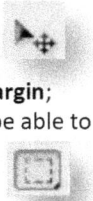

After the scaling click on one button lower:
now click YES when a dialogue window ask you to confirm the transformation.
After this, save the file.
Then click on the left tab, of the original file.
I fit worked well, it now will show the flag like for instance below;

If you are satisfied with the result, save a copy of the PSD [Save as] as a JPG (PNG). Use the standard file naming method: e.g.: [I_keyboard.jpg] in this case.
Rrrrready, now start making the next flag combination until you have done all flags from the table below. Mail me the files combined into one ZIP-file.
Or when too heavy via WeTransfer. Thanks for that!

Country Listing

Desired EU countries as PNG's or JPG's.

Belgium	Ireland	Portugal
Bulgaria	Italy	Romania
Cyprus	Croatia	Slovenia
Denmark	Latvia	Slovakia
Germany	Lithuania	Spain
Estonia	Luxembourg	Czech Republic
Finland	Malta	United Kingdom
France	Netherlands	Sweden
Greece	Austria	
Hungary	Poland	
-		

Desired World countries as PNG's or JPG's.

Argentina	Korea, South	Singapore
Australia	Lebanon	South Africa
Brazil	Malaysia	Suriname
Canada	Mexico	Switzerland
China	Morocco	Turkey
Colombia	New Zealand	Ukraine
Costa Rica	Nigeria	Unit. Arab Emirates
Egypt	Norway	United States
Georgia	Pakistan	Venezuela
Hong Kong	Qatar	Vietnam
India	Russia	
Indonesia	Saudi Arabia	
Japan	Serbia	
-		

38. Book review stream ❸

The Book Review assignment is a so-called 'stream assignment' for the semester Cross-Cultural Business Skills. As a student you are allowed to opt for this alternative track, if you wish to perform a somewhat more challenging task. You are asked to select, suggest and then read a book on one particular country, and to excerpt important country specific anecdotes, cultural peculiarities, points of interest for in the regular CCBS classes, and direct quotes of the writer or other mentioned sources. The text below explains you the assignment, the desired output, and the deliverable in PowerPoint. The Review assignment accounts for four (4) ECTS.

For whom?
This excellence/alternative research assignment is open to all joining the CCBS minor (i.e.: part-time, fulltime, exchange and Kies-Op-Maat students). Your learning outcome for this assignment is critical thinking and in-depth text analysis in order to select country specific cross-cultural pointers.

What is a good book?
We want you to find a book that offers a first-hand experience of living and/or working professionally as an expat/foreigner abroad. Therefore NO travel or touristic guides are acceptable, nor mainly political or historical oriented works. Your reading language choice is totally free, the review however must be in English.

Which country is allowed?
Anything you want or feel interested in. It does NOT have to be the same country as your team assignment by the way, the only restrictions are that the book has already been reviewed before, or that Sander doesn't feel the proposed book matches the content requirements set out for this assignment.

Where do I get my book?

The public or HvA library, buy an e-book or a hardcopy online, check Books 24x7 (for free), or simply ask your mom, grandpa, aunty, etc. etc.

Procedure

You will be contacted together with other participating students for a kick-off appointment and to receive a book of your interest. The books usually are private property of Sander, and therefore need to be returned clean and undamaged. It is not allowed to make notes, or folds in the book. Also the books don't drink any coffee, thanks for your kind understanding.

When ?

The assignment can be carried out at wish, during term one and/or two of the semester. The materials as well as the borrowed book need to be handed in before, the semester closure, and at the latest three weeks before the start of a new semester, in order to allow grades to be administered correctly.

First check

About one week after receiving the book, you will be invited for a first check. This is to assess whether you are on the right track. An appointment is either scheduled during a stream consult class, or via Skype. Of course you could also ask for coaching yourself.

Handing in deliverables

We ask you to mail the materials to your assignment coach, so no need here to upload anything on OneDrive. This is because we use OneDrive mainly for team assignments, and your book review assignment is an individual task.

Deliverables

1. Describe **15 FUN-FACTS**: interesting country specific anecdotes, habits or elements that an audience may find amusing, or nice to know. After selection, the CCBS lecturers may turn some of these into PowerPoint slides, to be used during country lessons.
    Weight 40% of grade - Hand in a MS Word file.

2. Direct quotes: find **30 RELEVANT QUOTES** on the country or culture.
    Weight 30% of grade - Hand in a MS Word file.

3. **BOOK OVERVIEW**: make one PPT slide with the book cover and its bibliographic information, as well as a small portrait of the writer, with a three line BIO.
    Weight 10% of grade - Hand in a MS PowerPoint file.

4. Overall **QUALITY** of the handed-in materials
    Weight 10% of grade

5. **Process**, punctuality, response to feedback and overall communication.
    Weight 10% of grade

Now let's look at the individual parts;

-

Fifteen (15) fun facts

Read the book and see if there are any funny topics, that you will only find in that country, or perhaps something invented there, someone famous, a funny kind of food, a scandal, in short: anything that may please the audience, and allow for some infotainment in between of the more dryer business skills.

Thirty (30) quotes

Besides the fun-facts we expect to find 30 quotes for the book review deliverable that you need to compile. Please read the whole chapter carefully. As you are reading the book, you may use typical useful remarks by the writer of the book, and of course also direct quotes used in the book. From our example book by Richard Hill we copied a page which you can see below.

Where the Dutch have evolved a supremely well structured and organised society, the Flemish are suspicious of authority (with reason) and often prefer to rely on their own wits and industry, supported by loyalty to their immediate circle. In the words of Dutch social psychologist Geert Hofstede: "There is more mutual trust between police and citizens in the Netherlands than in Belgium. Therefore in our country the police can rely more upon the help of the citizens in a crisis situation, and the citizens upon the police, than in Belgium."

In her book *The Fair Face of Flanders*, Patricia Carson makes the same point: "To the Dutchman, the Fleming is showy, wasteful and irresponsible. To the Fleming, the Dutchman is pompous, too well organised and, above all, too obedient to the state. To many Dutchmen the state is a friend, to the Fleming, if not an enemy; it is at least something to be avoided as much as possible."

This typically Belgian attitude, common also to Walloons, emerges moreover in a degree of passivity when dealing with authority, even at the humble and everyday level of the queue in the local post office. Bureaucracy, not just a monopoly of the Dutch culture, is accepted by Belgians with fatalism – but, compared with the Dutch, they are anarchists.

Suspicion of authority helps reinforce a remarkable feature of Belgian society that can perhaps be described as localism in microcosm: the continuing sense of family, something

158

> The section on Patricia Carson is useful.
> First copy the full text in a Word file.
> Also try to make a short version for later use in PowerPoint.
> Mention the page number, and the key topic in a key word.

Book Overview

Part of your deliverable is to mail your assignment coach one PPT slide with the book cover, as well as a small portrait of the writer, and in a textbox a three line BIO of the writer, plus some bibliographic information of the book.

It needs to look somewhat like the slide below. You can download the template PowerPoint from OneDrive from the folder: [Book Review].

Book Review assignment (BR)

Product (3 EC)

The criteria below are used for assessing the quality of individual work.

Criterion:		
30 quotes (40%)		**Score**
The level of the 30 quotes is adequate for professional use.		
Each quote focuses effectively on the specific country and/or a particular business skill.		
10 fun-facts (30%)		**Score**
The deliverables reflects in-depth reading, in a thorough way.		
They each represent enough material to make an interesting slide in PPT afterwards (by the lecturers).		
PowerPoint slide (10%)		**Score**
The PowerPoint slide follows the prescribed format (font, layout).		
ADDITIONAL GRADING CRITERIA		

Process (1 EC)

The criteria below are used for assessing the quality of individual work.

Criterion: (20%)	Evaluation specifications:
Coaching attendance and attitude.	
Availability & preparedness concerning Skype coaching meetings.	
Responsiveness to feedback.	
Mailed deliverables punctually.	
Time management.	

39. Ooopen lectures *by native students*

The essence of this elective course is to better understand different cultures. Now we have all sort of reading materials available, we conduct research by asking locals or expats for information, survey answers and even interview them. But there's one thing that beats it all: storytelling... Nothing is better remembered by people than honest human interaction. And we see that reflected in the semester evaluations. The expat student presentations are amongst the higher rated lessons. Besides it is much more convincing and charming to listen to someone explaining about their very own culture. It is therefore that we have decided to institutionalise such peer-learning, by scheduling so-called 'native presentations'. In order to allow people to bring along close ones or friends, we started with the Ooopen lecture concept recently, which was simply good fun. So here goes: we would like you to co-present for one evening lesson, and also conceptualise some kind of fun event management towards the end of the lesson. Furthermore we'll promote the lesson in-school.

Bonus point
You are entitled to a full bonus point on one of your grades at choice, (for an assignment/exam with a maximum of 4 EC's). Just let me know towards the end of the semester, which grade you want to use it for.

Duration
If you are alone a country presentation of about 30-45 minutes suffices. The larger groups with three to four people, are asked to present 75 minutes and co-organise (with the help of the event stream) a so-called 'Ooopen lecture'.

Ooopen lecture
This simply means, that we will communicate the lesson in the inner circle: which refers to in-school public relations and exchange student social media. We do not invite the outside circles, such as press or business communities (which we will host at the CCBS symposia), but anyone external is always

welcome of course. The Ooopen lectures will be made known in-school via A3 posters (at bulletin boards only), and invitation mailings. Translating Pierre Bourdieu's notion of **social capital** to: 'School's cool', the last part of the lesson may include something funny like a local dance, a local drink or bite. Anything that appeals to the senses and is fun for the audience; *"you can't just study cross-cultural, you gotta live it"*... So please feel free to come with a suggestion. Only issue is that we will have to smuggle things in, and make sure everything goes out in garbage bags again... Please check the details with the event-stream.

Copyright
Since the presentations may be made public via the website, we need to be 100% sure that all images, texts are free of copyright. Either ask for permission, or find creative commons images, that may be used publicly without permission. See for tips the paragraph in TXTBK on how to obtain free pictures. Of course copyright also has a more friendly side, namely your copyright. If it is your work, it will be seen as your work by future classes.

Business skills
Slides on the typical business and management skills will already be made (and presented) by Sander. This also includes the usual rankings, cultural dimension scores etc. etc. So just skip the square miles or kilometres, the capital, the climate, the organisational memberships, the religion, the currency and all those other 'usual suspects' in country presentations.

Available material
But Sander has an enormous amount of country related reference works, books, pdf files etc. etc. Just discuss with him, what is needed to prepare, we even can acquire specific books, materials or stock pictures if felt necessary.

Content related

Which elements can we best present? Well, you have by now a fair idea of what Sander's lessons usually are about. Take that as a guideline in gathering useful topics to present. The list below contains a lot of requests, suggestions and more. We realise that, and perhaps it is also based on a perfectionist desire to present your country in the most favourable way. So please take the following into account when choosing to co-present on your own country.

PERSONAL EXPERIENCE: 2 slides
You have been some time in the Netherlands now. Give us a listing of what most *shocked and disturbed* you. Have you changed your mind in between on this topic, and why (if applicable). What really *happily surprised* you and in what way is it different? Please try to also include some business skill related topics, if you can manage.

COUNTRY SPECIFIC KEYWORDS: 1 slide
I am looking for country specific keywords in the local language: e.g. *'Gründlichkeit'* in German, 'bella figura' in Italian, *'jeitinho brasileiro'* in Brazilian Portuguese, *'Neun-chi'* in Korean etc. etc. Could you seriously think about this one, and give me a short mini-definitions as well please?

POPMUSIC: selected YouTube links
I am looking for country specific pop stars, singing in the local language.

TOP THINGS: 2-3 slides in PPT
Your tip on two to three special local things to do or visit.
Example for Japan: 'Onsen'(hot springs), Finland: sauna, etc.

PHOTOGRAPHS: selected images
Copyright free (or own) pictures explaining typical elements of your country. We also ask your permission to reuse them for future presentations, or other use. Please think of the following:

- Preferably street signs in local language
- Businesses and professional situations
- Typical people (timeless)
- Landmarks (famous buildings or spots)
- Beautiful images related to country
- Newspaper stand or lots of magazines (showing local details).

TOP MODELS: selected list of people's names or even pictures
What are typical faces of people from your country? Who are famous people or just very handsome or pretty :-)

LOCAL DISHES: select some dishes: 2-3 slides in PPT
Your tip on two to three special local dishes, which are waking up the audience, and are either enjoyable to eat, or just very weird.

BUSINESS BLOOPERS: 2-3 slides in PPT
You must by now be used to the high vulgarity scores of Sander's bloopers. So you perfectly know what to look for here. Good luck with this important research task... :-)

BUSINESS CARDS: 1 slide in PPT
Do you have some business cards from your own country? Could you/we make a scan of that? We can change private data in Photoshop if you please.

MOVIES: 1-2 slides in PPT
Could mention three great movies (in the local language) from your country.

WEIRD THINGS: 2-3 slides in PPT
What typicalities exist in your country, that people can see hardly anywhere else? Thanks for including the local name and ideally an image and small in-text explanation.

TRANSLATIONS: please mail separately in an MS Word file

Can you please provide Sander with translations (include country specific alphabet letters also in your PowerPoint) of the following phrases or words:

English	Your language
Cross-Cultural Business Skills	
Sander Schroevers	**(only if different script, or first name: e.g. Sandro etc.)**
Introduction	
Cultural Measurements	
Economic key figures	
Currency	
Any questions?	
Expert Interview	
Communication patterns	
Coffee break: 15 minutes	
Top companies	
Personal experience	
Non-verbal / Gestures	
Linguistics	
Further reading	
Film tip	
Music selection	
Best time to visit	
Top things	

PRONUNCIATION: 1 slide in PPT

Sander would like to record two things during a Skype or telephone conversation. Firstly I am looking for one or two tongue twisters pronounced.

Secondly I would like to ask for a spoken translation of this introductory phrase: "ladies and gentlemen hello, my name is …, I will present on …".

And that concludes the content related questions for the presentation.

Now let's look on the work schedule and division.

Working method

Start on the basis of this guideline, and make a planning with Sander.

Download the necessary PowerPoint template, work in that look-and-feel.

- **Surf to OneDrive**
- **STREAMS**
- **Ooopen lectures**
- **___Tips & Tools**

Than some days before the presentation, check together with Sander the status of your PPT. He can show you what he has so far, and perhaps you can provide him with feedback on his slides. During this (Skype?) meeting we will try to make one final PPT, and decide who will present which parts.

Naturally you can also present less minutes, should you prefer so.

You do not need to present a full class, as Sander will take care of parts of the presentation. Most probably your part will take place after the coffee break. But simply discuss your preferences.

40.   Exam related remarks

There are two individual exam moments:
- the **Mid-term Exam** in term 1
- the **Final Exam** in term 2

Each exam is composed of a mixture of questions. You will receive detailed exam guidelines during the exam trainings (24/7 web lectures) for both exams. Besides you can read detailed explanations in the exam guidelines further in this book.

Just the book?
Indeed most of the questions are taken from TXTBK. But we also use selected web lectures as a direct question source. We ofer pdf versions of the lesson essentials. These are summaries of the PowerPoints, which are made available through OneDrive, in the folder 'Exam related'. Lastly, a small percentage of particular cross-cultural business knowledge might be covered in the lectures, and not in any published or online material. These may be used as an integral part of the exams. But please no worries about that as it hardly ever happens.

Computer-based exams
The exams are computerised exams, meaning that you will be sitting in a computer room. All questions can therefore be answered by simple mouse-clicks. With the ever larger amounts of CCBS participants, we were looking for a way to cut down on the huge piles of correctable exams. Computerised exams offered us that advantage. But also as a student you benefit, as it means no more waiting for grades. We now are able to upload your results a lot quicker.

But shouldn't exams consist of more than multiple-choice questions? Well, in our case actually *not*. This as both the Final Exam as well as the Midterm Exam only represent 5 credits. And as the semester's main assessments are for the Country Profile and the International Survey assignment, there is no (accreditation) need for any open questions in this case.

Review inzage

Exam papers may not be returned to students. This as the questions are taken from a tailormade 'Itembank' (database), meaning that questions always may return at any given exam. Specific results and/or questions can be verbally discussed at the discretion of the instructor. Review takes place on an appointment-only base.

Exam Time & Date

CCBS LessonPlan lists all regular exams and resits on its last page. Secondly an exam schedule showing the date and hours of examination for both regular and resit exams, is published each semester on the Faculty of Business and Economics intranet website. Thirdly it is also possible to check on mytimetable.hva.nl (or for Dutch: rooster.hva.nl) what time and date exams are scheduled, provided you check this choice after logging in. In general CCBS exams are timetabled in the evening's slots of Tuesdays or Thursdays starting at 19:30 hrs. Sometimes resit exams can be timetabled on Saturdays, when different starting times may apply. Try to arrive earlier, to check which class room you are listed for, and move to the correct floor. Be aware in case you aren't listed on the attendance list, this will also take up some time. People arriving late, may only enter as a group after 20 minutes.

Exam Locations, which room?

Other than the name of the building, not much can be said until the afternoon prior to the exam, when the exam rooms will be announced on the whiteboard on the first floor, just behind the escalators. On them you can see your name on one of the attendance lists, also indicating which class room. **Therefore please do NOT mail or call your lecturers, as they do NOT yet know this information.** Usually the first arriving students post a photo of the class room information on Facebook as a courtesy to the other students. Mind you that Sander usually is working abroad the very minute classes do not demand his AUAS presence...

Testing recommendations

All CCBS exams are made according to AUAS' testing standards, laid out in the *'Toetsafnameprotocol HvA - Digitale toets'*. Our questions database has been developed in close cooperation and guidance of the Coordinator Digital Testing of the Faculty of Business and Economics.

Teaching and Examination Regulations (OER)

All tasks and learning outcomes in this semester are based on the 'Teaching and Examination Regulations' or 'OER' as it is called in Dutch. This document includes all the regulations relating to the educational programme, the examinations and testimonials, testing and assessment.

EVC vrijstellingen

The part-time programmes are structured according to the principle of Competencies Acquired Elsewhere (in Dutch: 'EVC => vrijstellingen voor opleidings-onderdelen'). This means that on the basis of your work experience, you may qualify for certain exemptions. Based on your registration form, an interview will be held to determine whether or not you qualify for an exemption. An assessment will be made by two certified assessors and there are fees involved in this procedure. For further details, please see: www.evc.hva.nl

TDV Dyslexia

The purpose of TDV exam arrangements is to help disabled students, those with a specific learning difference or medical condition to perform to their full ability, without giving them an unfair advantage over other students.

At AUAS (HvA) there is extra-time allowance for dyslexic students, provided you are already registered as such at your own study AUAS (HvA) programme. If you are studying via a foreign partner institution, or via the Dutch Kies-Op-Maat system, you should in the first instance contact the Part-time Academy student counsellor Ms. Francis van HEKELEN [**f.van.hekelen@hva.nl**], Phone: +31-(0)6-21158339. She will need to have a written proof document, and will further process your TDV-status for both exams at the CCBS-minor.

What?
If eligible, you will be given extra time in minutes per hour of the exam and the additional minutes will be added to the overall standard time of the exam. For example: 15 minutes extra time per hour will increase the total time of a 2 hour exam to 2 hours 30 minutes. Additionally you are to be tested in an alternate class room: the 'TDV-room'. This room will be announced on the afternoon of the actual exam day itself, through the whiteboards near the escalator on the first floor. The lecturers do NOT know this, by the way. When entering the exam you are listed on the specific TDV-attendance list, or otherwise need to show a printed e-mail confirmation.

We advise you to make the necessary arrangements as early as possible in the semester. CCBS is part of the Part-time Academy at AUAS/HvA. Should you need to contact our own department please ask Ms. Petra LEUVEN [p.w.leuven@hva.nl] for further details.

Midterm Exam

The Midterm Exam is an obliged part of the semester Cross-Cultural Business Skills, given near the middle of the semester. This text explains you the concept, the reading material, and the exam itself. The Midterm Exam accounts for five (5) credits/ECTS. The exam will last exactly ONE (1) hour. It is meant for all officially joining the CCBS minor (i.e.: part-time, fulltime, Kies-Op-Maat, professionals-track, exchange students).

Exam content outline
The exam covers topics including effective cross-cultural communication for the national (business) cultures of France, India and Singapore. Furthermore it verifies your knowledge on applied research skills in the field of referencing, APA citation and academic writing style requirements. Below is a list of chapters that were used as a reference to create the Midterm Exam. If you read and study these chapters, making the exam should constitute no problem whatsoever.

Learning materials
TXTBK Cross Cultural Business Skills, by Schroevers & Dogan (Eds.), CCBS press. ISBN: 978-90-79646-28-9, only use the 2017 edition or more recent publications. From TXTBK just the following chapters need to be studied;

Chapter 23. Citing sources
NOTE: the beginning is most important, therefore study any tables just as passive knowledge.
Chapter 24. Style Guide
NOTE: just study this chapter in a light or uncomprehensive way.
Chapter 39. France
Chapter 40. India
Chapter 41. Singapore

Test design toetsmatrijs
The exam contains 30 questions to be answered in 1 hour. The approximate percentage of the examination devoted to each content area, is noted in the column called 'Weight'. The following table offers an outline of the learning goals and content areas covered in the examination.

LEARNING GOALS - the student can:	Remember	Apply	Analyse	Evaluate	Weight	Amount
1. Demonstrate the impact of given national cultures on a described management case.			2		6,7%	2
2. Distinguish principles of effective cross-cultural communication for the French culture.		2	3	2	23,3%	7
3. Distinguish principles of effective cross-cultural communication for the Indian culture.	2	2	3	3	33,3%	10
4. Distinguish principles of effective cross-cultural communication for the Singaporean culture.	1	1	3	2	23,3%	7
5. Employ research skills in the field of referencing, APA citation and academic writing style requirements.	2	2			13,3%	4
totals:	5	7	11	7	100%	30

Exam questions
All test questions are all in a multiple-choice style, of which the majority is according to the True/False format. A smaller amount of questions is in the A-B-C-D-format, with one correct answer and three incorrect options. Below you can see selected samples of the types of questions that may appear on the exam.

Grading scale criteria
Although CCBS works with a computer exam, we do first need to manually double-check all raw scores and percentage scores, to decide which questions need a second review. Furthermore we will need to discuss on the so-called cut-off score (*cesuur* in Dutch), only after which we can calculate the results and consequent grades. This is done following the so-called 'four-eyes-principle', meaning a second opinion. The grading of midterm exams in general is based on the below listed grading criteria (depending on the validity of questions).

Grade:	10	9	8	7	6	5	4	3	2	1
Correct nr. of questions	29-30	26-28	23-25	20-22	16-19	14-15	11-13	8-10	5-7	< 4

You will need to pass the exam with a minimum score of 5.5 points in order to qualify for credits. Normally (without disregarded questions) the minimum score for a pass is: 16 correct questions. Do it, do it, do it! The posting of grades will take place soon after the exam, via anonymised grade listings (by student number) which will be posted on OneDrive (folder: Exam related) and as a notification on the Facebook semester page.

MOCK EXAM FOPTENTAMEN

Please read carefully before starting your exam

Exam:	Cross Cultural Business Skills Minor
Module code:	MCCBS
Course no., SIS code:	6616MTEXTD
Date:	Tuesday 69 March 2051, 19.30-21.30 hrs
Exam duration:	One hour (60 minutes)
Authorised resources:	No books etc. allowed during this examination

Please read the following statements and/or options, and select the right answer.

Sample question 1:
In India it is always best to put, made business agreements on paper,
as contracts are a safe assurance and legally fairly binding documents.
- A) True
- B) False

Sample question 2:
The art of oratory skills, is much appreciated professionally in:
- I. France
- II. Singapore
- III. India

- A) All statements (I, II, and III) are correct.
- B) Statements I and II are correct, statement III is incorrect.
- C) Statement II is incorrect, statements I and III are correct.
- D) None of the above are correct.

Sample question 3:
In order to reproduce copyrighted material like photographs or graphic
charts, no prior permission from the author or copyright-owner is needed.
- A) True
- B) False

That's it for the samples, G☺od luck with the real exam !

SOURCE: TXTBK pp156-167. In the paragraph called 'Negotiations the value of the contract, it states clearly that Indians tend not to consider a contract as a binding document. Hence, the right answer here is B) False.

The right answer here is C) To come at this choice you need to have read all three country chapters, and compare them on a skill.

The right answer here is B). See the note on page 51 of TXTBK, bottom of the page.

Final Exam

The Final Exam is an obliged part of the semester Cross-Cultural Business Skills, given near the end of the lessons (the semester is longer for finishing stream tasks and so forth). This text explains you the concept, the reading material, and the exam itself. The Final Exam accounts for five (5) credits/ECTS. The exam will last exactly TWO (2) hours. It is meant for all officially joining the CCBS minor (i.e.: part-time, fulltime, Kies-Op-Maat, professionals-track, exchange students).

Exam content outline

The exam covers topics around effective cross-cultural business skills and the summaries of PowerPoints of selected evening lessons (in pdf on OneDrive). Furthermore it verifies your knowledge of three web lectures (direct URLs in WatchList.pdf on OneDrive). Below is a list of online video recorded classes that were used as a reference to create the Final Exam. If you read and study these web lectures and the aforementioned chapters, making the exam should constitute no problem whatsoever.

Learning materials

TXTBK Cross Cultural Business Skills, by Schroevers & Dogan (Eds.), CCBS press. ISBN: 978-90-79646-28-9, only use the 2017 edition or more recent publications. From TXTBK just the following chapters need to be studied;

- The entire Final Exam section of **TXTBK** (i.e. AFTER the three mid-term countries). So from chapter Negotiating internationally until the last chapter.

- Web lecture: '**Culture-shock + Stereotypes**' (49 minutes)
  http://hva.mediamission.nl/Mediasite/Play/278cdaf2e6b74c41a0c54ba3c44c8ef71d?
  catalog=8eec4c35-da6f-4ca9-8b28-16c2ce2b48c4

- Web lecture: '**Global leadership**' (33 minutes)
  http://hva.mediamission.nl/Mediasite/Play/572aeff4c1f1424fb4f64b05a2b80d6a1d

- Web lecture: '**German** business culture' (35 minutes)
  http://hva.mediamission.nl/Mediasite/Play/32c01fefe8454616b57c39898d53cb951d

Where? The Web Lectures

The web lectures can be reached easiest by clicking on the 'Watch-list' pdf we have uploaded in the root folder on OneDrive, or copy the URL's mentioned there. An alternative way is to surf to: www.hva.nl/webcolleges
=> click on 'Economie en Management', and there search for 'CCBS' or 'Schroevers'. When accessing outside the HvA school network, you will need to log-in first. To do so, click on the arrow in the right hand top corner, and choose 'Login'. This will lead you to a dialogue box, use your regular HvA account info. When opting for a web lecture, a second window opens. You can change the screen lay-out and size. You can pause, play the video faster or slower, and skip those slides you do not wish to hear explained, simply by clicking on the slide of your choice. Personally I really feel that this is innovative education.
24/7 available, and your teacher in silence, just whenever you want it ☺

Test design toetsmatrijs

The exam contains 40 questions to be answered in 2 hours. The approximate percentage of the examination devoted to each content area, is noted in the column called 'Weight'. The following table offers an outline of the learning goals and content areas covered in the examination.

Test Design (Toetsmatrijs)

Learning goals The student can:	Type of question					Weight	# Ques tions
	Reproduction	Production					
	Remember, Understand	Apply	Analyse	Evaluate	Create		
1. Describe principles of effective cross-cultural communication for given **national cultures**.	5	5	5			37,5%	15
2. Apply adapted cross-cultural scenarios for **business skills** that have been explained in class and/or written material.		5	5			25%	10
3. Giving advice on relevant **cross-cultural dimensions** in business and management scenarios.	2		3	3		20%	8
4. Demonstrate the impact of national cultures on a described **management** case.	3			4		17,5%	7
Totals	10	10	13	7		100%	40

Exam questions

All test questions are all in a multiple-choice style, of which the majority is according to the A-B-C-D-format, with one correct answer and three incorrect options. A smaller amount of questions is in the False True/ format. Below you can see selected samples of the types of questions that may appear on the exam.

Grading scale criteria

Although CCBS works with a computer exam, we do first need to manually double-check all raw scores and percentage scores, to decide which questions need a second review. Furthermore we will need to discuss on the so-called cut-off score (*cesuur* in Dutch), only after which we can calculate the results and consequent grades. This is done following the so-called 'four-eyes-principle', meaning a second opinion.

You will need to pass the exam with a minimum score of 5.5 points in order to qualify for credits. Normally (without disregarded questions) the minimum score for a pass is: 21 correct questions. Do it, do it, do it! The posting of grades will take place soon after the exam, via anonymised grade listings (by student number) which will be posted on **OneDrive** (folder: Exam related) and as a notification on the **Facebook semester page**.

Amsterdam University
of Applied Sciences

MOCK EXAM FOPTENTAMEN

Please read carefully before starting your exam

Exam:	Cross Cultural Business Skills Minor
Module code:	MCCBS
Course no., SIS code:	6616FIEXTD
Date:	Tuesday 69 March 2051, 19.30-21.30 hrs
Exam duration:	Two hours (120 min.)
Authorised resources:	No books etc. allowed during this examination

© the copyright of this exam is held by the AUAS (hva)

Please read the following statements and/or options, and select the right answer.

Sample question 1:
The academic GLOBE project by House et al, researched leadership differences across cultures by polling:

A)   Almost a thousand managers in Western-Europe.
B)   Almost 17,000 managers in some 60 countries.
C)   Almost a thousand managers worldwide.
D)   None of the above.

(The right answer here is B). To come at this choice you need to have studied the web lecture on leadership.

Sample question 2:
The adjacent placed gesture can be considered positively or not, depending on the country. Please choose the one alternative that you consider correct.

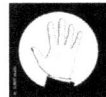

A)   Positive in Germany and Holland, negative in Greece and Souther
B)   Positive in Holland and the USA, negative in Malta and France.
C)   Positive in Japan and Spain, negative in Brazil and France.
D)   None of the above.

The right answer here is A). To come at this choice you need to have read the section Finger-talk of the chapter called GESTURES.

Sample question 3:
40% of expat assignments are considered unsuccessful due to the inability of expat and family to adjust to social and business life of a host country.

A) True
B) False

SOURCE: Web lecture on Culture Shock. In fact the amount in reality may be even higher than the mentioned 40%. Hence the right answer here is A) True

That's it for the samples, G☺od luck with the real exam !

165

Exam registration

As a general rule: all students of a present semester are automatically registered for the REGULAR EXAMS. Students doing a MINOR as a principle, do NEITHER need to register for that minor's RESIT EXAMS.
Just showing your AUAS student pass or an officially recognised ID will do, in order to be written down manually on the attendance list.

Nevertheless this takes time, and when nervous/focused this is something you perhaps do not want to do. Anyway it probably is better to check beforehand via the SIS administration site, whether you are listed for the regular (midterm + final) exams. In the case you're not and you'd still prefer to be listed, the following pointers give you a step-by-step approach. The enrolment period for exams starts about a month before the actual exam, and it runs for three weeks. You can verify your exam enrolments and/or enroll for resits via SIS (SIS is AUAS' online course and grade administration system). Should you have any questions or encounter problems when enrolling for a resit, during the enrolment periods you may stop by the Service-point on the 1st floor of Wibauthuis. Service-point opening hours: Mon-Thu between 08-20 hrs, Fri 08-17 hrs, Sat 09-14 hrs. For more elaborate exam registration questions you can contact the Education Office via onderwijsbureau.fbe@hva.nl or via www.hva.nl/digitalservicepoint. Mind you, they tend to be busy before exam periods, so better to plan ahead.

Exam Protocol

The following rules on conduct apply to students sitting CCBS computer-based exams. To get access to your exam room you will need to identify yourself with your AUAS (HvA) student card. In case you haven't brought (or received) your AUAS (HvA) student card, bring your passport, ID card or driver's license. Without any of the aforementioned identification ways, unfortunately no entrance to the exam is allowed. When entering the computer class-room you will need to sign the attendance list. Standard all official participants are registered for the regular exam, but NOT for a resit exam. In case you did NOT register for the exam beforehand. It is allowed in the case of a minor course to register manually. However this takes time from the present invigilator, who needs to also organize many other things. Therefore do not risk to have to start twenty minutes later, and simply register beforehand when necessary (i.e. in case of a resit exam).

You are required to comply in all respects with instructions issued by the exam invigilators, before and during the exam. Students are asked to leave all personal items, including watches, cell phones, laptops, bags, or backpacks in a designated place. Students may not sit for an examination if they bring personal items to their computer table. Furthermore hats with brims or bills (e.g. baseball caps), and/or coats may not be worn during the examination. The allocation of seats is according to instructions issued by the exam invigilators. Each computer is surrounded by privacy screens, which must remain in place for the duration of the examination. Candidates must not talk to, or attempt to communicate with, other candidates during the exam under any circumstances. You are not allowed to use, or attempt to use, or intend to use, any unauthorised materials while the exam is in progress. Going to the rest room is only permitted after finalising your exam. Unless you have a medical statement about visiting rest-rooms (yes, that exists...). Only thirty (30) minutes after the official start of the exam, is it possible to leave the computer exam room.

Listen carefully to the instructions which the invigilator will read out and make sure you follow the instructions on your computer screen. If you have any questions, raise your hand to ask for help. Mind you that most present invigilators aren't regular lecturers, but external hired trained exam invigilators. They are instructed by a colleague from the central exam organisation. In fact your lecturers have almost NO role in this all.

Late?
There is just one moment when students that have arrived late are allowed to enter, namely twenty (20) minutes after the start. Extra time, beyond the scheduled end of the examination will not be granted to make up for students arriving late. Anyone arriving after the twenty-minutes entrance possibility, is not allowed to sit for an examination anymore.

Computer-based Exams

Below is an introduction on some practical aspects of sitting a computer-based exam. Reading this section may help you to concentrate on what really matters: namely making a good exam, instead of being distracted by all kind of more technical issues. Once you have been assigned a seat, (after leaving all not allowed things, at a designated spot). You can start the exam preparations.

Step 1: **Logging in to the exam mode**
- The PC is in the 'Secure Test Environment'
- You will need to click on the icon on the desktop: 'HvA concern desktop'.
- Preparing the image will take some 10 seconds.
- Now log-in with your usual AUAS/HvA username + password combination.

Step 2: **Opening the exam software**
- Now you need to log on to the exam software.
- Type your AUAS/HvA student number
- And a password that you will be given.
- Here you choose the exam it concerns.
- Now wait for the invigilator to manually enter a password.
- Once **submit** is entered, a time registration starts running.
- After that you just follow the on-screen instructions.
- You can always make changes in any answers, during the exam.
- You can navigate between the questions, via a small square in the upper left corner,
- If you have any questions: raise your hand in the air, (this as asking attention verbally isn't allowed).

Step 3: **Logging off correctly**
- Ask one of the invigilators to check your exit screen.
- Now click on the Windows button on the keyboard.
- Click on the Exam Manager icon.
- Click TWO TIMES on '**Submit** Exam'

PREPARATORY **TEST TAKING TIPS**

- Read the above guidelines or watch the online video.
- Send your boy- or girlfriend (or spouse) on safari.
- Study according to the tips and mock exam above.
- Forget Facebook, switch off your phone, Spotify and Netflix.
- Headache? Well that usually goes away after 5 minutes.
- Study 2,5 hours per day section (meaning: 10 hours a day). You can always sleep when you're dead.
- After the exam don't forget to celebrate a good result. In other words: work harder => party harder

ACING **THE CCBS EXAMS**

- If you read the many paragraphs you will manage easily. The way Sander makes a question is just by reading the text sections, and asking what could be a question here. Simple as that. If you prepare accordingly, you can't go wrong.
- Brainstorm possible questions with other CCBS students also taking the course.
- Begin studying early, because multiple choice exams tend to focus on details, and you cannot retain many details effectively in short-term memory.
- Read each statement carefully, and pay attention to the qualifiers and keywords

- Better to divide work and play. Quite a bit of research suggests that spaced study practice is generally superior to massed study practice. For example, you'll get better results out of three 2-hour blocks, than one 6-hour block.
- Because multiple choice exams contain many questions, it forces you to be familiar with a much broader range of material than open question exams do .
- It's been demonstrated that when you create extra emotional pressure, performance suffers. The most constructive approach is to put in as much time as you can afford.
- A certain amount of anxiety is normal (or even useful). Once the test begins slow down. Take your time over the directions and make sure you are clear on what you're being asked to do.
- Try not to forget to check the clock, don't spend too much time on difficult items.
- First answers are often correct! But don't be afraid to change your original answer upon reflection. For example, a 2005 study found that when students changed their answers, they went from wrong to right 51% of the time, right to wrong 25% of the

time, and wrong to a different wrong answer 23% of the time (Journal of Personality and Social Psychology, Vol. 88).

- If the test answer is only partly true or is true only under certain narrow conditions, then it's probably not the right answer. Don't be trapped by double negatives.
- No exam items are intended as a trick question, or to be deceptive. We do fair play.
- If any part of the question is false, then the entire statement is false but just because part of a statement is true doesn't necessarily make the entire statement true.
- Usually on most tests there are more true answers, than false ones.
- Try taking a few breaks during the exam by stopping for a moment, shutting your eyes, and taking some deep breaths. Periodically clearing your head in this way can help you stay fresh during the exam session.
- If you try to do several things at once, you increase the probability of a mistake.
- If you've just finished the last question with time to spare, take the opportunity to check for mistakes like skipped questions or misread items. You might recall a new detail and pick up some additional points. Remember, you get no points for being the first person to finish the exam. Keep your cool for the dance-floor.
- All righty, these were some strategies for maximising your success, but the best way to improve your chances, is to study like a mad-man before the exam! Go, go, go!!!

Good luck!

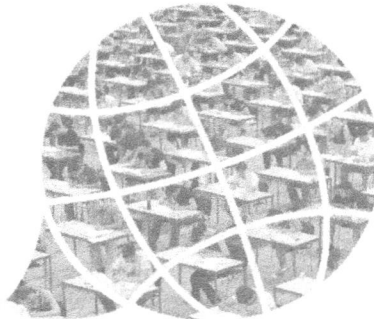

CCBS TXTBK

41. Grades

Please be aware of the fact that doing a minor at a school as large as the AUAS will have some administrative consequences. We'll try to keep any administrative issues to a minimum for you, but at times it could involve an extra little step. Also please realise that all grades are entered AT ONCE in the final weeks of the semester, meaning AFTER the book party. In case of alternative assignments or resits, the entering week may differ of course. For exchange students with a known need, we are willing to make a tailor made solution.

Grade calculator tool

Sometimes you want to know exactly what you need to score for an exam or assignment in order to still make a higher mark possible as final result of a course, right? Well this simple tool in Excel does exactly that.
Besides, it is a quick way to know your final result for the CCBS minor as well. Log-in to OneDrive and click on: **=> Downloads => GradeCalculator** and download the Excel file to your computer, to log your own grades, should you be interested.

Exams reader

Tentamenbundel

Excerpt from THT Culture Compass

42. France

Introduction

Most French managers do not simply work for achievement, as it is considered too individualistic a quality. Individuals should not aim to single out their own contributions, but rather use their visionary powers to benefit their group. Individual achievement is, therefore, lost in the interest of the group, though not the individual's ability to guide the group. Not everything that makes money or produces profit is worth achieving in the first place. French managers go beneath achievement to ask, "What is the purpose of our effort?" "To what should we ascribe value in the first place?" A key characteristic of French businessmen is their extreme status-consciousness. It is extremely hard for the French to disdain social stereotypes. They are vivid and affect social interaction. Social status in larger organizations protects autonomy but involves many restrictions. Educational credentials are considered to be verifiable discriminators of organizational hierarchies, expressed in salary and position. At the top is the autocrat or patriarch - often referred to as le patron - who is the *Président-Directeur Général* (PDG, or chairman and chief-executive-officer rolled into one). The separation of functions, increasingly common in some Western European countries, is still rare in France, though the established organizational hierarchy in France is something that even the French find amusing. The political structure of the country serves as a model for business. Vertical administration, clear-cut divisions, ordered hierarchies, central planning are important features of companies. Education plays a key role in determining status. Age too is a great determiner. Though age in itself does not guarantee power, older people are certainly treated with due deference.

Personalities

Before meeting with an employee of a French corporation, you should invest plenty of time in studying the structure of the organization, its interests, and most importantly, who is in charge. Take a look, too, at its history. Relationships are very particular in French society, and therefore, you should make the right connection at the right moment. It is very important that you take the time to get to know your counterpart, and what he/she wants. Don't forget, however, that the French feel that rules should be flexible. So just when you think you know their plan, it could be changed to adapt to a different circumstance. Be prepared for this particularism.

Secrecy And Privacy
French corporations tend to be more secretive than American corporations. Agreements reached are typically private unless there is an agreement to release details. This is part of the particularistic ethic. Our agreement is entre nous, between us, special to the two parties, who have unique access to each other. This kind of understanding is more advantageous if others do not know about it. So strong is the ethic of secrecy that Michelin, for example, will not patent its products since this invites scrutiny of its innovations. In part, the reason for privacy is so corporations make more money. To boast of this is to invite envy and dislike. In any case, it is considered vulgar. There is a tradition to be discrete about making money.

Intellectual Capacity, More Important Than Work, Results Or Money
In meetings with French managers, you might encounter the "mental gymnastics" that strike many foreigners as excessive. Yet, for most French managers, the ultimate worth of an individual is not so much in what can be substantiated, such as his/her track record, profit indices, etcetera but in his/her special intellectual capacity or ability to organize knowledge in incomparable and unique ways. In French culture, the intellectual is still respected. Being an intellectual is a profession, a calling in life.

Private Deals
In private meetings, French managers may suggest a private deal, a personal understanding that is not put on the record. Americans may prefer a more public or formalized promise that may be used, if necessary, to seek legal compliance. French preferences for private understandings should not be taken for untrustworthiness but understood as cultural custom. Privacy may even make the obligation stronger.

You're On Your Own
Meeting the French can become rather annoying in the sense that they feel that their organization is pitted against yours. Both groups have interests, which need to be defended. And since the French like to fight out their differences, they may

seem rude and aggressive. If your organization normally sends one, or at best two, representatives, you might encounter even more difficulties; you will most probably feel like you are on your own since a French delegation usually consists of more than three people. Regardless of whether you go alone or with a team, you should be prepared and try to remain calm. Study the goals of the organization you're dealing with and try to convince your counterparts of your good will. You should make an effort to make a good impression, especially in the beginning of the meeting, and show them that your interests coincide.

Everybody Agrees

Unlike individualistic cultures, the French would rather not vote in order to reach a decision. That is not to say that they never vote. They simply prefer to come to a consensus. By French definition, a group of people from the same organization has the same needs and interests. How could it be possible that one or two from that group should not agree with a proposal? A group should be so tight and close that it becomes one entity that cannot be divided. Since the French prefer consensus, you might get annoyed with the sheer length of the decision making process. Though you may prefer to vote, they would rather argue until they all agree. They will also try to convince you of the fact that you have made the right decision. Do not try to interfere and don't get upset. In the end you will get there anyway, whether you vote or not. The final decision, however, will be made by the patron. Consensus may exist within each group, but the highest echelon will eventually impose a decision on the lower ones.

Shall We Have Lunch?

A French business lunch can take more than two hours. Your French partner wants to eat his way graciously and cautiously to a few business remarks with coffee. After initial informal conversation, business issues are usually discussed during the main course, or even later, towards the end of the meal. Occasionally, a shorter, simpler lunch is preferred, perhaps only with one glass of wine or just mineral water. This is more a matter of changing generations and regional differences. No Frenchman can digest a new business proposal until dessert, or as the French put it entre la poire et le fromage, between the pear and the cheese (Unlike some other culinary traditions, according to French gastronomy, after the main entrée, it is best to present a fruit dish before the cheese tray). A meeting over a meal may not even seem to have a particular agenda; people just talk with the idea of building rapport or getting better acquainted with other people. It is a sort of preliminary "feeling out", and this frequently takes place over a few lunches or meetings. If your business lunch has been arranged in the executive dining room of the company, it is a special honor, giving a clear indication how much importance your hosts attach to your visit.

Let's Beat Around The Bush

What other cultures consider to be beating around the bush, the French consider to be necessary preliminaries. You must listen very attentively to the opening statements in a French colleague's discussion, in order to decode its implicit meaning, even though the French can be very revealing to those who know how to read them. In France, an eloquent and witty colleague, one who can present an opinion in an interesting, challenging and also entertaining way, is much appreciated. A little theatrical touch, a dramatic edge and preferably a solution left to the imagination is what defines a good French discussion. "We are seduced by brilliance," Claude Bébéar told Polly Platt. "French people look for solutions which are the most brilliant and the most elegant, not the most pragmatic or efficient." French managers are cocorico, they crow like roosters. Each individual aime paraître, "loves to show off". Many Americans get very impatient with this tendency. They hear a vast amount of talk but no conclusions or decisions. But for the French, that is not the purpose of the meeting. It is to enrich and develop a shared context that members of the group can use to improve their work. This is more important to French managers than pledging themselves publicly to achieving specific tasks. French managers have complained that they can never get a sophisticated answer from Americans. American managers have complained that they can never get a simple answer from French managers.

Infuriating Ambiguity

Cultures that are diffuse and high-context (having an indirect, circuitous communication style) are also very ambiguous by the standards of most English-speaking people. If A is qualified by B, C and D and if there is tension with X, which is part of the overall pattern, then it becomes hard to speak plainly and tell which side is up. Subtleties, nuances, hints, meaningful silences, things not said, enigmatic gestures, or understatement - all these aspects strike American managers as evasive, if not deceptive. Yet the result of such intense relationships may be agreements to disagree, different interpretations of the same event, deniability of unlawful acts, official ignorance and unofficial understandings. It is a tangled web indeed that is woven by many diffuse cultures. People from specific cultures are often confused because they tend to focus more on explicit messages rather than implicit messages.

Getting The "Look" From French Men Or Women

Although French managers and other citizens are not generally friendly to strangers, they will "look you over" if they find you attractive. It is not a glance of friendship. It is rarely an attempt to pick you up or solicit you. It is a look of approval and admiration. French people give and receive these sorts of looks freely, and all concerned enjoy one another's beauty without embarrassment. A man may also tell a woman how ravissante she is without a sexual agenda. It is simply spontaneous admiration of someone else's grace and elegance. You can accept the compliment and go your way. Although women may appraise handsome men without being thought forward, they should not speak first to strange men. That would be taken as soliciting. When a man and woman pass each other and both look back, it may make both feel good all day long!

Etiquette

Etiquette is a French word and an important one. The typical office-day in France begins in the morning with a handshake and a greeting. If you are greeting, say Jacques Moreau, you should say, "Bonjour Monsieur Moreau", or if you know him well, "Bonjour Jacques". You would be wise to greet people in the shop where you usually buy provisions. Personal greetings are far more welcome than impersonal ones (See Universalism-Particularism). If you know it is Madame Blazot, then use her name. "Au revoir Madame Blazot." Nothing gets Americans and Britons into more trouble than getting down to business before issuing diffuse greetings. You must establish at least minimal rapport before making demands of people. If the person addressed does not respond to your request but says "Bonjour" instead, you are being reproved for being "mal elevé" (badly raised). Nearly all French women, even quite young ones, may be called Madame, which is more formal than Mademoiselle. The higher status person usually extends his/her hand first, so if you do not extend your hand to subordinates, neither will they. But then they may consider you mal elevé. Do not shake hands with the same person twice. It is a sure sign that you don't remember doing so earlier and that your initial greeting was therefore insincere. "It is," as one American put it, "as if you were running for Mayor of New York."

Overlapping Communication

An impression of emotional intensity in French people comes not simply from their physical proximity, their vivid gestures and their volatility, but from the fact that they seem unable or unwilling to wait for the end of your sentence. A very visible desire to interrupt and an extraordinary series of expressions is going on while you speak, just inches in front of you. Foreigners who are not accustomed to this style of communication may lose their own train of thought or complain about being constantly interrupted. In this respect, French communication patterns follow the Latin style. In France, conversation is viewed more like fencing, with thrust and parry and all the excitement of verbal conflict. Viewpoints are supposed to clash, and interruption and face-work are seen as ways of contributing to an elegant fencing match. The idea is to enjoy yourself, not drag your point of view to some glorious culmination. You win by being clever and à pointe, to the point, not by running unchecked down the football field to score your goal.

Passionate Commitment

A young American manager who had recently been assigned to the Paris office of a banking conglomerate complained to a colleague about French meetings. "Everyone emotes about some pet item on the agenda and then we go on to the next one. Nothing is ever decided. What I have noticed is that people are asked to do what they are most animated about. That way they get to do what they really want. You have to endure this intellectual fireworks display, but it does appear to have logic. People volunteer to do what they feel most passionately about. It works after a fashion although the idea itself and the passion are much more admired than the result. We rarely look at the results of last month's terrific performance in meetings." The underlying logic is the belief that people will do well when they care passionately about something, especially if they have committed themselves by their behavior during public meetings. Every solution should be personalized. Every protagonist should be inspired by rigorous intellectual conviction. Opposition will tend to increase passion and increase commitment.

They Shoot You Down In Flames

There can be some misunderstanding about the purpose of French meetings. Decisions are not made in meetings nor are solutions accepted. Everyone competes with everyone else in offering exciting ideas, which are assailed from every side by counter-arguments that test these propositions to the breaking point. The task is usually allotted to the person whose conception was the most brilliant, thereby testing people's passion for their own ideas. It may appear that they are "shooting you down in flames", as one American electronics engineer put it. He told a consultant that during a meeting, the French came up with a dozen alternatives to his solution, but that his boss afterwards informed him that they had found his idea brilliant. Still, they had to attack his proposition in order to test it and to have an exciting meeting.

Courtesy
To greet someone in France implies not only shaking hands but also saying a few polite words. Shaking hands with everyone both when meeting and when parting is mandatory, regardless of how time consuming this process may be. Not to do so may give offense. To say a general "hello" to everybody in the room is simply impolite. The order in which you greet people is decided by general rules of social precedence. At the workplace, every colleague is greeted with a handshake in the morning and, in most cases, also when leaving in the afternoon. There are slight variations in this practice, which you can observe easily. At the same time, however, any other form of bodily contact is not appreciated.

One Step Between Love And Hate
The French have a well-known expression, de la haine à l'amour il n'y a qu'un pas, ("From hate to love is just one step.") Good friends and close relations can get furiously angry with each other almost out of the blue and show great affection the next moment as if nothing had happened. This sudden volatility can alarm foreigners, but it is considered quite normal to most French people. This strongly contrasts with Anglo-American practice, which views affection as "good" and anger as "bad". By comparison, French managers may never really be at ease with you until you show evidence of disliking something or someone. What they admire is a wide range of emotional expression, and someone who pretends to be "happy" all the time is not trusted. The French are much less likely to talk about feelings. They will not calmly say, "I am feeling angry." They will radiate anger.

Do You Speak French? Parlez-vous français?
Although many modern-day French executives have a good command of English, they may prefer not to use it. It may be a matter of national pride or fear of making mistakes and looking foolish, or it may simply be strategic. The French prefer to stick to French and their knowledge of other languages, apart from Roman languages, is limited. (Remember that this is a stereotype and your business colleague in France may speak the Queen's English, as well as other

languages.). The French value eloquence highly. A polished and grammatically correct language is taken for granted by most people. Expressing oneself brilliantly, making use of a rich vocabulary, never exhausting one's resources in a discussion, all of these are highly valued by the French. Since eloquence is so positively valued, it follows that a person of few words or one who is taciturn is regarded with suspicion. Silence may also be interpreted as a sign of intellectual inferiority. A cultivated gentleman in France is someone who can carry on a sophisticated conversation on almost any topic in any situation. This explains the dilemma of the French when it comes to making conversation in English. Not being able to use French and its power of persuasion makes many French people feel somewhat awkward and disadvantaged. To refrain from participating in discussions or conversations, however, is an equally threatening idea; one does not wish to give the impression of not having an opinion. All these attitudes have become more flexible recently, because of increasing globalization, particularly in business.

The Senior Person Knows Everything
One of the consequences of taking knowledge, reasoning and intellectuality seriously is that the leader becomes the repository of all these contributions and is responsible for intellectual coordination. André Laurent asked managers from different nations if they agreed with this statement: "It is important for a manager to have at hand precise answers to most of the questions that his subordinates may raise about their work." The percentage of managers who agreed follows:

- Italy 66%
- France 53%
- Germany 46%
- Belgium 44%
- Switzerland 38%
- UK 27%
- Denmark 23%
- USA 18%
- Sweden 10%

The French superior is expected to have "conceptual mastery" over subordinates to an extent greater than most other countries. If you ascribe life-long aptitude to your best scholars, they must live up to their billing.

Reason Transcends

Reasoning power, as we have seen, is the supreme virtue. Talleyrand said of Napoleon's assassination of the Duc d'Enghien, "C'est pire qu'un crime, c'est une faute" (It is worse than a crime; it is a fault). Faulty reasoning is a more serious defect than criminal propensity! In French meetings much can be gained by inviting participants to share the same reasoning processes. Take time to state your premises clearly and then invite participants to deduce the logical conclusions from these premises. What should be avoided at all costs is rival deductions from different premises leading to opposite conclusions. If you are believed to be accusing a French person of being illogical, the fat may be truly in the fire.

Perfect Solutions

Senior managers, to whom logical reasoning has been ascribed, often aim for the perfect "scientific" solution. Science as conducted in the grandes écoles is the ideal. It is deductive, moving from theory to application. The theory must first be perfected and so become part of the wisdom ascribed to top managers.

There is much less of the American fly-by-the-seat-of-your-pants approach. If it works, Americans do not always need to know why. They think inductively from good results to generalizations, and they want to get to the market first, even if the theory is left behind.

French managers prefer to take longer, get the theory perfect and leave its application to subordinates, thereby maintaining the hierarchy. The most important value is to create intellectual coherence. Perfect applications are believed to spring from perfectly coherent work. The French generally dislike short cuts and regard high risk as the result of inadequate reasoning. If you are clever enough, you should be sure your theory works.

The French View On Time

The French view of time has real implications for the foreign visitor. Having to wait, for example, may be seen as one side's tactical weapons for negotiation; the people who have to wait are put in their place. All of this notwithstanding, once the French dedicate their time to you, they really dedicate it to you. You will not be sent off in a quarter of an hour. If you are to become their new business partner, client, or supplier, they would like to cultivate a good relationship.

Processes That Intermingle And Jostle Each Other

Edward Koster, an English engineer, just having completed a year with Elf

Aquitaine, had this to say about meetings in France. "Our meetings are curiously similar to chaotic political gatherings in which this or that cheering section reacts excitedly to the speakers and heckles them. I had always assumed that the speeches and applause had been rehearsed and were faked, but now I'm not sure. Because even after the show is over and the meeting comes to an end, they leave together, continuing the discussion. Meetings neither plan, nor decide, nor commit. It's as if they were running ideas in parallel and celebrating the connections they discover. In some strange way, it all works out as processes intermingle and jostle each other enthusiastically". Running processes in parallel during meetings increases the chance of fortuitous, lateral connections, or synchrony among processes. This also occurs between conversations, developing almost simultaneously while facilitating connections. The connections and the overlap between parallel processes will eventually allow the task to be performed rapidly; a second phase starts before the first is completed and so on.

Endless Objections Sabotage Deadlines
"I explained that the deadline was important," Steve Bronson was telling American friends in the coffee room. "So then I went around the room trying to get these French guys to commit. After all, it's a German client. There are penalty clauses! But I only got objections. No one, but no one, would promise to deliver by the 15th. If anything, they were competing with each other with fancy excuses." "What goes on with you lot?" I asked Gaspard, after the meeting. He's worked in the UK some years and I rely on him to explain the mysteries of French culture. "You have to talk it through with each person before the meeting," he said. "Consider their objections and discuss ways to get around them. The meeting is the place to announce agreements, not to create them. The trick is to present them in such a way that the participants can discuss and accept them. The real decision is usually made outside, before or after the meeting. Each one of them expects to have your ear first. Time is an agreed rendezvous, not an imposed deadline."

Cerebral Orientation
French inner-direction is "of the mind". The ideal is to get a concept into the public realm through skillful exposition. Products are not of themselves considered great ideas, unless they are complex and grand. Hence De Gaulle could ask a group of businessmen after World War II "Who are you, messieurs?" The implication being that though some of them had collaborated, but they had still done little to forge an identity for themselves. Making useful objects is not

enough and nor is making money. The closer you operate to the top of the abstraction ladder, the higher your status in France. Hence financial analysts and electronic engineers are considered superior to production managers and mechanical engineers. The greater the immateriality of your the task, the higher your standing. An ideal object gets its reputation more from the elegance of the idea than from its usefulness, although it should have both.

Representatives
When dealing with the French, you are advised to send representatives of equal or higher status, or with a similar educational background, rather than just experts in the field. It will save you a lot of time and could spare you the embarrassment of getting lost in the jungle of French hierarchy. It is necessary in order to facilitate the desired relationship building process. When you negotiate with a group, it is advisable to address first the most senior person. There is a very simple three-fold rule of social precedence that applies in all French interpersonal interactions: women before men, older people before younger ones, and superiors before subordinates. Of course, there is nothing exclusively French about these rules, but they are adhered to on just about every business or private occasion in France. Young people tend to be a bit less traditional in this respect.

Status Consciousness
Social status in France depends primarily on one's social origins, type of education and especially, on one's school. For years, in order to be somebody at the higher executive levels you had to have been trained at one of the prestigious grandes écoles. Once graduated, the privileged, self-confident meritocrats are well aware of their own value. In France, educational qualifications indicate status and competence in much the same way that salary indicates status in the USA. In most countries one's diploma is only of value during the first two to five years of one's career. In France, the value of a diploma lasts significantly longer.

Le Patron
There is a wide expectation for le patron, the boss, to be decisive, fearless but also formal, polite, good mannered. He is expected to have a better understanding of everything that goes on in the company than any subordinate, to have a firm opinion on every issue, even the most trivial, affecting the business, thereby showing interest and involvement in the work of others. At the

same time, he is expected to keep his distance, respect the hierarchical levels and generally display his position; anything else would create uneasiness and embarrassment. Against this background it becomes immediately obvious why it is so important to make sure in advance that initial contacts in France are established at the right hierarchical level.

The Classic Career Path

In France, a classic career path usually leads from civil service to industry. Routes to the top are limited and well-trodden. The preponderance of former civil servants in the higher échelons of management can be summed up in a couple of keywords. Elitism is one; dirigisme (interventionism) is another. The French civil service is where dirigisme and elitism meet. As huge sections of the French economy are still controlled by the state, the public service extends its influence to the private sector. Fifteen of the chairmen of France's top twenty-five companies (excluding banks and insurance companies) are former civil servants. A further eight are either the founders or the inheritors of family firms. Top executives are more likely to be parachuted into the top, than to work their way to the higher échelons of management through business performance or other achievements.

Does Our Reasoning Concur?

The process of ascribing status among French managers has much to do with sharing the same reasoning processes. If we seek to understand why sometimes French managers do as they have been asked to by their superiors, and on other occasions defy that authority, we can find the answer in whether the managers' raison has been convinced.

For French managers it is extremely important that their reasoning powers concur with those of their superiors. Comparison with other countries shows an extreme difference in compliance and defiance of orders.

Le Cadre

The notion of cadre, the French equivalent for senior management, is still quite close to its original meaning, a select group of military experts with a high degree of technical competence. It is not surprising that they have a hands-on approach to management. On the other hand, workers' rights and privileges are rigidly protected, reducing the scope for flexibility in meeting changing markets, manufacturing or other conditions. There has recently been a gradual adoption by the government of more flexible forms of employment, such as part-time employment, which is still low by European standards, and short working periods.

Getting The Right Office In France

An American manager was sent to France and had the following account. "When I came to Toulouse they asked me what type of office I needed. When I gave them some ideas, they told me to talk to the plant manager. But immediately they added that I could go around all that and talk to the guy in charge of the layout. It seems that if you go around the formal system, it all goes faster. When I talked to the guy in charge, I discovered that in Toulouse, ALL the managers are on the fourth (top) floor. They stick together and nobody cares if they are close to their people; the French view is that you should be close to the people who have at least the same amount of power as you have. They could be 600 miles from the people they are managing."

Management By Subjectives

A Dutch consultant was discussing the process of management of change to an international group of MBA students at Erasmus University in Rotterdam. He described a situation where a young Process Controller from the West Indies kept checking with his English boss to make sure that every little thing that he did was OK. The boss did not understand why the Process Controller did this. He was obviously very capable of making decisions on his own when his boss was not around. The Dutch consultant then asked the students to get into groups composed of the same nationality. Their task was to discuss the case and to suggest some possible ways to change the situation for the better. The French students thought the problem was obvious. The ascribed-status orientation of the West Indian man kept him from taking responsibility when his boss was around. The French understood very well that when the boss was around a respectful subordinate could not claim any authority. However, for them the solution was simple. They suggested, "You need to talk with the subordinate and change his job title so he can take responsibility even in cases when his boss is around." In the literature this stereotypical French posture is known as MBS (Management by Subjectives). This type of response is quite normal in the power oriented French culture.

Les Grandes Ecoles

Attendance at one of Les Grandes Ecoles, The Great Schools, is the basis of much ascribed status among French managers. To have attended a certain school is more important than how you got there. Transcripts of grades are often unavailable. Your attendance and graduation guarantees your caliber as a person and assures you of a lifetime of networking with other outstanding persons.

Among the most prestigious Grandes Ecoles are:
Ecole Polytechnique, (also known as "X"); Ecole Nationale d'Administration (known as ENA); Ecole des Arts et Métiers (CNAM); Ecole des Hautes Etudes Commerciales (HEC); Ecole Supérieure de Commerce de Paris (ESCP); Ecole Supérieure des Sciences Economiques et Commerciales (ESSEC). The old boys' network does in effect ascribe status to one another. Authority is very personal in France, representing as it does the superior reasoning power of the fonctionnaire and all those who reason in a like manner. The French word honneur, honor, stands for this personal sense of tightness and reasoning integrity. People get angry when criticized because their honneur is affronted. You are insulting not only them, but their academic lineage, their deductive capability, their raison d'être, reason for being. You ascribe status not as realistic feedback on prior accomplishment but because you believe in yourself and your ability to reason is a necessary precondition for achieving anything worthwhile.

Conclusions
French meetings seem oddly inconclusive to foreigners, especially to Americans. People are forever emoting, propounding, presenting, but there is a curious lack of a firm conclusion. Everyone present takes pride in a personal inner-directed power of deductive reasoning. Since everyone is "rational", it follows that one only needs to clarify issues, expound methods, and let "reason take its course". It may insult the intelligence of others to do this for them. Everyone's inner-directedness must be respected. In contrast, Americans often take pride in forcing others to agree by the irrefutable logic of their arguments. They present the data and then push others into drawing the same conclusion, thereby overcoming "sales resistance". This may antagonize French managers, as they take their own cerebral orientation seriously. It also makes hard sell inappropriate.

Excerpt from THT Culture Compass

43. India

Introduction

India is a land of extremes, with extreme differences across regions, religions, languages, customs, geography and socio-economic levels. To describe it as a land of contrasts is simply stating the obvious; there are few places that can match the scale of diversity that India has to offer. Indians themselves view their country as unique, as do many other nationalities, but they carry that view further and tend to believe that a global mind set will not begin to address the complexities of India. It seems hardly surprising then that business practices here are highly particularistic, with contrasting solutions to contrasting situations. Indeed, it is difficult to compare sensibly the agrarian economy, which still accounts for about a quarter of India's GDP, with the new economies of information technology. It is just as difficult to draw comparisons between the rigid and slow-moving government bureaucracy and the fast-changing savvy business environment that has gripped some of the major cities in India. To do business in India, it is best to come with a flexible attitude. Many times, that is what the visitor will receive in return, though he or she must also be prepared for the myriad complexities of an over-developed and extremely rule-bound bureaucracy.

Before the meeting

You should invest some energy in making sure that you are meeting the right person for the job you intend to undertake. A personal introduction to the right person will be of immense value and will go a long way in removing obstacles. Identifying the right person for the job may in itself present a few challenges as initially you may find that everyone is willing to lend an ear, even if they are not in a position to take part in anything beyond an initial conversation. You will not hear many no's, but you may hear quite a few "acha's" (all right). There are indications that some sectors of the economy are changing. Indeed, the technology hubs of India can seem astonishingly Western in their approach. Even here, however, the right introduction to the person with the appropriate status and position will be a huge asset.

Investing in the relationship

The power of a particular relationship will go extremely far in India. Indeed, that is the normal way that much of the economy operates. There are many businesses that are entirely relationship driven and do not adhere to more universal standards. An example could be the domestic tailoring industry. Despite the huge garment industry that is mainly directed at the export market, most Indians will still visit the tailor for their individual needs. The depth of relationship with the tailor will determine the end quality of the product; a collar that rubs the wrong way will be obligingly corrected and an expanding waistline will be accommodated with grace. A good relationship with the tailor can also result in clothes being made ready in record-breaking time. Naturally this means that one may need to be oriented towards many details.

Establishing Rapport

Indians cope very well with diversity and difference of viewpoint, particularly in the political and social arenas. You can see evidence of this in a free and highly critical press. A lively, opinionated discussion is something most Indians enjoy and indeed this would even go some way in strengthening rapport and building relationships. Naturally, the visitor should exercise normal caution in being critical on a sensitive matter, but there is no reason to not enjoy a good conversation on a topic unrelated to work. If you are from a cricketing nation, be prepared to know the names of your cricket team! The idiosyncrasies of cricket are perfectly suited to the particularistic people of India and it is the rare Indian who is not an ardent cricket fan.

How the government operates

For much of its post-independence history, India has run a socialist economy and it only began to open up in the 1990s, when significant privatization took place and the country became more open to direct foreign investment. But the presence of the government is still quite heavy and impenetrable. A foreigner seeking to do business with the state and national governments will most likely be baffled by the countless regulations and be daunted by the obstacles. The rigidity of government regulations can, in fact, be seen as a sign of extreme universalism. There are ways out of the impenetrability but these particularistic solutions are often no more than instances of corruption.

Negotiations The value of the contract

Indians tend not to consider a contract as a binding document. Points of a contract can always be revisited and renegotiated: A shift in circumstances will invite a second look at what was initially agreed and parties are expected to be flexible enough to accommodate change. Don't take something you agreed on yesterday to be still holding today. An unyielding adherence to the contract on the part of the visitor will be a deterrent to a good business relationship. Indeed, the visitor should even use the flexibility to work for his or her own changing needs. The advice here would be not to get bogged down by a missed deadline or goal but to work around these to reach perhaps an even finer conclusion. One needs to be flexible regarding specific terms, mode of payment, timelines etc. Again, this will be different if a visitor is dealing with the government. Bureaucrats here, as in many other countries, are less open to suggestion and are generally resistant to change. They tend to display flexibility only during times of crises. For example, it was a severe foreign exchange problem that led India to negotiate with the International Monetary Fund in a speedy and relatively flexible manner. A similar assessment could of course be made of many government bureaucracies.

The role of entertaining

Food has great symbolic value in India. In a country where many are undernourished, a meal together carries almost ritualistic importance. Meal times are respected and the food itself is considered important. Indians are also highly social people and meal times are a good opportunity to relax and talk, often about food and cuisine! Be prepared to join in the conversation. A foreign visitor will invariably be invited out to dinner in the course of negotiations. A good time enjoyed by all will go a long way in building a good personal relationship.

Management Delegation - choosing a team for your task

Faith and relationship play a huge role here. For lack of a more universal standard, you may find that you need to base your choice of personnel and partners just as much on the person behind the job as on the specifications of the job description and suitability of qualifications. Should things take an unexpected turn, you will find that you will rely on factors of personality to bail you out, rather than depending on machinery that is ill-equipped to address grievances and breaches of etiquette.

Nepotism I

The strength of the particularist orientation in Indian culture can be detected in the way staff is recruited, in many industries and businesses. In some areas such as the IT industry and the fast changing finance sector, particularly where businesses are based in the metropolitan cities, the foreign visitor to India from a universalist oriented society will recognize merit/achievement based recruitment procedures such as assessment centers. However, in many other businesses recruitment decisions are often made as much on the basis of relationships as of purely narrowly job specific competences. In most cultures, hiring decisions in family-owned companies are of course affected by relationships. A study by Grant Thornton on family owned businesses showed that 22% of North Americans, and 24% of Europeans owners of family businesses indeed felt that their successor should come from their family, whereas 46% of Indian business people wished to keep control within the family circle.

Contemporary Issues Indian English

India is arguably "the most chattery country in the world", as writer and traveler Pico Iyer maintains "coming at you in almost 200 languages, 1652 dialects, and a million signs on every hoarding, car hailer and passing shop." However, the visiting foreigner, confronted by such a multitude of languages, many of them mutually incomprehensible, finds solace in the fact that English is widely spoken. India has taken over from the United States to become the world's largest English-speaking population, and English is the common medium for university education. A survey in 1997 found that about one third of the population was able to carry out a conversation in English, up from about four or five percent in the 1980s. Since 1997, as language expert David Crystal argues, the number of Indians who speak English has probably reached at least 350 million, as English is taught in more and more schools, and is seen as essential for upward mobility. Although the influence of British English is pervasive (including Scots English, where the use of the word 'stay' for 'live' is echoed in the question "and where do you stay in Delhi/Chennai/London/New York?"), Indian English has developed into a vibrant and colourful version of the mother tongue. It is influenced by Indian languages, both in its vocabulary (a 'lakh' is a hundred thousand, a crore is ten lakhs), and in its idioms and distinctive usages - "What is your good name?", "they gave the children one one sweet" (one each). David Crystal also records some distinctive usages, such as 'near and dear numbers' (the phone numbers of friends and family), and 'kitchen platform' for the work surface in the kitchen. Humour and word play is a feature that delights the visitor: Crystal talks about "A review headline about a critical book on Jane Austen begins 'Austensibly, it's about Jane', [with the 'o' of 'ostensibly' spelled 'Au']. Be Ecofriendly, says a sign in Delhi, but it spells the second word 'Ecofriendelhi'." Rhymes are common and much appreciated - of course a road sign saying 'slow down' does the job, but 'hurry hurry spoils the curry' is much more memorable. The influence of English on India has been large, so, though, has the influence of Indian languages on English. When you are wearing pyjamas or a cashmere shawl, living in a bungalow, eating a mango, or watching a juggernaught go past, you are using terms 'imported' to the language from India.

Negotiations Emotions and reason cannot be separated
Indians can be quite emotional. Amartya Sen in his book "The Argumentative Indian " talks about the vast history and philosophy of Indians that make them argumentative. When discussing a point it's natural to gesticulate a lot and express emotions freely. Westerners are amazed as to how Indians can shout at each other at the workplace one day and yet be perfectly civil the next day. A rather unemotional westerner can be misinterpreted as one who doesn't have a real and deeper interest in the business. It can give an Indian the impression that you don't care enough about the success of the venture. One can get emotional about various things. One can get emotional about an increase in tariff rates, about religion, about a pay increase as well as a promotion. One can get emotional at a board meeting, in the lift or even at home. That doesn't mean that it clouds one's way of thinking and reasoning. It means very often just involvement and motivation. It has been observed that for any statement made about India, the opposite is also true. Emotional display is common in the workplace, there are even bosses who browbeat their juniors and shout and scream to proclaim their position. However, there are also bosses who are do not show much emotion and show a cool exterior. This is interpreted as showing superiority as he knows best and is a father figure and arbitrator. This apparent indifference to the concerns of other 'mere mortals' is not uncommon amongst officials and bureaucrats.

Importance of face/national pride
It happens sometimes that foreigners feel that Indians cannot deliver what they promised. One of the reasons for this may be their inability to say "no". Saying "no" amounts to a loss of face. This is not just a loss of face for the Indian who has to admit that he can't do something that has been asked of him, it's also a loss of face for the person who has asked him to do it. It means insulting the boss

or the superior to his face. A way of trying to maintain face is to use the expression "I'll try" - the wise foreigner will interpret it as a probable "no", and consider alternative ways of questioning so as to find out what is possible. Many Indians have a huge ego and will not compromise on what anything that hurts this. Even threats like "then we'll take the business elsewhere" may have no effect. Indians will freely criticize aspects of their country - government, roads, officialdom, corruption etc. However, if an outsider echoes the same sentiments, it will probably be construed as grossly insulting (as well as very discourteous. Indeed, few people welcome criticism from guests in their countries) Indians have a huge pride in their history, civilization, religion, food, culture and cricket.

The boss is the boss
The Indian boss outside the work environment is definitely still the boss. The persona of the boss is big and extends over and beyond office hours and the employee will always treat the boss with loyalty and respect. This phenomenon may be slightly different in the new industries in India, Youngsters in high tech industries are more likely to seek egalitarian relationships within their work environment. The head's position will always be distinct, but the office atmosphere here may be more convivial.

Business Topics Introduction
Indians are an emotional people. Indian films, produced by the dozen in "Bollywood" (India's Hollywood), amply prove that Indians don't shy away from emotions. Emotions, certainly on screen, are embraced, heightened and celebrated. This is evident even in daily interaction. Visitors to the country can find this overt expression of sentiment slightly embarrassing. The raised tones seem to indicate a misplaced excitement and it may be puzzling to see this excitement dissipate as soon as it is generated. On the other hand, business dealings and official language can be surprisingly dry and emotionless. There seems to be a dichotomy that is baffling and hard to penetrate. It is difficult to understand how two sides of the same coin can be so very different.

Meetings The importance of the social connection
Business meetings in India can seem almost emotionless. High up in the business hierarchy, people will come across as contained and reserved. This is especially true if you are meeting independent of any kind of social introduction. The hand of friendship and trust is extended only when the visitor has been appraised and accepted as part of the inner circle. Things change very quickly when there is a

social connection. Business will take place in a much more open and relaxed environment and people will readily let down their guard and show what they feel. In familiar settings, emotions can be a sign of trust and sincerity.

Reading the response
Inevitably, there is some kind of emotional response in a meeting. But this is not always a true indicator of feelings. A neutral reaction may actually disguise a negative reaction. An extremely positive reaction may actually only indicate a slightly favourable view. In general, it is probably safest to read an emotion that is one notch lower than what is professed because Indians can be quite reluctant to demonstrate a negative reaction clearly. Saying a direct no to a visitor would be considered as on the rude side. Subsequent meetings will make the response more clear.

The visitor's mood
Complete neutrality on the part of the visitor is not always perceived with sympathy. A dispassionate, entirely rational viewpoint can be construed as being rooted in disinterestedness. In this case, the visitor risks being seen as rude and condescending. On the other hand, too much emotion will not be seen as sincere, and will be understood as a barefaced attempt to go to whatever extent to land the business. There is therefore a level of complexity in the way the foreign visitor should pitch his mood. Invest some time in subsequent meetings for the communication to get more overt.

Greetings
The traditional Indian greeting is the 'namaste.' The word is pronounced while your hands are brought together, fingers pointing upwards. It means literally, 'the spirit within me greets the spirit within you' and it would be completely appropriate at a formal party given by your host, for example. At a business meeting, Indian men would simply shake hands with the foreign visitor. But it would be best if you waited for an Indian woman to offer her hand for a handshake before you reached out yours. If she does not offer her hand, simply acknowledge her with a smile and a nod. Age is respected in India in a fairly overt manner, such as introducing the most senior member of the entourage first. Women too are treated with a respectful physical distance. Be aware though that hierarchy of position and title can supersede courtesies of age and gender. People in senior positions wear their power very openly and like to be treated according to rank. Similarly, people with titles may want their titles to be

acknowledged in the open. (See also the dimension Achievement - Ascription for more background on the importance of seniority)

Negotiations Taste for debate

Indians love the power of conversation and logic. On the street corner and in the boardroom, Indians love to demonstrate their flair for argument, discussion and opinion. In contract negotiations, the minutes of points can be given enormous discussion and attention, simply to prove a fine point of logic and settle a matter of pride. Logic is often followed relentlessly, at the cost of practicality and time.

Concept of face

The concept of face is incredibly important in India and has been discussed in the context of other dimensions as well. Indians can be extremely touchy and in that sense highly emotional. Direct rebuke or criticism is taken very much to heart and can shatter the person on the receiving end. So be very careful as to how you make your critical comments. A blunt and unflattering appraisal can destroy a relationship entirely with no grounds for renewal.

High peer pressure in corporate structure

Old-fashioned corporate structures in India are very intense. There is quite a lot of competition within the corporation, the structure of which is hierarchical and inflexible. This gives rise to a fairly rigid sense of peer pressure and peer competition, which is not at all conducive to the free flow of emotions. Senior managers in these old-fashioned firms are unlikely to share or exhibit their emotions.

Emotional Bargaining

In the final stages of a negotiation for a Joint Venture between a Western European and an Indian financial company a group of 8 Senior Personnel had flown down from Europe for the final discussions on the percentage of share-holding etc. They went into the first day of the2 day negotiation thinking that they had sealed the deal. Some of the Europeans at this meeting were from departments that had up to now not been involved in the initial stages. To their surprise their Indian JV partners brought up newer issues with a lot of emotion. The Europeans were shocked and found such a display of emotion in the business context highly unprofessional. When they said this, the Indian partners staged a walk out and left their European counterparts totally perplexed. They sought advice from a cross-cultural consultant, who told them that they should attend the 2nd day of the meeting as if nothing had happened. Indians can use a lot of emotional language and persuasive powers particularly as a bargaining tool and this is the way they show that they are really involved with the project. The Europeans with not too much confidence went to the meeting the next day and their Indian partners were there, friendly, and carried on as if nothing had happened the previous day. To the surprise of the Europeans, the deal was signed with no further ado, and the company is a successful business venture today.

Logic, reasoning and public persuasion

Early examples of neutral behaviour. India has a long tradition of analysis. This goes back to the sciences of astronomy and mathematics. Observations made of the position of the stars and the planets thousands of years ago continue to amaze modern mathematicians. India also boasts great thinkers and rulers and among them is Ashoka Maurya, of the Mauryan kingdom, who came to be king in 274 BC. At the beginning of his rule, Ashoka was intent on expanding his kingdom and he did this with a fair amount of cruelty. After many massacres, Ashoka grew to wonder what good he had done for his people and his kingdom, as many of them had died in the acquisition of land and kingdoms. He came to embrace Buddhism and became an instrumental figure in the reputation and character of India for centuries to follow. He wished to bring about "a practice of social behavior so broad and benevolent in its scope that no person, no matter what his religion, could reasonably object to it." With words like that, Ashoka could sound like a modern, enlightened politician. And indeed, India is hugely indebted to the legacy of Ashoka Maurya. In his aim of establishing a "law of moral, religious and civil obligation" he was probably one of the first rulers in the world who took enormous measures to introduce public debate in the kingdom. His famous "Ashoka pillars" were erected in the far reaches of the kingdom. Inscribed on these pillars were his ideas on religion, harmony and the rule of the kingdom. But by making this part of public discourse, he encouraged public debate and involvement. He wanted a public that was open to reason and enlightened thinking. Open up the editorial page of any leading big city newspaper and you see the modern inheritors of ancient figures such as Ashoka. Some Indian newspapers are extremely cerebral, with quality editorials that demonstrate high levels of thinking. Able and sharp-witted television journalists have also transformed political debate on the screen, affecting profoundly the functioning of democracy in this country. And indeed, political debate is alive in every sphere of society. It is an extreme minority that is not involved and committed to exercising political franchise. Indians love to argue, debate and express opinion. As the inheritors of old traditions, they do so with impassioned reason.

Meetings Mirrored expectations
It can be difficult for a visitor to gauge the reality of a business meeting in India, a fact that we have discussed in relation to other dimensions. But the relevance here is that Indians can have a tendency to react according to your expectations. Anything will be said in order to keep you happy. This is especially important to keep in mind if you are approaching an Indian company as a client. You may find your Indian partner in business to be tremendously optimistic about what he can offer you. Be aware that this may not actually be the case. You will need to therefore schedule consequent meetings to reassess what can actually be achieved. This is even truer at the micro level. The tailor will tell you that the clothing will be ready on the day you want and the contractor will promise you that all deadlines will be met. The chances that this will happen without any further intervention are very slim indeed.

Negotiations Flexible agenda
Indians are flexible negotiators. Very rarely is an agenda followed to its minute detail. Rather, agendas will evolve as circumstances dictate. Because the process of a negotiation is rarely set in stone, the foreign visitor must be prepared to be somewhat flexible, adapting to new situations, as does his Indian counterpart. This approach, though it does have its extremely creative side, can strike the western negotiator as frustrating.

Range of influences on decisions
In his book " Doing Business in India", Rajesh Kumar quotes a Danish manager: "I feel that the most difficult thing is that the Indians will tell you one thing, think another, and do a third thing, what is not what a Dane would do." Indians show a high degree of sensitivity to different aspects of the context. Decision-making may be influenced by a wide range of factors, in addition to 'purely' commercial ones. Such factors may include astrology (dates for signing contracts may be fixed for auspicious days), the views and influence of family or friends, who are often treated as trusted advisers, or national or community concerns. This sensitivity to a broad range of influences in the environment (as Kumar explains the desh or place, the kal or time, and the patra, person) often makes interactions rather fluid, and "may make the notion of finality irrelevant. Since situations are always evolving, nothing can be set in stone." Although many

agreements are adhered to in the form in which they were agreed, it may also happen that Indian counterparts may expect changes in agreements to follow from changes in circumstances.

Management Try first, plan later

Pavan Varma, in his book "Being Indian" talks about the Indian ability for "creative improvisation". This often consists of taking an established product and finding new or different ways to use it, then improving it a little more, then maybe deciding that it might look better with this modification or that..... While valuing the creativity thus displayed, many foreigners find this approach of first doing, and then improving, rather frustrating. They would prefer a process of planning, followed by implementation, accepting that although the final product may not be the most creative, at least they will be able to predict what it is. Indeed, this is not unique to foreign managers. The (Indian) marketing head of a major Indian multinational has impressed upon his team that when he has signed off a project, he expects what he has agreed to be delivered. With no surprises. He has, however, knowing that his young and talented staff will have plenty of ideas for the improvements, suggested that they documented these, so that they can be put into practice on the next project.

The push and pull of circumstance

The visitor may find his Indian partners to be incredibly adaptable when it comes to business goals and strategy. Modern Indian managers, as opposed to bureaucrats mired in miles and miles of government policy, can be very open to new ideas and opportunities. They will be happy to learn about new methods and are eager learners. In this respect, they are very able to use outside circumstances to their benefit and profit. But when things go wrong, there is a certain tendency to push the blame back on to circumstances. For example, a project could not be completed according to deadline because such and such happened. These circumstances are taken to be beyond control and therefore inevitable. This can be frustrating for the foreign visitor, who may see this as a kind of dead end. The advice here would be to wait the lull out and then go on to the next step. There generally is one.

We'll do our best

A subsidiary was set up in Bangalore by a Dutch company to develop software. The work was project based, and in the highly competitive market timelines were crucial. The Dutch manager of the software developers was impressed by the technical ability of his team, and the fact that they were willing to put in long hours, including working evenings and weekends, to complete the work. However, he found discussions with his team about deadlines to be quite frustrating. Admittedly, the deadlines were tight, however, what he needed from his team was a firm commitment that they would meet them, which he could then convey with confidence to Headquarters. In the discussions, however, team members often pointed out that meeting the deadlines would be difficult, however, "we'll do our best". The Dutchman felt that it was within the power of the team members themselves to meet the stretch targets by committing to the work. Team members, willing to commit to hard work and long hours, nonetheless realized that factors outside their control may impact achieving their goals. They pointed to recent examples: disruption of traffic caused by a Ministerial visit to the city (in which in any case traffic is notoriously bad), the absence of a key team member who had to attend the funeral of a close relative, the need for another team member to attend an interview for his child to gain admission to a good school.

Karma, dharma and maya
Many scholars have noted that Hinduism, the faith of more than 80% of Indians, is difficult to define precisely. There is a large body of religious literature and philosophical thought, which includes some key beliefs such as karma, dharma, and maya. The doctrine of karma asserts that, in a future life, a person will be rewarded for good deeds performed in this life, and punished for bad deeds. Good deeds are rewarded by rebirth in a better social situation, bad karma will lead to rebirth in a lower status, and more difficulty in achieving the ultimate aim, moksha, being united with the ultimate reality, and escaping the maya, the illusory world which we experience. Dharma is the concept that refers to morally appropriate behaviour, or duty. There is a universal dharma, but also dharmas focusing on appropriate behaviour for women, elders, individuals at different stages in their life, etc. One of the challenges for each individual is to decide which duty (as an elder, or as a woman, for example) is the most important at a particular time.

Meetings Family businesses are cornerstones of industry
There are a great many family businesses in India that are highly successful with histories that are intertwined with the industrialization of India. The foreign visitor may very well be interacting with such a family-held enterprise. Many, like Tata, Birla and Reliance, are among the biggest business empires in India.

But their sheer size means that they function as publicly held businesses, with recognizable corporate hierarchies and channels of communication. There is a particularly strong sense of community and allegiance in this type of company. When dealing with Tata, the mega-corporation, for example, the foreign visitor will come to know about the town Jamshedpur (erstwhile known as Tatanagar, the city of Tata), founded by the man behind the company. Certain guidelines laid down by the founder will be sacrosanct and everyone, even the foreigner, will be expected to respect these.

Negotiations Indirect speech
Years of living in an extended community have had the tendency of making Indians rather indirect in their speech. If one lives in an extended community, one cannot always say and do exactly as one feels. One always has to consider the impact on society. Communication is very much of an implicit art and there are many shades of meaning in the choice of words. Indians are therefore quite subtle communicators. This may be seen by a foreign visitor as a lack of transparency, but, in contrast, Indians may perceive total frankness as bordering on the rude. The subtlety and implicit nature of speech here can make contract negotiations a fairly abstruse process and the foreign visitor may need to invest some time in order to get a clearer and fuller picture. Time invested will also bring you closer into the community and will bring about a better understanding.

Management Teamwork
Indian teamwork, particularly at the higher level, can be a problem. The higher up the corporate ladder, the more difficult it is to create a team that works well. Senior managers here have high opinions of themselves and come to the job with a strong sense of their own perspective. This seems odd in such a highly communitarian society, but can be explained by looking at individuals outside their own community. A communitarian society does not mean that the individual ego is not developed. It is just that it develops differently. The individual outside of the community, particularly a privileged individual brought up in a privileged community, is no longer that model community player. He or she can be as individualistic as the best of them. Neither is there a suppression of creativity and talent at this level. Sales positions in India of course vary in terms of economic reward, but generally speaking, sales departments work according to individualised incentive packages. Whether you are selling cars, or insurance, this type of model has been accepted and embraced. Lower down the corporate echelon, the team spirit becomes stronger and more reliable. It is fairly easy to

motivate and manage people at the middle-management level. They respond well to group directives and, within the group, there can be a strong sense of loyalty and similarity of purpose.

Success is not an individual thing

A rising star in Bollywood (India's Hollywood) recently had a very good year. He directed two major feature films and both were highly popular. So, at the awards ceremony for Bollywood movies, he was called to the podium again and again to receive his various prizes. Each time he came on stage, he brought his proud mother with him. The mother did not say anything but stood glowing in the background while her son made his speeches of acceptance. His mother was such a big part of his identity that the son could not conceive of his success without his mother.

Nepotism II

The quality of your life in India, besides being dependent on obvious things such as money, will depend absolutely on who you know. If you want to visit a doctor, or get your house painted, you would not first consult the yellow pages. You would instead ask a friend, who would ask a friend and you would soon have your answer. Everything is based on your community connections. This can work very well, but it does create clear divisions between communities that are less connected and those that are obviously privileged. There is also a distinct whiff of nepotism in the extent of community networking that takes place. Admissions to schools and colleges, lucrative jobs, even government postings are all influenced by one's connections in community.

High degree of tolerance

Even affluent Indians choose to live in groups. It is really not an ambition to be completely self-sustaining. Young children do not feel compelled to leave home as soon as they are financially independent; neither are they encouraged to do so. Similarly, elderly parents will choose to live with one of their children, rather than maintain an independent household. Things are changing very fast, with moving populations and more job-related mobility, but still, the joint family is very much the ideal. Indians like the idea of many generations living under one roof and accommodating to the various needs of the various members of the family is not considered a real issue.

Meetings Corporate India

A walk down the street in any major Indian city and the differences in the level of status hit you in the face. A visitor might well find it difficult to function comfortably with these differences, but they are something that every Indian is brought up with and indeed comes to absorb: one's level of status is part of one's definition of self. In corporate India, however, things are really changing quickly. Even though there is huge awareness of status, this is a rather dynamic segment of society and there is much more opportunity that is available to many more people. It is up to the individual to reach out and take it, either through excellent work or through outstanding education or by riding on a very bright idea. So there is certainly movement. Do well and you will rise. Talent will be noticed and rewarded. But even here, the halo of the boss, once in place, is really rather bright and really quite self-evident. If the foreign visitor wishes to engage with an Indian company, a good relationship with the boss is the right place to start. You cannot discount hierarchy completely. Bear in mind also that in any discussion of corporate India, we are automatically talking about the upper echelons of society. Ascription thus plays a silent but enormous role.

Outward signs of status

A person of higher status at the workplace is often one who wears a suit or is more formally dressed. He/she gets preference even when in the queue for the elevator. The body language is more assertive while his juniors are more deferential. Those lower down in the pecking order may avert their eyes and not make direct eye contact (as this is considered to be impertinent). The boss at work often has his laptop/ briefcase brought in to his office by his driver/staff. If he is carrying anything that looks a bit unwieldy it's immediately taken from him by someone in the office. He/ she are often referred to as "Sir "or "Sahib" or "Madam" in the Indian context. One doesn't really disagree with him/her and his opinion is not contradicted. In the more dynamic environment where MNCs (multinational corporations) or new companies are the norm, such behaviour is being frowned upon and a corporate culture of being open or allowing all to speak is being encouraged. It's up to the Corporation to instill, with training, new patterns of behaviour. To a society brought up to be "yes " men to the person in authority, whether at the family level or at the workplace, it requires a lot of training.

Meetings The business card

Indians are at heart quite status conscious. At any business meeting, there is likely to be an eager exchange of business cards. People like to be assured that they are meeting someone of the appropriate rank or status. People are also intensely interested in the roles of others. There is a good deal of healthy curiosity.

Negotiations The negotiating team, composition and strategies

Age and status are respected in Indian society. So a young 28 year old who comes in to negotiate is often treated as an upstart with no experience. In a negotiating team it is wise to send senior people, age and position in the corporation are important. If a middle level executive is sent to negotiate with the MD then he will very often get to meet with those lower down the rung. No decision will be made as decisions are taken at the top. It will be a futile meeting and only when the senior person arrives will it be taken seriously. The senior most should be addressed mainly and the juniors very often will stay silent. They certainly will not offer anything different from what the Boss says. Again the seating arrangements should be such that the seniors sit at the head of the table. They could often arrive a little bit late and the others of their negotiating team could praise their boss and his judgment. Yet all this is in the process of change with foreign companies coming in and Indian companies going global and trying to change the mindset of the people who work for them in India. Meetings do not necessarily start on time, which may be simply a matter of differing attitudes to time, but is also occasionally a demonstration of power and status - who waits for whom is an indication relative status. A lot of small talk can be indulged in without getting to the point. Once the personal relationship has been established then the business discussion can take place.

Ego

Indians are well known for their egos and any sign of disrespect or trying to put them down would not be taken lightly. He would prefer to lose the deal than to have his ego hurt. It would be wise to be a good listener and show interest and respect for religion. The nature of the Indian is to be hospitable and to go overboard in order to please his guest but in no way does that mean that he is a fool and will do anything. Out of politeness he may say yes to his guest but the Indian is a tough negotiator and bargains with a hard nose.

Women in your negotiation team

Though India has a reputation of being a male-dominated society, in corporate India this is really not an issue. There are countless examples of women in power and countless examples of women shining in education, journalism, advertising, science, medicine and indeed any industry you may care to name. Here, education and capability are key. As a female foreign visitor, you probably won't encounter particular obstacles though it may be wise to be prepared for slightly different cultural norms. Though individual women can be very successful, the male sense of ego is still rather high. Indian men don't take very well to an openly aggressive manner, particularly from women. Try and get maximum leverage with a more muted sense of strength. Also be prepared for fairly direct questions about your marital status, whether or not you have children, etc. These come simply from curiosity and indeed may be directed at men and women. Indians don't as yet have such a pronounced notion of what is or what is not politically correct. Western women, however, may feel particularly ill at ease with this kind of conversation. Things again are very different outside corporate India. The foreign visitor is probably aware of the international perception of the plight of Indian women; this is self-evident when one visits a rural setting, for example.

Women in the workplace

Women in the workplace are not an unusual sight these days. Previously women worked purely as secretaries, teachers (considered a noble profession for women) or as domestic helpers. Occasionally one found doctors or even lawyers who were women but they were few and far between. Nowadays there are many professional and technically qualified women especially in urban India. Trains and buses are full of women going to work in the mornings. There are quotas for women in politics, and education (some states even have free college education for women). Those who come from educated backgrounds have the advantage of a good education. In most middle class families girls have equal opportunities with their brothers. However this in not the case with the lower income group. Here girls are discriminated against and their brothers' have all the benefits. Nowadays the offices of banks and MNCs in many of the big cities employ many well educated, capable women, who are making their mark along with their male colleagues, but this may not be the case elsewhere.

Gender discrimination

There is still gender discrimination in many workplaces, reflecting the lower status of women in many parts of Indian society. From denial of advancement opportunities, to verbal harassment, the Indian woman may experience considerable discrimination. While in cities like Mumbai and Bangalore Western dress at work is common for women, in many areas women are expected to dress in the traditional style. The higher the level in the hierarchy, the more one is expected to dress in a sari/ salwar kameez (Indian tunic and trousers) in order to be taken seriously. In many parts of rural India women have very little status, and are disadvantaged in terms of health, access to education, and economic independence. The purdah or veil system exists in some parts of India even today.

Management Seniority
Age is respected in India. It is the obligation of the young to be respectful towards elders, and it is a theme that is often visited in the ancient Indian classics. In modern reality, there are obvious signs that this is not the case, but still respect towards the elderly is an idealised notion. This is carried over to old-fashioned work environments, where promotion is dependent on how long you have served at a company. We have the example of the Indian arm of a British organisation, where executives are all engineers, all similarly qualified. There is no attempt to single out the most competent person to serve as leader. Instead, the most coveted positions are doled out on the basis of seniority. It is very different in modern industries, where competence to lead is more a factor than age. But even so, the way you treat elders is always important. Two senior expatriate Dutch bankers in Mumbai decided to celebrate St Nicholas Day for the Dutch and Belgian community based in Mumbai. The older banker dressed up as St Nicholas and the younger one as Black Peter. St Nicholas, who did not live too far away from the venue of the party, decided to walk the 5 minutes along a busy junction. He had on a white robe, beard and long white hair. As he started walking along the Breach Candy Road he noticed the people staring at him and slowly a crowd started gathering around him. People got out of cars and taxis and began to touch his feet (asking for his blessings) and even the police, who arrived to see what the commotion and traffic jam was all about, folded their hands and bowed before him. No one for one moment realized that it could have been a fancy dress. Fortunately Black Peter who lived far away travelled by car otherwise his fate would have been one of taken into police custody. This goes to show how much respect is given to religion, age and holy men.

Clubs
The clubs in some of the major cities of India are relics of a bygone age.

For example, Kolkata's Tollygunge Club, established by the British, boasts massive green fields, golf facilities, tennis, swimming and gracious dining in a beautiful and spacious setting, despite the density of population of the city around it. You enter the gates of the club and you are literally transported back by a century and a half. Even wild animals dare to roam here. Membership to the club is strictly a matter of ascription. Most likely, it is inherited; otherwise it may be arranged through clout and connection. Needless to say, it is highly coveted, as spots are limited and demand is high. Ten years ago, the clubs established by the British were the only clubs in town. This is partly explained by a matter of real estate. There were only a few areas in town that were considered acceptable places to live and the old clubs had the clear advantage of location. But even this is slowly changing. As cities grow physically, newer areas are coming into the limelight and money is being spent outside the old centres. New clubs, with huge ambitions, are cropping up in the suburbs. In cities such as Mumbai, this change is especially apparent. Though demand for the old clubs remains fierce, the growing moneyed class can buy into a similar level of pampering. It's not only the lucky inheritors who can enjoy a poolside bar-b-q after a game of tennis.

Competition at schools

Indian graduate schools are highly competitive simply because we are talking about a country with an enormous population. If one just considers the top to middle economic bracket of society, the percentage may be small but the numbers will be large and will warrant a level of competition that is indeed very real and intense. And in this segment of the population, achievement is what matters. Importantly, it is basically this level of society we are talking about when we talk about corporate and entrepreneurial India. It is probably fairly safe to say that the foreign visitor is more likely to interact with this level of society, even though his or her business may be directed at the country at large. Things are changing evidently and changing very fast, and not only in the socio-economic group just mentioned. In the last decade, for example, more and more Indians of modest means have transformed their economic health by joining the ranks of double-income families. Slowly seeping into the collective consciousness, especially among the urban poor, is the need for smaller families. The result then is greater income dispersed among fewer dependants and greater ambitions. This demand for more - in terms of goods and education and levels of living - has of course a profound impact on India's domestic market and on society in general. Aspirations are high and appetite for goods and services is soaring. There is a huge middle class in the making.

44. Singapore

Excerpt from THT Culture Compass online

Introduction

Your first impression of the Singaporean business environment may be that Western business values have been adopted. However, Singaporeans are proud to have their own unique system; they are pragmatic and tend to incorporate whatever works best. They don't like to have universalistic values imposed on them. An important concept for doing business in Singapore is guanxi. Guanxi is a Chinese term that can be translated as "connections" or "personal relationships". The importance of guanxi in Chinese culture has been extended to business dealings. Singaporean business has historically been dominated by networks of Chinese entrepreneurs. Although modern Singaporean companies tend to be less paternalistic and centralized than businesses in China, networks based on personal relationships and guanxi still play an important role. The Singaporean business networks are sometimes not transparent to outsiders. The party in power determines what is acceptable in the negotiation process, not some abstract universal norm. Singaporeans have gotten used to Western ways of working, including the extensive use of written contracts. For present-day Chinese entrepreneurs, who are doing business internationally more and more, the dilemma is that they may actually still prefer to work based on relationships of trust, but they are forced to rely more and more on written contracts. Another first impression of Singapore may be that it is a country of many rules. However, in business, flexibility is the keyword. Rules and systems are obeyed as long as they lead to results and a healthy economy. Singaporeans are extremely results oriented and pragmatic. Having said that, they are quite used to dealing with business entities from many different cultures and are generally able to deal with all of them.

Multicultural History

Singapore's particularism is closely related to its multicultural history. Not long after Britain's Sir Stamford Raffles landed on the island of Singapore on January 29, 1819, he reached an agreement to found a settlement with the local Malay ruler, and Singapore became a multi-ethnic society. It was established as a trading post and a free port, and migrants came by the thousands. The Chinese soon became the largest group. As the multiethnic society developed, the different groups began to cluster in different neighborhoods such as Chinatown and Little India. The Japanese invasion in 1942 imposed yet another cultural influence on Singapore. When Singapore got internal autonomy within the British colony in 1959, Lee Kuan Yew was the leader of PAP (the People's Action Party), which was the party in power. In 1963 Singapore joined the newly independent Federation of Malaya, together with Malaysia. However, after Singapore was dispelled from the federation in 1965, Lee Kuan Yew became the first Prime Minister of the city-state of Singapore.

Meetings Many Ways To Do The Same Thing
A Singaporean business tycoon often repeats this saying in staff meetings, "In business there are a hundred and one ways to do the same thing." This statement reflects the Singaporeans' particularistic approach to business.

Meetings Addressing People
There is not one universal way to address people in Singapore. The Chinese may use Western first names or initials. Malays may use Mr. followed by their first name. Indians may use their first name preceded by their father's first initial, and they may abbreviate their name if it is complicated. To be on the safe side, always ask a person how he or she wishes to be addressed. This is an issue that confuses Singaporeans as well.

Negotiations Particularly Shrewd Negotiators
The history of the Chinese in Southeast Asia has led to stereotypes of the ethnic Chinese as "opportunistic transients" and shrewd negotiators who can manipulate a deal in their favour. The position of the Chinese in Southeast Asia has always been somewhat uncertain, and this has led to the need to get the best out of each and every deal in order to survive. It is important to realize that the attainment of self-rule in Singapore meant that for the first time in the history of the Chinese in Southeast Asia, a group of Chinese could actually settle in a reasonably secure environment. The stereotype of "opportunistic transients" can therefore not be justified in Singapore. Nevertheless, it is true that the Chinese Singaporeans can be very effective negotiators because of their particularistic approach. The party in power determines what is acceptable in the negotiation process, not some abstract universal norm. It is perfectly acceptable to make use of the weaknesses of the other party. Therefore, especially if they

are buying, they will do anything to get a good deal, including discovering your weaknesses. If you are buying, they will expect you to do the same thing.

Negotiations The Role Of The Economic Development Board

Singapore's Economic Development Board (EDB) has played an important role in the economic strategy of Singapore, a strategy that has been described as "Strategic Pragmatism". Negotiations with foreign companies have played an important role in this strategy. By negotiating with multinational companies on how a company based in Singapore could best allocate its resources, the EDB has been the architect of business in Singapore. The EDB has typically taken a very pragmatic, particularistic approach towards negotiations with multinationals. The EDB has provided many different types of support, depending on the particular needs of the multinational company in question. For example, the EDB has served as a broker of relationships; they have provided or helped companies to obtain financing; they have managed the industrial park; they have helped to find joint venture partners; they have arranged for the requisite technology; and they have provided the "software" or mental programming needed to industrialize. The EDB has an investment budget and has invested in joint ventures with multinationals. They weren't motivated solely by the opportunity to make a profit; they wanted to give their corporate partners the confidence to proceed, to share the risks and to cement the relationships. As a condition for admittance into Singapore, companies had to share their plans with the EDB and other agencies, who then made sure that the skills, the training and the informational support were in place and that partnerships were created. The EDB has always negotiated with the aim of serving the particular goals of both parties. Singapore's primary goal was to enhance knowledge and become "The Learning Nation". The primary goal of the multinationals was to establish investments that were well integrated into the Singaporean network. The main idea behind "strategic pragmatism" is that through sharing risks, sharing interests and building relationships, everyone wins.

Management Chinese Family Business

The Chinese family business has been the core and drive of Singaporean enterprises. In this type of organization, the top people have absolute control and the ability to make quick decisions. The management style tends to be paternalistic. Employees are expected to be loyal and are rewarded for their loyalty. Chinese family businesses grow through networks and some have grown into large conglomerates. Networks extend to other conglomerates, governments and other authorities. These networks may not always be apparent to outsiders. Although modern Singaporean companies tend to be less paternalistic and centralized than they were in the past, networks based on personal relationships and guanxi still play an important role (See Presence of the Past, Guanxi and the Importance of Networks). The term "guanxi" is for instance the motto of Silk Route Ventures, a company that assists clients in designing and maintaining web sites, in marketing products and services on the Internet and in setting up Internet facilities for internal office use. The Chinese characters for "guanxi" are framed and mounted on the wall behind the desk of the CEO of Silk Route Ventures to remind staff and visitors of the vital role of "personal relationships". The CEO sees guanxi as vital for building a global business network.

Bargaining For Jobs
Bargaining is a popular Singaporean pastime, so the Singaporean bank OCBC started an experiment to make bargaining part of the recruitment process. The bank employed 34 graduate trainees for job-rotation training on a temporary contract. Upon the completion of the training, 10 out of the batch of 34 trainees were allowed to negotiate for the positions they wanted within the bank. The bank informed the trainees as to what positions were available. Managers who had worked with them were given the opportunity to make bids for the trainees that they wanted to work for them. The recruits also stated their preferences and reasons for wanting a particular job or department. The bank announced the experiment under the motto "Let new recruits bargain for the jobs they prefer instead of pushing them into vacancies." As a result of this method of filling positions, the bank was able to retain recruits.

Management Free Of Corruption
People who are universalists often believe that particularists are corrupt. This is definitely not true for Singapore. Singaporean politicians are financially incorruptible. Business is virtually free of corruption, and even small-scale bribery leads to arrest.

Case Developing Training Materials
A Singaporean company, part of a British conglomerate, wanted to start a technical training institute. The project team responsible for developing training materials consisted of two British consultants from the head office of the conglomerate, both specialists in developing training materials, and three

experienced technical instructors, all Chinese Singaporeans. At the first meeting, the British consultants proposed starting with a detailed analysis and outline before designing the actual training materials. The Singaporeans, on the other hand, wanted to start writing the training materials right away. The detailed analysis was redundant in their perception. However, the first meeting was dominated by the British who said that they had done the same type of projects in other parts of the world and that they had always started with a detailed analysis. Subsequently, the formal meetings during the first weeks of the project were spent on discussing the analysis. During the meetings, there was a formal agenda, decisions were made and minutes were taken. Meanwhile the Singaporeans had informal meetings to develop training materials. When the analysis was complete and decisions had been made about the outline, the British consultants wanted to start with the second phase, translating the outlines into a teaching syllabus. The Singaporeans said that they had already developed the materials and only needed a framework to grade and link the materials. The British consultants replied that the completed materials were useful only as illustrations of theory they had discussed. The syllabus could only now begin to be designed, and the design should be governed by the analysis and the outlines. The meeting ended in a complete deadlock.

Mr. Kiasu

Mr Kiasu is an extremely popular cartoon figure in Singapore. He expresses Singapore's particularism in his war cry "Everything also I want." Mr. Kiasu is a single young urban professional. Some of his followers have bumper stickers on their car that read "Graduated from Kiasu College". Mr. Kiasu's survival strategy is reflected in his attitude that he has "the right to have everything". He bargains and tries to get discounts on everything. If he is only buying one ounce of taugeh (soy sprouts) at the market, he still thinks he has the right to select the best ones. Getting free drinks and free samples of food is one of his favorite pastimes. One of the Mr. Kiasu comic books contains a "How to get things for free" list. Young Singaporeans interpret Mr. Kiasu's message as this: "The system will not take care of you in modern Singapore. If you want your particular needs to be fulfilled, you have to take care of yourself."

Meetings Ways Of Dressing

The climate in Singapore is characterized by high temperatures and high humidity throughout the year. As a result, people tend to dress casually and informally; they only dress formally when they go to work. When attending business meetings in Singapore it is important to keep the following Chinese expression in mind: "They respect your clothing first. Then they respect you." Office dress is conservative but fashionable. Singaporeans value designer brands, but they don't dress too ostentatiously. Female business dress should not be showy or flowery. Plain, feminine looking clothes are the rule. With the exception of important meetings and formal events, an air of grace is more important than the right "power suit". Neutral colours are the rule, especially for higher-level management. Generally speaking, a jacket is not necessary. A shirt with long sleeves and a tie is considered formal. It is perhaps most important to look neat, to wear well-ironed clothes, and to have your hair neatly combed.

Introductions
Introductions are important in Singapore because it is important to assess another person's status. It's best to have yourself introduced by a higher-ranking person in your company, someone who already knows the people you will be dealing with. A meeting normally starts with the exchange of business cards. This is not as formal a ceremony as it is in Japan. Still, it is important to show respect for people's business cards. In addition to the person's name, business cards will give the person's title and have a company logo. The card can be in English; Mandarin on the other side is only necessary when visiting Chinese-owned companies. It helps to have prestigious looking business cards with an impressive sounding title on them.

The Position Of Women
Singaporean women are well educated and can be found at all levels of business. However, the highest concentration of female managers in Singapore is in personnel, public relations, administration, and consumer affairs. Support staff is usually female. Singapore is a power-oriented business culture, and women may have more difficulty exercising their power in the Singaporean business environment. Business establishments and business clubs can be quite male oriented. A lot of business is done on the golf course. Inner circles are very tight and consequently, it may be more difficult for women to build networks. Western businesswomen are readily accepted, but it's important to take into account that building networks may be more difficult for Western businesswomen as well.

Negotiations Credibility Of Female Negotiators
A female team leader may experience a problem establishing her credibility

unless team members clearly show that she is the top-ranking member of the negotiating team. Singaporeans might have a tendency to address the men on the team more than the women. Seating arrangements that put the female in the lead position will help. Western men need to be aware that the tendency to jump in and answer questions, especially when a woman is speaking, may undermine her authority. When a question is asked to a male member that should have been directed to the female leader, it is best to redirect the question to the female team leader. This can be done by saying that she is the best person to answer that question. (See "Cases", Establishing Credibility)

Meetings Respect
Singaporeans show respect for ascribed status and expect others to acknowledge status as well. Seating at meetings is often arranged in a hierarchical manner. Therefore it is important to supply a list of the names and titles of the people on your team, with those of highest rank at the top of the list. Elderly people are accorded great respect in Singapore. It is important to show respect for business partners by ensuring that meeting materials (handouts, information leaflets, etc.) are of top quality. Foreigners are also expected to show respect for Singapore. Discussion of sensitive subjects should be avoided.

Negotiations Use Of Titles
In Singapore, hierarchy is respected, and it is important to address people by their correct title. Teachers are referred to as "Sir" or "Madam" by their students. Younger people are not supposed to address their elders by name; it is a sign of disrespect. People of status are referred to by their title, such as President or Dr., followed by their family name.

In spite of these apparent formalities, Singaporeans seem to have a love for shortening forms of address. For example, Malaysia's Prime Minister Mahathir Mohammed is addressed in Singaporean newspapers as Dr. M. Prime Minister Goh is addressed as PM Goh. After he resigned, the former Prime Minister received the title of Senior Minister, and he is now addressed as SM Lee. Lee Kuan Yew's sons, who both have the title of Brigadier General, are addressed as "BG". Hierarchical relations are respected in business, and it is important to address people with the right title. When negotiating with Singaporeans, you should address them with their title and their name. Keep in mind also that the first name mentioned is the family name, such that Chang Chu Chin, should be addressed as Engineer Chang, or Madame Chang if she does not have a professional title, but not Engineer Chin. Those with impressive titles will be treated differently and what they have to say will carry more weight. It is wise to pay attention to people's titles and to find out where they rank in the hierarchy.

A Fine Country

Singapore is sometimes referred to as "a fine country" because you seem to get fined for everything. Spitting in a public place, smoking in a prohibited area, or littering all carry a maximum fine of $1000. Having an unlicensed dog or selling chewing gum have a maximum fine of $2000. Jaywalking or creating conditions that are favorable to the procreation of disease carrying mosquitoes, such as allowing water to stagnate in roof gutters for example, also carry heavy fines and are considered to be serious offenses.

In Singapore, the ascribed status of authority is still respected. Punishment is severe. Judges send strong signals to deter profiteers from committing offences, as in the case of a 54-year-old retired person who bought 150 Viagra pills in the USA and smuggled them into Singapore. He got a $20,000 fine. Another case is a 53-year-old man who stole his neighbour's panties, which had been hung out to dry. The offender got a $500 fine, and the newspaper published his name, photo, and the street name and block number where he lived. A first offense may be punished by a fine, which you have to pay at a place far outside the city limits. There are usually long lines with many people waiting in front of you in the burning sun. Recidivism may be punished by making the offender pick up garbage in a public park for a week. A third offense may mean caning, a certain number of hits with a 2-meter-long cane. Canings are feared by all as they are said to be extremely painful, and they leave lifelong scars. Drugs smugglers can get the death penalty. Many people are proud of the result of the tough punishments. People are disciplined, crime is pretty well controlled, and the streets are cleaner than in Switzerland.

Status Symbols

Singapore is proud to be a meritocracy, where success is based on merit, not on connections and birth alone. Status, however, remains as important as ever although the status symbols may have changed. It's still important to impress people. Modern status symbols are cars, houses and the schools children attend. The younger generation talks about the 5 C's: car, condominium, credit card, cash and country club membership.

Prestige

Perhaps the most prestigious scholarships are the Lee Kuan Yew Scholarships, postgraduate scholarships that are intended to allow outstanding Singaporeans to pursue a Masters or Ph.D. program overseas or locally. The eligibility requirements for these scholarships are interesting. Recipients must have an outstanding academic record as well as strong leadership qualities. In addition, they must be active in social or community services or sports. Singapore wants leaders who are not just outstanding in their fields but who are also community-minded.

Servants
Having a live-in servant is a status symbol in Singapore. Among professionals, it is fairly common to have a servant especially if both the husband and wife are working and have a certain level of income. Nowadays, most servants are women from the Philippines and Indonesia. In the morning, you can see them carrying their master's briefcase to the car. In the evening, you see them waiting for their master to come home. Some carry the children's book bags to school. The Singaporean Sunday Times contains several pages of advertisements for maids.

Meetings Modesty
Singaporeans tend to downplay their talents. Singaporeans say, "Only a fool brags and boasts." Being modest and reserved is appreciated and boasting is frowned upon. An American human resource trainer on a two-month assignment in the Singaporean branch of her company introduced herself to the team by boasting about her experience, expertise and success. She continued to talk about her accomplishments in subsequent team building meetings. Within two weeks her behavior had raised such serious doubts about her ability among the local employees that the team distanced themselves from her. As a result, she was unable to function effectively in her job because local staff members were not willing to open up and accept her. Among the local employees, they nicknamed her "daalaapa" (big trumpet in Chinese/Mandarin). They commented, "She must have no wares to show. That's why she is so loud."

Meetings Presentation Style
Women in Singapore tend to be soft spoken. They use very few gestures and are not openly expressive. For that reason, women from cultures that are characterized by broader gestures and a greater variation in intonation may be viewed negatively. Speaking loudly and laughing a lot will usually be considered uncouth. It's important to have a style you are comfortable with, but you may be more effective if you tone it down a little bit when presenting to Singaporeans.

This will help people to pay attention to what you are saying rather than being distracted by your movements.

Negotiations Non-confrontational Style
The negotiation style of Singaporeans tends to be non-confrontational. It is important to tone down your voice since a loud voice can be interpreted as being aggressive or angry. If your Singaporean counterparts have a negative view of you, they are unlikely to want to continue to negotiate with you.

Management Feng Shui
Feng shui is one of the most ancient Chinese philosophies. This theory of the importance of harmony between heaven, earth and people has influence on modern business life in Singapore. Good feng shui will enhance the energy flow not just in your house but also in your business. A proper beam of energy flow can prevent bad spirits or negative energy from entering. Property developers in Singapore often have feng shui reports made before deciding to buy land, build a house, or buy a house. Feng shui practicioners observed a sharp increase in their business when the East Asian crisis started to emerge in 1997. The essence of feng shui is to do the right thing in the right place at the right time. Recently, there has been an enormous increase in interest in feng shui in Australia, the USA and the UK. Feng shui columns in woman's magazines reflect a "do-it –yourself approach", and the expectations of instant results can lead to disappointment. Singaporeans will tell you that learning to practice real feng shui takes time. A good feng shui consultant has a long history of practicing the art.

There are foreign companies in Singapore that try to adapt to local culture by making use of feng shui. When the Dutch bank ABN Amro set up its head office of its Asian Pacific operations in Singapore some years ago, they hired a feng shui master. The feng shui master He concluded that the two flows of traffic, along Chulia Street and along Singapore River would bring luck to the 15-story high-rise office building in downtown Singapore's business center. The Dutch management did not really believe in it, but it was a part of their effort to show that ABN Amro was not just a Dutch bank. As an international bank with a worldwide network of offices, they wanted to show that they had knowledge of and respect for Asian people and customs. Furthermore, they realized that the locals would feel more at ease conducting business in an environment that was in a good position to attract prosperity.

Aiyah!

You may notice that Singaporeans frequently exclaim "Aiyah!" when they are conversing among themselves. "Aiyah!" is used at the end of a sentence to indicate that the speaker or someone they are talking about has had (or has almost had) some form of setback. It is used by Chinese, Malays and Indians and shows their awareness of the risks and threats that the environment imposes on them. The exclamation serves the purpose of making people feel better and is a way of expressing one's worries or sorrows. Another exclamation that you will frequently hear is Wallah! It indicates surprise because something unexpected has happened.

Meetings Being In Control

The business etiquette in Singapore is to stay cool, calm, and courteous under all circumstances. It is important never to shout or swear, or to act openly confrontational. A person who openly shows their emotions is thought to be out of control. A person who cannot control his or her emotions is considered to be inferior and not trustworthy.

Singaporean Neutrality Sometimes Seen As Rudeness

Singaporeans can sometimes be considered as rude by other Southeast Asians. In a Thai – Singaporean joint venture, this caused serious problems between the Thais and the Singaporeans. It turned out that the problem was caused by the Singaporeans' neutral behavior during meetings. The Chinese Singaporeans were seen as unfriendly workaholics.

Silence Is Golden

In the Singaporean communication style, listening before speaking is highly valued. Moreover, Singaporeans tend to maintain a brief period of silence after someone stops speaking. This period of silence shows respect for the person who has just finished speaking. Differences in communication style between Singaporeans and Americans led to problems in the Singaporean subsidiary of an American company. The Americans did not understand that silence was a way of showing respect. They interpreted the silence as well as the Singaporean custom of listening first and then talking to indicate a lack of knowledge, initiative and motivation. The Singaporeans felt insulted and used. Among themselves, they described their American colleagues as "a half of a pail of water" (meaning that there is a lot of empty space in the pail, so it makes noise), and they said things like "empty cans make more noise" and "big heads have no brains". Hence, in order to be respectful and to gain respect when meeting with Singaporeans, it may be wise to listen more and talk less.

Negotiations Display Of Emotion
Singapore's neutral orientation can lead to a tough negotiation style. Singaporean negotiators can put the other party under great pressure while keeping a poker face. They generally avoid displays of emotion during negotiations because it may be viewed as a loss of self-control. They expect the same behavior of their counterparts. It is also important to maintain more neutral facial expressions and limit gestures when negotiating with Singaporeans. They may end up watching your arms moving about and stop listening to what you are saying.

Possible Misunderstandings
The neutral orientation of Singaporeans can result in cross-cultural misunderstandings. For example, although Singaporeans have a neutral orientation, they smile a lot. For this reason, they may think that people from other neutral cultures such as Northern Europeans don't smile enough. The neutral orientation of Singaporeans can also lead to problems in interacting with very affective people. For example, Singaporeans tend to be somewhat reserved in conversation, so they may think that people from Latin cultures talk too much. If your communication style is different from that of the Singaporeans, it is important to make it clear to them that although your behaviour is different, your goals may be the same. For example, Singaporeans may say, "We do not talk much but we smile a lot out of respect for the relationship." But by the same token, a Northern European may say, "I don't smile because I have respect for the relationship." People from Latin cultures may say, "We talk a lot because of our respect for the relationship."

Negotiations The Singaporean Style Of Conflict Management
Singaporeans prefer to avoid emotional issues and use a professional approach to diagnose and resolve conflicts. They tend to verbally agree with people in an effort to maintain harmony and avoid confrontation, but that does not mean that they always avoid conflict. Nods of the head and murmurs of agreement may only signify that you have been heard and understood. They don't necessarily indicate agreement. Anger and frustration may be expressed in a controlled way through the use of nonverbal communication. Especially after big meetings it is

necessary to clarify if everybody agrees with you.

Expressing Negative Feelings

Singaporeans will rarely show anger and frustration openly but may express their feelings about management in a more neutral way. For example, at one American company in Singapore, some Chinese Singaporean employees were not at all happy with the American expatriates who were working there. They had written the following message in Chinese on their whiteboard: "You have a big head but no brains. Even if you have brains you use them to grow grass." The message expressed the feelings of the Singaporean employees who felt that the expatriates were aloof and stayed away from the local staff. Since the American staff could not read Chinese, the message was also a way of saying that the expatriate staff did not really know what was going on. The local staff felt no need to express their feelings in a more open way.

No Boisterous Laughter

A neutral, controlled way of behaving is very much valued in Singapore. This is expressed through politeness in language and in non-verbal communication. Smiling is important, but loud or hearty laughter is uncommon. Those who do it are thought to be uncultured and to have no class or self-control. Women who laugh loudly are considered to be intentionally seeking attention. Not only are they perceived as ill-behaved, they are also perceived as not respectable, not intelligent, "short-circuited" (emotionally unstable) and/or not trustworthy. The ability to be silent when it is appropriate is considered a virtue. Especially for people in top leadership positions, an extreme show of emotion is considered to be a sign of lack of stability. People in a leadership position don't laugh; they smile.

Meetings Greeting

Greeting another person in Singapore is more than just saying "Good morning. How are you?" Singaporeans complain about Westerners greet them but do not acknowledge them. Greeting another person by saying, "Good morning. How are you?" and then walking away before the other person can answer, may be an acceptable form of greeting in Western countries, but it may offend Singaporeans. In greeting someone in Singapore, eye contact is important. Facing the person, acknowledging that you actually see him or her, and giving the other the opportunity to acknowledge you is vital. Greeting someone should be more than a standard "Good morning. How are you?" Just a smile will be seen as more friendly. A genuine "How are you?" and/or "How are your kids?" or complimenting the person's appearance will make a positive impression. In Singapore, it is not unusual for formal greetings such as "good morning", "good afternoon" or "good evening" to be replaced by questions such as "Going out?" "Have you eaten?", "Going home?" etc. Westerners who are not accustomed to these types of inquiries may feel that it is none of the other party's business to ask. It's important to realize that these types of questions are not attempts to pry into one's personal life nor does the asker expect a detailed response. They are just a way of showing familiarity or acceptance.

Trust
In Singapore, it is extremely important to be considered trustworthy, and people will start accessing your trustworthiness during the first meeting. Singaporeans tend to be more implicit, subtle and indirect than Americans and Europeans. Singaporeans rely more on gut feelings and instinct. They pay particular attention to certain types of body language such as frequent blinking, rolling one's eyes, or lack of eye contact. Not making eye contact or frequent blinking, unless it is a physical impairment, will be interpreted as meaning that the person has something to hide; such a person is not to be trusted. After this initial screening process, one can begin building trust. Trust is built through sharing, showing respect, keeping promises and acknowledging obligations.

Meetings No Open Disagreement Or Criticism
If a subordinate argues or openly disagrees with a superior, this means loss of face for the superior. A subordinate may therefore agree with his boss in a meeting, but say things like "It will be difficult" or give subtle nonverbal signs (like hissing inwardly through the teeth) to show disagreement. Therefore, it's extremely important to learn to interpret subtle differences. Agreement is frequently verbally voiced while disagreement is usually shown through silence or subtle body language. In general, Singaporeans won't criticize someone in public. For instance, superiors generally do not reprimand their subordinates publicly. If they do so, it can have negative consequences for the superiors themselves (See "Cases", Open and Direct Feedback Causes Problems).

Negotiations Polite Negotiators
Saving face and giving face are extremely important in Singapore. If Singaporeans want to stop a negotiation or end a business relationship, they will do so without losing face.

Even in a situation where the underlying sentiment is "good riddance to bad rubbish", Singaporeans will handle the situation with honor and face.
When negotiating with Singaporeans, do not mistake deference and hospitality as demonstrations of trust in you. You are an outsider until you have won their trust. Lack of trust may result in over-politeness and in the withholding of information. During meetings, there is normally no need for excessive small talk because in a serious business relationship, other social events such as cocktail parties, banquets, sightseeing tours, etc. will be planned. These are good opportunities to build a diffuse relationship, but don't let it oblige you to give in. There are benefits and risks in getting involved in a diffuse relationship. Feel free to politely decline to participate in any activity you find offensive.

Negotiations Giving Face
Giving face is an important prerequisite for business success in Singapore. When asked for the reasons behind the success of a Singaporean tycoon, a rival banker said, "His willingness to accept invitations impresses others. In an Asian society, this is important. He gives face to everybody." Attending receptions and dinners is not just socializing, it is also the most effective way to pick up business intelligence. In general, there is not a big separation between the private and the corporate spheres. Therefore, when negotiating with Singaporeans, it is a good idea to take time to socialize with them.

Management Open Office
The CEO of a European company in Singapore had an office with glass walls. He could see people from his office and others could see him. The staff liked it because they felt that it was similar to an open-office arrangement. When a new CEO came, he immediately closed all the blinds so that people could not look in. Moreover, he expanded his office by taking over the room next to it, which had been used as a conference room for small group meetings and for receiving guests. He wanted a room specifically dedicated to receiving his guests. The Singaporean staff saw this step as a sign of unfriendliness. They felt that the CEO was imposing his power on them. They wondered if he might be doing things he didn't want the locals to know about. Their interpretation was that he had things to hide and, therefore, was not trustworthy.

Personal Relationships
A diffuse leadership style should not be confused with being nice and gentle. Chinese Singaporean managers may shout at their staff when they are doing

something wrong, but they will also show their diffuse orientation by making it clear that they care about their staff. They will for instance visit them in the hospital when they are sick, come forward and try to take care of them when they have problems at home, and attend the wake or the funeral of a relative of an employee. Singaporean bosses tend to treat their personnel like family.

Open And Direct Feedback Causes Problems

An Australian supervisor wanted to be genuinely fair to her subordinates and colleagues. She practiced speaking her mind during meetings and not taking matters out of the meeting room. During meetings she praised and reprimanded her staff openly and directly. She did the same with her colleagues during cross-team meetings. Soon she found that her staff was extremely quiet during meetings and that her subordinates and colleagues started to avoid her. She found the situation unpleasant and could not understand why her staff and colleagues gave her the cold shoulder. She decided to ask her secretary. After a great deal of coaxing and promising not to disclose who had told her, her secretary finally explained what had gone wrong; public criticism resulted in a loss of face for her Singaporean staff. The Australian woman immediately stopped reprimanding her staff during meetings and started telling them about their mistakes in private. Still, it took some time before her staff started to speak out during meetings and people stopped avoiding her.

Dealing With Conflict Indirectly

A European senior manager was advised that Asians do not like open confrontation and that it is better to handle the conflicting parties separately. When he took a position in the organization's Singapore branch office, he sensed that there were interpersonal problems within his management team. Putting the advice he had received into practice, he called in his staff one at a time to get their individual opinions. He tried to address the interpersonal problems separately but he ended up with a bigger mess. All of the staff member voiced their "grievances" about the others but asked not to be quoted. Each person hoped that the others would be reprimanded. The manager thought things over for a while but could find no way to resolve the problems in the usual setting. He decided to try role-playing. By reframing the problems in a role-play, he was able to resolve some of the conflict. Having a third party act as an intermediary and set up meetings can also be quite effective, especially if the intermediary has quanxi (connections). By having a third person act as a go-between, your Singaporean partners do not have to lose face.

Ambiguity As A Tool

Singaporeans know how to use indirectness and ambiguity. They know how to never say "no" and how to use intermediaries to communicate a difficult message. In South East Asia, indirectness and ambiguity are important tools in diplomacy. They are frequently used to solve issues in ASEAN (the Association of South East Asian Nations). Although Westerners find ambiguity confusing, it is part of the magic that makes ASEAN work. In South East Asia, ambiguity provides room for people to save face and to accommodate one another.

An example of an indirect communication can be seen in the use of silence. In meetings and discussions, silence can mean either agreement or disagreement. Silence has to be interpreted in conjunction with the combination of subtle body language and facial expressions that accompany it. Silence combined with a nod of consent will probably mean agreement. Silence combined with a cynical smile, on the other hand, means disagreement. In order to communicate effectively with Singaporeans, it is important to learn how to interpret these subtle messages.

Personal Questions

An American expatriate was living in an apartment building in Singapore. Every morning when the man was leaving the building, the Malay security guard would ask him, "Where are you going?" During the first week, the American answered, "I'm going to work." But as time went on, he started to get annoyed because he felt the question was an intrusion on his privacy. He did not realize that "Nak pergi mana" (literally translated by the guard as "where are you going") is a friendly way to greet another person in Malay.

Getting To Know You

Visitors to Singapore sometimes get the impression that Singaporeans are very direct. Singaporeans might ask you questions about your salary, whether you are you married, how many children you have, etc. The reason they ask these kinds of questions is that they want to get to know you. For Singaporeans, it is important to build a diffuse relationship, which entails discovering what you have in common. If they think that certain questions would be acceptable in your society, they may even ask you things that they would not ask another Singaporean. It is not always necessary to give a complete answer as long as you use the opportunity to start a conversation that will help them to get to know you.

Meetings Punctuality

Singapore has a synchronic time orientation but that does not mean that Singaporeans are not punctual. Arriving late for social events is fine; however, Singaporeans are very punctual when it comes to being on time for business appointments, and they expect guests to be punctual as well. Even though Singaporeans are punctual when it comes to the start of meetings, the end of a meeting is often not that clearly defined. Meetings may go on for a while and include discussions about items that are not on the agenda. Furthermore, it is important to be prepared for spontaneous meetings and introductions. If a scheduled meeting is going well, your Singaporean hosts may improvise additional meetings on the spot and introduce you to other people within the company.

Negotiations Patience

Negotiating business deals with Singaporeans may require numerous meetings and several visits to Singapore. Patience is important. The Singaporeans will typically not want to finalize anything until they have had time to build a personal relationship with you. Therefore it is important to think twice before replacing representatives. Sending a new representative to meetings with your Singaporean counterparts may delay the negotiation process.

Language And Time

Different ways of viewing time are reflected in language. In English, verbs can be used in many different tenses to indicate when an action takes place (i.e. present, past, future, present perfect, past perfect, future perfect, etc.). In Chinese and Malay, these tenses do not exist. From a western perspective, verbs in these languages use the present tense only. In order to indicate the time of an action in Chinese and Malay, the speaker would use a time expression. For example, you might say something like "I go tomorrow. I cannot yesterday."

== End of text = =

45. Negotiating internationally

Sander Schroevers

Globalisation, not to mention the European single market, has strongly influenced the way we work. As a consequence, we find ourselves communicating more and more with people from other countries.

This chapter will introduce some of the communication functions that play an essential role in international negotiating. Recent research shows that international managers spend approximately twenty percent of their time on some sort of negotiation activity. Because negotiating is to a large extent communicating, it seems only logical that local differences influence the communication process. Most books on international negotiating seem to depart from the idea that there is one universal way of negotiating. Here I try to describe how adapting the usual negotiating tactics in line with particular cross-cultural differences will most probably improve the results of the negotiation.

Potential pitfalls

Techniques that work well at home may fail in another country where the expectations of a negotiation party may simply be very different. The usual focus on *win-win* or *win-lose* outcomes cannot solve expectations in the fields of:

- Behaviours related to eye contact, interruption, intonation etc.
- Terms for making convincing arguments,
- Normal bargaining techniques,
- Expectations with regard to seniority,
- Ideas about hierarchy or decision-making authority,
- Use of time.

A recent European study (*Elucidate*) clearly shows that around forty percent of the international negotiations in a European programme failed because of comparable cross-cultural conflicts. The problem is that most people who need to negotiate internationally have not been schooled in that area. Usually only governments or large multinational corporations have specialists in that field. For most companies, negotiations abroad are carried out by those in middle management positions or by technical specialists. They will probably, therefore, need to improvise, which in terms of risk management can, of course, be a challenge.

Unspoken codes
There are various ways to express differences. Many of these are unspoken codes, or subtle distinctions. Differences that for foreigners can be hard to distinguish. The point is that we are often taught certain values during our upbringing. Cultural groups such as, for instance, the Germans, Swiss, Scandinavians or Dutch tend to be quite direct in their communication and usually express exactly what is meant. Scientific research has shown that the way in which the Dutch express their thoughts can be quite to-the-point. The problem is that other cultures sometimes may perceive this directness as just plain bluntness. Native English speakers tend to opt for the much more scripted language of request-making. The majority of requests take the form of:

- **Could you,**
- **Would you,**
- **Would you mind ~ing ...**

Therefore, try to be aware that specific levels of directness appropriate for given situations might differ cross-culturally. And remember that languages such as Dutch or German tend to use more direct-level requests than, for instance, British English. The table below shows selected cultures and their levels of directness in communication. The ranking of the United Kingdom explains the differences described above.

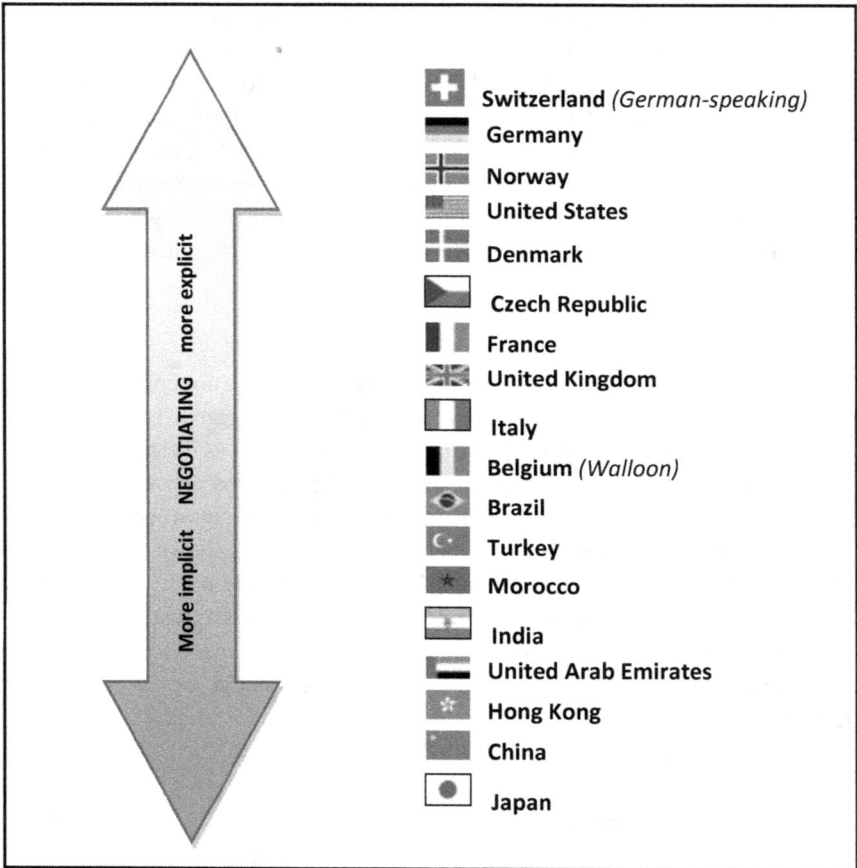

Levels of directness in negotiations, by country

The table also makes clear why Americans generally use more direct and explicit communication. And indeed, British English can seem vague at times to people from the cultures positioned higher in the table. But there is a very simple reason for that: vagueness is used to maintain politeness, saving face and thus avoid confrontation. The same applies to friendly small talk, humour and understatement, which are all normally used to soften style. Humour comes in many varieties in Britain, and can often be used for many different situations: humour, self-mockery, criticism, paying a compliment, awkward moments etc.

Timing differs

When is the right moment to start the negotiating process? Do all cultures follow the same timing pattern as in, for instance, the Netherlands? The answer must be: absolutely not. Even people in neighbouring countries such as Belgium and the Netherlands have different ideas on this. When, for example, would be the right moment to make an offer during a business lunch (dînatoire) in France? The answer here is: probably close to the time a small coffee or desert is being served. It is often felt that starting business any earlier could be too blunt. The overview below shows us which selected trade cultures open their talks immediately and which cultures indulge in more small talk, when starting straight away would be considered less well-mannered;

Country	Early	Half	Late
China			☑
Czech Republic	☑		
Denmark	☑		
Emirates			☑
France		☑	
Germany	☑		
Hong Kong		☑	
India			☑
Italy		☑	
Japan			☑
Morocco			☑
Netherlands	☑		
Turkey			☑
United Kingdom		☑	
United States	☑		

Using interpreters

For most of the cultures mentioned below, people will either fall back on speaking English or on using an interpreter. It is of great importance to prepare an interpreter or translator beforehand. This is done at a small pre-meeting by exchanging lists of jargon, key-terms, common abbreviations or, for example, brand names. When negotiating with an interpreter, try to maintain eye-contact with your negotiating counterpart, not with the interpreter. An interesting anecdote about how a senior Russian negotiator obtained an advantage in his negotiations with an American, concerned his use of the interpreter. Despite the fact that the Russian spoke English adequately, he still made use of an interpreter but for an entirely different reason: while the interpreter was translating, the Russian could study the American's non-verbal communication without hindrance and when the American spoke, the Russian had twice the response time.

Different goals

Scientist interviewed negotiating teams from, amongst others, countries such as Japan, Brazil and the United States about their expectations for specific negotiations. The analysis showed that culture does indeed influence the expectation of a negotiation. The Japanese for instance were much more focused on the long term relationship, whilst the Americans were mainly concerned with the short-term deal. The principal goals of the different negotiators also showed significant differences; where the Brazilian chief negotiator was concerned with achieving a respectable negotiation outcome, the Japanese negotiator was mainly focused on market share, and the American on short-term high profit. It is fair to say that some knowledge of specific Asian, Latin or Western expectations will lead to better results.

Local negotiation techniques

Scientist have studied negotiation techniques in Japan, Brazil and the United States in a combined research of Universities from those same countries. They interviewed various participants and analysed many hours of video recordings. The results showed some remarkable differences;

Behaviour tactics			
SILENT PERIODS (Number of silent periods greater than 10 seconds, per 30 minutes)	5,5	2,5	0
OVERLAPS (Number per 10 minutes)	12,6	10,3	28,6
FACIAL LOOKING (Minutes of gazing per 10 min.)	1,2	3,4	5,6
TOUCHING (Not including handshaking, per 30 min.)	0	0	4,7

The Japanese, for instance, can maintain several seconds of total silence. If a negotiator is not aware of this, he or she may be influenced by such a silence in that they may perceive it to mean something other than intended. In Mediterranean cultures, on the other hand, people can overlap in their conversation, meaning that people can talk simultaneously. The same applies when interrupting people. This is considered rude in North-Western European cultures but in more Southern cultures it is quite normal, and as such, thought of as a form of active listening. The table above also shows us that Brazilian negotiators touch their counterparts much more. The so-called comfort-zone between people in Brazil is also much smaller than, for instance, in Holland. Latin people feel that they want to stand closer to each other, especially when talking about confidential matters. Northern people, however, usually feel uncomfortable with close proximity to others and try to create space, often by stepping back a bit. It can sometimes lead to amusing movement patterns by the participants at international summits.

Compromises

Making a compromise is considered positive in certain cultures but not in others. For instance, Dutchmen, Belgians or Swedes learn to compromise from a young age, whereas Russians, Spaniards or French, for instance, have developed their skills in other directions. A Spaniard, for example, generally believes that a compromise might damage honour (*pundonor*). Some knowledge of such cultural differences can help to prepare differently, and probably negotiate with more success.

Look me in the eyes

As the table above shows, direct eye-contact amounts to only twelve percent of the total time in a country like Japan. Indeed, in Asian cultures continued eye-contact is generally seen as too assertive or emphatic. Many people in the West would not trust someone who avoids at least some kind of eye contact and people in the Middle-East even use much more intense eye contact in negotiations.

Strategic negotiating framework

Stephen Weiss examined cultural aspects of the international negotiating process. He concluded, after studying many negotiation cases, that for successful outcomes it mattered that negotiators reflected on their own cultural negotiation script as well as on that of the other parties involved. By choosing strategies accordingly, better results were achieved. A choice of negotiation sequences or scripts could be made, depending on the level of knowledge each party has of the other party's culture. The scale of such awareness will determine which of four possible scripts can be chosen for an optimal international negotiating outcome. The model on the following page shows the four options of the Weiss framework;

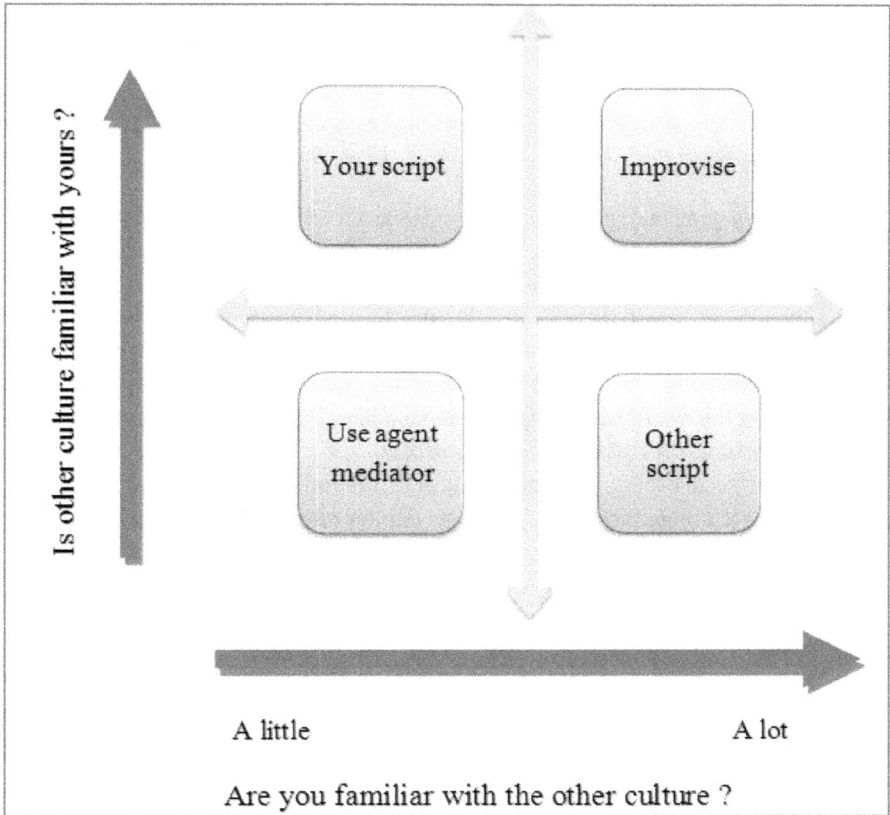

Image: Weiss framework

46.   Cultural Rankings

Jaime Offermans and Roy Gerritsen (CCBS alumni)

In some ways all human beings are alike, in some ways everybody is a unique individual, and in some ways everybody is very similar to a certain group of people within a country. The latter similarities would be considered culture as defined in the Oxford Dictionaries (2013): "the ideas, customs, and social behaviour of a particular people or society". When people from different cultural backgrounds meet, those different beliefs and customs also come together, increasing the risk of potential misunderstandings. The same simple hand gesture can represent something positive in one culture, but be considered very disrespectful in others. With increasing globalization there has been an increase of cultural clashes, over time creating a need for better cultural understanding. To answer these needs different anthropologists and cross-cultural researchers have done a lot of work to develop systems for comparing cultures in one way or another. While there are many, three of them stand out compared to the others in terms of the impact of their work on the field:, the Dutch academic author, public speaker and consultant in the field of cross-cultural communication Fons Trompenaars, the American anthropologist Edward T. Hall and the Dutch cross-cultural researcher Geert Hofstede.

Fons Trompenaars and Charles Hampden-Turner

Fons Trompenaars and Charles Hampden-Turner are the founders of the Trompenaars Hampden-Turner consulting firm which specialises in many corporate issues, among them cross-cultural dilemmas. Fons Trompenaars is a consultant who earned his spot at number 42 in the 2011 "Thinkers50" as one of the most influential management thinkers. He has worked with many of the top Fortune 500 companies and helped them solve their cultural dilemmas. He teamed up with Charles Hampden-Turner, who is a British management philosopher, and together they have turned out to be a powerful combination in the world of international management consultancy. They are responsible for developing a model for measuring cultural aspects based on seven different dimensions, where the first five dimensions are based on Parsons' five relational orientations, thus based on people's attitudes towards other persons (how humans deal with each other). The sixth dimension is about people's attitudes towards time, and the last one is about people's attitudes towards the environment (Trompenaars and Hampden-Turner, 1997).

Universalism versus particularism (rules versus relationship)

Trompenaars' first dimension is about how people judge other people's behaviour. A universalistic culture is one where people will judge other people's behaviour based on written or unwritten rules. In a particularistic culture people judge behaviour based on the influence that someone has on a personal level. They are more focused on personal relationships, adapting to the circumstances, and having respect for other people's needs. In a particularistic society people will value personal influence more than rules or regulations. Imagine yourself being in a meeting where the rules say that eating is not allowed and you haven't eaten anything all day to the point where sick are feeling sick. In a universalistic society people will have the opinion that you should have eaten before the meeting as the rules say you can't eat during the meeting, and therefore it is your own fault. In a particularistic society people will feel for you and will consider it fine for you to eat something during this meeting since it affects you this much. In business, both universalistic and particularistic differences are also very present. Contracts by definition favour the universalistic thinker since they are full of rules and regulations. In contrast, a contract can come off as very distrusting to a very particularistic person; they can feel that your wanting a signed contract means you think one party will try to cheat on the other party. So if you come from a universalistic background and are trying to finalise business agreements with particularistic people, it might not be the best idea to bring your lawyers and heavy contracts to sign and expect that way to close the final deal. Another big difference regards the timing of things: particularistic people will more likely than not withdraw from situations where they feel hurried. When dealing with particularistic people you do not want to set heavy deadlines. Instead, you want to take your time to make them feel comfortable.

This also means that when it comes to time perception if you compare particularistic versus universalistic societies, the universalistic societies will most likely show signs of a monochronic time perception to use Hall's term, and particularistic societies will probably show signs of a more polychronic time perception.

Individualism versus communitarianism (the individual or the group)
In this dimension, individualism is an aspect of a culture where personal achievements and freedom are respected and people are expected to take care of themselves, as opposed to communitarian cultures where the group you belong to is more important than the individual and your loyalty to the group provides a safety net where you are taken care of. It is basically about how people within a culture perceive themselves, either as an individual or as part of a group. This dimension is basically the same as Hofstede's "individualism versus collectivism", the only real difference being that it seems as if Hofstede looks at how the culture tends to be from the outsider's point of view, and Trompenaars looks at how the people in that culture perceive themselves.

Neutral versus affective (neutral versus emotional)
This dimension ranks cultures based on how accepted it is that people express emotions in public. In a neutral culture rational reasoning comes before emotions when deciding or taking action, and expressing emotions tends to be less accepted, thus people will be less apt to express what they think or feel. On the other hand there are affective cultures where expressing emotion is very accepted and often even encouraged. The use of emotions to communicate in these cultures is a big part of their everyday life.
Whether people are more neutral or more affective in the way they are used to dealing with each other is something that affects business meetings a lot. Affective people will be looking for emotional connections much more in these settings than neutral people, and when they get no emotional response from them they might consider this as disinterest. This also works the other way around where emotionally neutral people might consider a heavy positive emotional response from the other ones as a sign that they have already agreed to the proposal, while in reality this may not be the case. Also for neutral people,

a calm and collected posture will be more respected, while the affective people are very used to honest emotional displays and often will be using more physical contact, which in return can make the neutral people feel very uncomfortable. When dealing with the other side of the spectrum in a business context, know what to expect and try to move as close as you comfortably can towards the other party's customs, as this will cause less friction and will greatly benefit the chances that your business meetings will be successful.

Specific versus diffuse

Whether a specific culture is considered specific or diffuse depends on how deeply the members of a culture get involved with each other on an emotional level. Consider multiple layers into how deeply you can be involved with somebody, from knowing who the other one is (acquaintance) to being a close and personal friend. In very specific cultures, the layer reached in the relationship between two people will be very specific to the goal or task at hand. There won't be an emotional connection unless the goal of the relationship between the two people requires this, whereas in a diffuse culture multiple layers of the level of engagement with one another will be reached whenever two people get involved with each other.

For business this often means that people in a specific culture will only get involved in the layer that is necessary for business and the business can easily only involved mere technical facts and economic aspects. In a diffuse culture, on the other hand, there is a need for personal relationships between the individuals doing business before any kind of cooperation can be established. Where specific cultures will expect productivity and profitability to come from technical aspects, diffuse cultures will expect success to come from a good personal relationship between business partners. This means that when dealing with people from specific-oriented cultures, a successful strategy will be to focus on the technical aspects and profitability expectations, and when dealing with diffuse-oriented people, that would be to establish a good personal relationship with them first.

Achievement versus ascription

This dimension describes how status is assigned within a culture: do people acquire status by means of their achievements or by ascription? The big difference is that in cultures where status is achieved, status is assigned from their having done something, while in cultures where status is ascribed, it is assigned based on their being someone or something. A practical example for this is that in an ascription-oriented culture, you can have a higher status based on age, class, gender or the like, while in an achievement-oriented culture, status will be given based on experience and achievement.

In business this means that people will value different aspects about someone when deciding his or her level of authority. Business people used to an ascription-oriented culture will value the older person's opinion more compared to the person with a better track record of results, while for businesspeople from an achievement-oriented culture the exact opposite will be true.

Sequential time versus synchronous time

Where the previous five dimensions were oriented towards personal relationships, this dimension is about how people in a certain culture manage time. In a sequential-oriented culture, people will view time as a natural sequence of events that follow each other. They will work towards a schedule to reach a certain goal step by step. In cultures with a synchronous-time orientation, people view events in time as being interrelated. Each event has a past, present and future that are all interrelated to each other.

In a synchronous-time orientated culture, people can work towards a goal by being able to work on different aspects parallel to each other at the same time. The sequential-time orientation from is very similar to Hall's monochronic time-orientation, and the synchronous-time orientation is very similar to Hall's polychronic time-orientation.

Internal control versus outer control

This last dimension is about how people relate to their environment. It basically means that on one side there is internal control, where people perceive the environment as something that can be controlled, and the end result is much more in their own hands. With outer control, on the other hand, people perceive the end result to be due to the circumstances beyond their control. People from internal-control-oriented cultures will lean more towards feeling they are in control of their own destiny, whereas people from outer-control-oriented cultures will feel like their future is determined by circumstances. In business, internal control cultures will adopt a more dominant attitude towards the environment: the focus will be on their own business and they will be uncomfortable with the idea that things are out of their control. Outer-control-oriented business cultures will be oriented much more towards the outer world, the other party, the customer, the potential business partner. They will be much more flexible and willing to compromise to keep the peace, and will be very comfortable with a changing environment if they perceive this to be natural.

Edward T. Hall's key cultural factors

In the field of anthropology and cross-cultural research, Edward Twitch Hall Jr. (16 May 1914 – 20 July 2009) was known for developing the concepts of "high-context" and "low-context" and "monochronic" and "polychronic" to describe cultures (Hall, 1976). Hall's work has influenced many researchers after him and he is generally considered to be one of the founders of the field of cross-cultural research. Hall started as a professor teaching at different universities, but the real start of Hall's intercultural work started in World War II when he served in the US Army in Europe and the Philippines. Later on Hall worked for the US government teaching intercultural skills. It is important to note that Hall did not provide us with any information as to where specific cultures rank on in terms of his concepts, but he did provide those theoretical factors to help compare cultures. Other people after Hall have continued to use his system to rank specific cultures.

High context versus low context
This cultural factor is about communication between members of a culture. It can be looked at as a measurement from being very direct (low context) to being more indirect (high context) when communicating. In a high-context culture the words and body language used can have a much bigger or different message attached to them, whereas in a low-context culture the words used are generally

very similar to the message meant to be given. This also means that in a high-context culture the impact of a single word can be much more significant than in a low-context culture. Knowing where a country ranks on the spectrum of high context versus low context cultures can be very helpful when attending a business meeting with potential partners from that country's culture. When you know that the people you are about to meet come from a high-context culture, you can prepare yourself by knowing what to expect and how to communicate with them. When for example an American businessman (the US is considered low context) attends a Japanese business meeting (Japan is considered high context), the American would be wise not to be too direct when communicating, because this can be considered very rude by a Japanese person. The American would also need to know the specifics in terms of what the Japanese counterparts say or do not say, and what they generally mean when they say certain things. Basically what it boils down to is when you communicate with people from a high-context culture, you need to figure out what the underlying message is when they say certain things, while at the same time knowing what the perceived message for them could be if you yourself use certain words.

Monochronic time versus polychronic time
Monochronic and polychronic are terms used to describe how people in a certain culture use and perceive time. A monochronic orientation is a very organised, step by step approach to time management, where everything is done according to a schedule and done one thing at the time. On the other hand, in the polychronic orientation, time management and the specifics are much less formal. More things can be done at the same time and dealing with time is much more dynamic and fluid. People from polychronic societies place much more value in personal relationships as opposed to getting the job done, which is much more indicative of the monochronic orientation towards time. The specific time orientation of a culture is very important for business meetings in the sense that if you are from a monochronic culture like Germany, you will generally expect a business meeting to start more or less exactly on time, but when meeting with people from a polychronic cultural background, for example Mexicans, you can expect people not to be there at the exact time. When you know these things

before you meet with people from a different background, you can set your expectations to a realistic level so you will not be surprised.

Geert Hofstede's theory of cultural dimensions

Geert Hofstede, born in 1928, is a well-known Dutch cross-cultural researcher. He is considered the founder of comparative intercultural research, and in any case a pioneer in the field. Hofstede developed a theory of cultural dimensions, which was the first more elaborate system to compare and rank different quantifiable cultural aspects. Hofstede's theory is still widely used either as a basis of cross-cultural comparison or as an influence and inspiration for other theories. His system originally started with four dimensions, later on two more dimensions were added, the last one as recently as 2010. Hofstede originally graduated with a technical engineering degree, but later on received his PhD (cum laude) in social psychology. The foundation of his cross-cultural work was laid when he worked at IBM where he gathered an enormous amount of information on people's behaviour in large companies all around the world. It was when he took a sabbatical from his work at IBM that he finally had the time to actually conduct some research based on that information. This ultimately led to him publishing his theory in 1980 in his book called *Culture's Consequences.* His ideas were further developed in *Cultures and Organizations: Software of the Mind* (Hofstede, Hofstede and Minkov, 2010).

Power distance
This dimension explains how people in a culture accept the way power is distributed in society, from the bottom up. This means that it measures how the people lower in the hierarchy accept and expect how unequally the power is divided. In cultures with a large power distance, everybody has their own place in the hierarchy and there is obedience towards authority. On the other hand the cultures with a smaller power distance expect much more equality in the distribution of power and don't always settle for or verbally agree with what somebody tells them to do, even if that person is in a much higher position. When people from significantly different power-distance backgrounds meet, it can cause friction. It is generally not accepted in a high-power-distance society

that you as a floor manager for example should have direct contact with the CEO of another company when trying to do business. Basically roughly knowing how a culture scores on power distance can help you in deciding who to approach from your position, or sometimes, if you want to get something done, who from your company should approach them in order to be successful.

Individualism versus collectivism
A highly individualistic culture is explained to be one where people are seen as individuals and expected to take care of only themselves and their immediate family. Decisions are made based on individual wants and needs. In an individualistic culture people tend to think in terms of "I", in contrast to a collectivistic culture where it would be in terms of "we" and where people are born as a part of a family or extended family. Within these collectivistic families, members will always be protected by their family and unconditional loyalty is expected of them. Members of a collectivistic culture base their well-being and achievements on external factors like meeting the expectations that are set by the group they belong to. Group loyalty and coherence are the biggest parameter for collectivistic cultures. When doing business with collectivistic cultures, you should never expect a single individual to be able to make any real final decisions. Usually people from collectivistic cultures will need the approval of the group before any changes can be made. Generally when attending a meeting with people from a collectivistic culture, you can expect to meet with a higher number of people, and rarely if ever with a single individual.

Masculinity versus femininity
The masculinity dimension that Hofstede has proposed measures the level of assertiveness compared to that of modesty. It is called masculinity versus femininity because modesty is considered more of a feminine value and assertive more of a masculine value. Research has shown that women's values are actually very similar from one society to another, making the comparison of a whole society more of a comparison between the men's values from one society to another. Meaning in a feminine society the men's values will be much closer to the women's values, and thus the society as a whole will be much more modest. In a masculine society the gap between the men's values and the women's values

will be bigger, making society as a whole more assertive. So what Hofstede did was to measure assertiveness and modesty and conceptualise those as an equation of average masculine values compared to average feminine values of a society. The smaller the difference, the more modest the society will be. But what is really happening is that they are basically only looking at the men in a society and at how modest or assertive their combined values are. A masculine society is likely to be more competitive, materialistic and focused on recognition and accomplishments, while a feminine society will be very modest and caring. When doing business with a very feminine society you ideally want to be more modest even in business. This means not overselling your product or service, as this will likely come off as arrogance. When dealing with a very masculine society, you would actually do want to do precisely that. Basically on one side of the spectrum praising yourself can be the way to go, and on the other side this can only push your potential business partners away. If you know which side to lean to, you know which strategy is more likely to be successful.

Uncertainty avoidance

This dimension measures how tolerant a society is towards uncertainty and to what extent the society is programmed to avoid situations with high uncertainty. In a society with high-uncertainty avoidance among their members, life will be very structured and there will be very strict laws and religion. Since members of a high-uncertainty avoidance society will be used to living under these structured conditions, they will generally be much less comfortable with uncertainty, unstructured situations and adjusting to changes. On the other side societies with low scores for uncertainty avoidance will be programmed to be much more dynamic, risk taking, and will prefer as few rules and regulations as possible. There is also a big difference in emotional expression, where people in high-uncertainty avoidance societies will be much more emotional in general, and people in societies scoring lower will be expected to not express themselves in an emotional manner. When you are dealing with people from high-uncertainty-avoidance cultures, in order to keep them feeling comfortable you will want to be very structured in your approach. If you are very clear in scheduling appointments with them, and respect those appointments, they will feel much more at ease with you. Do not expect people from high-uncertainty-avoidance societies to be very flexible. They are not the ones where it is alright to cancel a day before and ask if it is alright to reschedule, because although it may be accepted and alright, it will cause them to feel much more uncomfortable with you. Take more time to consider something before you agree with it, as agreeing today and coming back on the matter in one week because you have changed your mind will affect these people much more than it would people from a low-uncertainty-avoidance culture. While obviously it is never a good idea in any business relationship to agree on something and then change your mind later, the effect on the business relationship will be much more significant with people from high-uncertainty-avoidance societies.

Long-term orientation versus short-term orientation
Hofstede added this fifth dimension his theory in 1991. In this dimension, the members of long-term oriented societies are oriented towards future rewards, adapting to changes, and persistence, while members of short-term oriented societies are focused more on the past and the present. The latter will highly value tradition, integrity, national pride and social obligations towards society and their family. Being a short- or long-term oriented society also translates into business. Naturally long-term oriented societies seem more fit for successful business because of their orientation towards the future and achieving goals, while in short-term oriented societies the focus lies more on the past and the present. It is always recommended to keep in mind what the nature is of the people you are about to do business with. If they are short-term oriented, you will want to respect their traditions, integrity and national pride.

Indulgence versus restraint
In Hofstede's last dimension, indulgence shows how freely a society can satisfy its members' personal needs which relate to enjoying life. In a restrained society the satisfaction of personal needs is suppressed, controlled and regulated by social customs. This dimension has relatively little influence on doing business itself, but it can have a big influence on the ways used to establish a personal relationship with people from societies at one end of the spectrum or the other.

47.   Defining Culture

Fons Trompenaars & Peter Woolliams

When we are living and working in another culture, we are usually very aware of obvious differences in dress, food, and basic behaviours. Much more important for effective integration are differences at a deeper, implicit level, which we are less likely to be aware of.

Analyzing the structure of culture
The culture of any society around the world can be compared to an onion. It has layers, which can be peeled off. Three distinct layers can be distinguished:

- the outer layer
- the middle layer
- the inner layer.

The outer layer contains those elements that people primarily associate with culture: the visual reality of behaviour, clothes, food, language, architecture, and so on. Wherever they are, they will readily recognize differences from what they are familiar with at home. This is the level of explicit culture. The middle layer refers to the norms and values that a community holds: what is considered right and wrong (norms), or good and bad (values). Norms are often external: each society superimposes them on its members, reinforced by measure of social control. Values tend to be more internal than norms, and most societies do not have many means of controlling their enforcement. Values and norms structure the way people in a particular culture behave. But they are not visible, despite their influence on what happens at the observable surface, in the outer layer of culture.

The inner layer is the deepest: the level of implicit culture. Understanding the core of the culture onion is the key to working successfully with other cultures. The core consists of basic assumptions, series of rules, and methods that a society has developed to deal with the regular problems that it faces. These methods of problem-solving have become so basic that, like breathing, people no longer think about how they do it. For an outsider, these basic assumptions can be very difficult to recognize.

Understanding the different meanings

On arrival in your foreign destination to begin your professional assignment, you will immediately be aware of differences arising from the outer and the middle layers of culture. The importance of the inner layer of culture is that different cultures may give a different meaning to the same thing. You are likely to find differences in the following areas, among others:

- the status accorded to older people
- the relationship between men and women
- the respect given to the law (and even simple rules)
- the degree to which your working relationship is or becomes more personal.

It is very important that you do not make the mistake of assuming that cultural differences are just about such visible elements as clothes, food, and houses. You may embarrass yourself, or your host, because you give different meaning to the same things. If you have some understanding of these differences, and learn how to cope with them, your whole experience of working in a different culture can be enhanced and made much more effective – and enjoyable.

Understanding the basic assumptions

Every culture has developed its own set of basic assumptions, which can be categorized into different dimensions. In dealing with universal human problems, each cultural dimension can be seen as a continuum: at one end there is a basic value, which contrasts with the value at the other end. The continuum will cover every possible combination between the two contrasting basic values. All cultures need to deal with the challenge of these extreme choices. They face a continuous series of dilemmas, because by itself each alternative is either unsatisfactory or insufficient. In business, for example, do we go only for the short term or the long term? For stability or change? For market-led or technology-led products? For rewarding individuals or teams? Transnational organizations respond to these dilemmas in different ways, according to how they stand on each separate dimension derived from their cultural heritage. Seven cultural dimensions can be distinguished, as follows.

Universalistic versus Particularistic

People in universalistic cultures share the belief that general rules, codes, values, and standards take precedence over particular needs and claims of friends and relations. In such a society, the rules apply equally to the whole "universe" of members. Any exception weakens the rule. For example, the rule that you should bear truthful witness in a court of law, or give an honest account of an accident to an insurance company before it pays out, is more important here than particular ties of friendship or family obligations. This does not mean that, in universalistic cultures, particular ties are completely unimportant. But the universal truth –that is, the law – is considered logically more significant than these relationships. The United States is a notable example of a universalistic culture, which explains the high number of lawyers per head of population. Conversely, particularistic cultures see the ideal culture in terms of human friendship, extraordinary achievements and situations, and in a network of intimate relationships. The "spirit of the law" is deemed more important than the "letter of the law". Obviously there are rules and laws in particularistic cultures, but these merely codify how people relate to each other. Rules are needed, if only so that people can make exceptions to them for particular cases, but generally individuals need to be able to count on the support of their friends. South America and parts of Africa are examples of cultures where, typically, relationships between friends and family members are deemed more important than the letter of the law.

Individualistic versus Communitarian

In predominantly individualistic cultures, people place the individual before the community. The pace is set by individual happiness, welfare, and fulfilment. People are expected to decide matters largely on their own, and to take care primarily of themselves and their immediate family. The quality of life for all members of society is seen as directly dependent on opportunities for individual freedom and development. The community is judged by the extent to which it serves the interest of individual members. The United Kingdom and, to a greater extent, the United States, are examples of cultures that encourage the individual. Pay and performance systems in organizations are often based on this. At the other end of the continuum, a predominantly communitarian culture places the community before the individual. It is the responsibility of the individual to act in ways that serve society. By doing so, individual needs will be taken care of naturally. The quality of life for the individual is seen as directly dependent on the degree to which he or she takes care of fellow members, even at the cost of individual freedom. People are judged by the extent to which they serve the interest of the community. For example, in both China and Japan, working in a team and contributing to the group or society have a higher priority than individual performance.

Specific versus diffuse

People from specific cultures start with the elements, the specifics. First they analyse them separately, and then they put them back together again. In specific cultures, the whole is the sum of its parts. Each person's life is divided into many components: as a newcomer, you can enter only one component at a time. Interactions between people are highly purposeful and well defined. The public part of specific individuals' make-up is much larger than their private space. People are easily accepted into the public area, but it is very difficult to get into the private space, since each area in which two people encounter each other is considered separate from the other, a specific case. Individuals within a culture that is specifically oriented tend to concentrate on hard facts, standards, measures, contracts. In specific cultures (such as the United States or Australia) business can be done without individuals having to form a relationship first. People from cultures that are diffusely oriented start with the whole and see each element in perspective to the total. All elements are related to each other. These relationships are more important than each separate element; so the whole is more than just the sum of its elements. Diffuse individuals have a large private space and a small public one. Newcomers are not easily accepted into either. But once they have been accepted, they are admitted into all layers of the individual's life. A friend is a friend in all respects: at work, in sports, in domestic life, and so on. The various roles that someone might play in your life are not separated. Diffuse cultures cherish such qualities as style, demeanour, empathy, trust, and understanding. In diffuse cultures such as in the Gulf countries, you have to develop a relationship first before you can do business. A high level of involvement is required as a precursor.

Affective versus neutral
In an affective culture, people do not object to a display of emotions. It is not considered necessary to hide moods and feelings and to keep them bottled up. Affective cultures may interpret the less explicit signals of a neutral culture as less important. They may be ignored or even go unnoticed. For example, Italian and French cultures display their emotions – expressed, some would say, particularly in flamboyant driving! But this cultural bias is also revealed in their beautiful car designs and haute couture. In a neutral culture, people are taught that it is incorrect to show one's feelings overtly. This does not mean they do not have feelings; it just means that the degree to which feelings may show is limited. They accept and are aware of feelings, but are in control of them. Neutral cultures may think the louder signals of an affective culture too excited, and over-emotional. In neutral cultures, showing too much emotion may erode your power to interest people. For example, it may be difficult to tell what business partners in Japan are thinking, as they are likely to exhibit little body language.

Universalistic 49%	Particularistic 51%	
Individualistic 28%	Communitarian 72%	
Specific 70%	Diffuse 30%	
Neutral 49%	Affective 51%	
Achieved 63%	Ascribed 37%	
Sequential 20%	Synchronic 80%	
Internal 10%	External 90%	

100 90 80 70 60 50 40 30 20 10 0 10 20 30 40 50 60 70 80 90 100

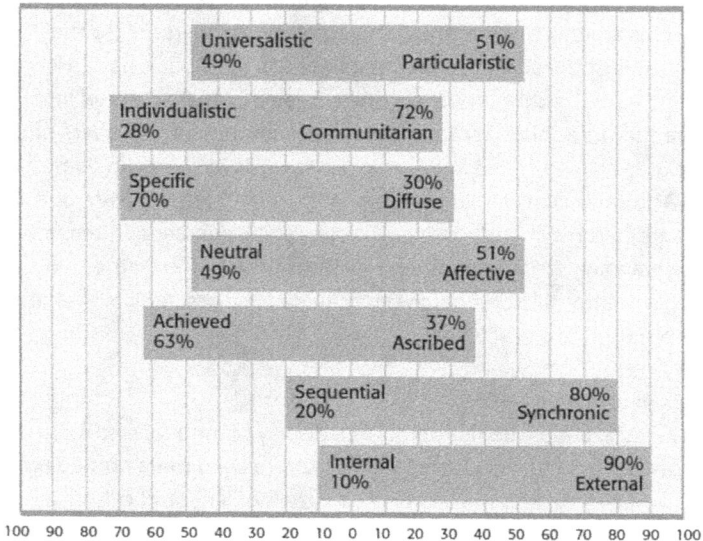

Achieved versus ascribed

Achieved status is a reflection of what an individual does and has accomplished. In cultures that are achievement-oriented, individuals derive their status from what they have accomplished. An individual with achieved status has to prove what he or she is worth over and over again: status is accorded and maintained on the basis of his or her actions. The Dutch culture is a good example of one that encourages people to achieve results, while family background is less important. It is what the individual does that is significant. Ascribed status is a reflection of what an individual is and how others relate to his or her position in the community, in society as a whole, or in an organization. In an ascriptive culture, people derive their status from birth, age, gender, or wealth. People with ascribed status do not have to achieve results to retain status: it is accorded to them on the basis of their being. In the Middle East and Far East, for example, who you are has to be taken very much into consideration.

MATCHING CULTURAL NORMS TO BUSINESS ACTION

The way that people in different societies interact with each other has important repercussions for business practice. To take an everyday example, consider buying food at a delicatessen. If you are in, for example, the United States, the United Kingdom or the Netherlands, you might collect a numbered ticket that shows your place in the queue. You patiently wait your turn, in the orderly, sequential queue. The sales assistant serves you with everything you need before the next customer, and this is an efficient system.

But if you are in, say, Italy, and you ask the assistant for salami, he or she will serve you and then shout, "Who else wants salami?" Other customers will then be served accordingly, before the assistant again asks you what else you want. This is also an efficient system. The salami is unwrapped just once, and the knife does not have to be washed again. This process also promotes social interaction between the cluster of customers who have a common bond (in this case, a need for salami).

Now imagine that you are running the computer services for a global hotel chain. You commission a computerized database system for the check-out system, which has been written by a US-based software house employing programmers with an Indian ethnic/cultural background. The desk clerk asks guests for their room number and retrieves their accounts from the database. This is a sequential system that works well in the United States, the United Kingdom, Germany, and other countries.

But this system is not customer-friendly in the synchronic cultures of South America, Spain, or Italy. Here, the desk clerk and one guest expect to examine the account for extras (telephone, mini bar, and so on) while the guest in front is paying and the guest behind is shouting their room number. Sequential culture is actually built into the internal architecture of database software that originates in sequential cultures. It is difficult to make such a database work in synchronic contexts.

Sequential versus synchronic

Every culture has developed its own response to time. The time-orientation dimension has two aspects: a culture's approach to structuring time, and the relative importance it gives to the past, present, and future. Time can be structured in two ways. In the sequentialist approach, time moves forward, second by second, minute by minute, hour by hour, in a straight line. In the synchronistic approach, time moves round in cycles: of minutes, hours, days, weeks, months, and years. People structuring time sequentially tend to do one thing at a time. They view time as a narrow line of distinct, consecutive segments. Sequential people view time as tangible and divisible. They strongly prefer planning and keeping to plans once they have been made, rather than extemporizing and adapting. Time commitments are taken seriously, and staying on schedule is a must. Sequential cultures include Canada, Australia, and Switzerland.

Conversely, people structuring time synchronically usually do several things at a time. To them, time is a wide ribbon, allowing many things to take place simultaneously. Time is intangible and flexible. Time commitments are desirable rather than absolute. Plans are easily changed. Synchronic people especially value the satisfactory completion of interactions with others. Promptness depends on the type of relationship. The whole philosophy of 'Just in Time' management derived from the highly synchronic Japanese.

Past-oriented cultures
If a culture is predominantly oriented towards the past, the future is seen as a repetition of past experiences. Respect for ancestors and collective historical experiences are characteristic of a past oriented culture.

Present-oriented cultures
A culture that is predominantly oriented towards the present will not attach much value to common past experiences, nor to future prospects. Rather, day-by-day experiences tend to direct people's thinking and action.

Future-oriented cultures
In a future-oriented culture, most human activities are directed towards future prospects. Generally, the past is not considered to be vitally significant to a future state of affairs. Detailed planning constitutes a major activity in futureoriented cultures.

Internally or externally controlled
This dimension is concerned with relationships to nature. Every culture has developed an attitude towards the natural environment. Survival has meant acting with or against it. The way people relate to their environment – internalistically or externalistically – is linked to the way they seek to have control over their own lives and over their destiny. Internalistic people tend to have a mechanistic view of nature. They see nature as a complex machine, and machines can be controlled if you have the right expertise. Internalistic people do not believe in luck or predestination. They are "inner-directed": one's personal resolution is the starting point for every action. You can live the life you want to

live if you take advantage of the opportunities. People can dominate nature, if they makes the effort. Many Israeli people, for example, are highly internally controlled. Externalistic people have a more organic view of nature. Mankind is one of nature's forces, so should operate in harmony with the environment. Man should subjugate himself to nature and go along with its forces. Externalistic people do not believe that they can shape their own destiny. "Nature moves in mysterious ways", and therefore you never know what will happen to you. The actions of externalistic people are "outer-directed": adapted to external circumstances. Russians and Singaporeans are notably externally controlled.

48. Presentations in English

Sander Schroevers

Humour and jokes

Anglophone speakers make more and easier use of humour than for example German or Scandinavian speakers. A French or Russian speaker will probably prefer *not* to make any jokes, as that damages the desired image. Finding the correct type of humour in your presentation is somewhat tricky, as humour doesn't always travel well. In Asian countries, humour types like sarcasm, satire and parody aren't always understood or appreciated. On the other hand, I remember all the serious warnings I got when lecturing in the Middle East or Far East, but much to my surprise I saw the whole crowd laughing out loud. It confirmed my believe that certain cultural differences seem to be getting smaller and smaller, despite all those that stay different. And isn't that somehow less surprising, now that people are watching the same movies, wearing the same clothing brands and so forth?

Listening habits

The way you set up your presentation should take into account which audience you are addressing. Research shows that the way specific cultures listen (and watch) differs to a great extent. Just like cultures use speech in different ways, so do they listen alternatively. An example: Dutch, German, Swedes and Finnish business cultures put great emphasis on factual information and they know how to listen well to that. Spaniards, French or Italians according to their expectations prefer an imaginative talker, using eloquent phrases and knowing how to present oneself. They much rather hear things brought with flair or grandeur, than those dry facts or technical details. The same applies for the listening span, which can be relatively shorter. Being Dutch or Flemish, one is used to a very data orientated and linear build-up of presentations. Mind you that not every audience will react in the same way. The best solution is to be able to jump between the different units within your presentation. You should also know how to deal flexibly with interruptions or delays. In certain countries you will find yourself being photographed endlessly with members of the audience. That's probably why the VIP-rooms usually can be found behind the stage.

Nonverbal communication
There exist international differences in the way people understand certain information. This may involve elements you don't always think of, like certain gestures you are used to make, or the use of certain colours, images etcetera. For instance, in China red and yellow (or gold) bring luck and prosperity, but the same colours in Mexico can mean death. Chinese also really care about numbers: where in our culture financial amounts will end at comma 99, or comma 00, Chinese prefer the use of lucky numbers and will try to avoid the unlucky numbers. Take a look at the flight numbers when you book a seat for a Chinese destination, know how certain floors in buildings never seem to be on the elevator buttons, and so forth. Another unexpected element of talking abroad is the gestures you use. My worst own experience concerns two gestures: the OK-sign (thumb up) and the perfect-sign (thumb to forefinger, making a circle). Because they can mean the most horrible things in other cultures. May I here refer to the chapter called: 'Gestures the world at hand' further in this book? It is funny to read...
When doing business with someone from a different cultural background, it is worth preparing this often overlooked element of communication.
Then of course there may be religious influences as well, certain animals aren't liked, or on the contrary liked more than we expected. I remember at an international conference that I wasn't allowed to show certain images, because these showed too much woman's skin (the upper arm in fact). Things you actually know, but simply forget since you are perhaps too
used to it. In short, when presenting abroad, it is worth to critically go through your slides, based on the points mentioned above.

49.   Thinking in dilemma's

Trompenaars Hampden-Turner

Cultural diversity expresses itself in viewpoints and values, in operational priorities, and in ways of doing things. In our research and experience in working with international organizations, issues rooted in differences in (cultural) values often take on the character of basic strategic dilemmas.

Our approach is to help organizations recognize, respect and reconcile these differences. A dilemma can be defined as two propositions that are in apparent tension. A dilemma describes a situation where one has to choose between two good or desirable options. For example, on the one hand we need to centralize (global), while on the other hand we also need to decentralize (local). There are several options to resolve the apparent conflicting propositions:

Stick firm to your views.
One response is to stick to your own viewpoint and reject the other orientation. In other words, you take the 'head office wants to centralize decisions' approach.

Abandon your own views.
Another possible response is to abandon your own viewpoint and 'go native'. Here you adopt a 'when in Rome, do as Romans do' approach.

Compromise.
A compromise is sacrificing decentralizing to centralization or visa versa. It is splitting the difference. It frustrates the values of both parties.

Reconcile both views.
What is needed is an approach where the two opposing views can be synergized so that instead of 'either-or' thinking, there is 'and-and' thinking. So, instead of trying to look for pros and cons, we look for new value in both and then reconcile the dilemma to create innovative results. Thus, for instance, the ability to take

centralization and decentralization and reconcile both is the beauty and the strength of reconciling dilemmas! Dilemma reconciliation is a unique way of looking at problem solving, and it is a skill that can be developed. Let us illustrate the steps we take when reconciling different values. Below, two values are in opposition. It is quite natural for us to see these value differences and look at the pros and the cons. Does the corporation risk disintegrating or does it suffer from over-control? The "rope" is frequently stretched between rival factions as in a tug-of-war, each believing that to "save" the company it needs more centralization or more decentralization.

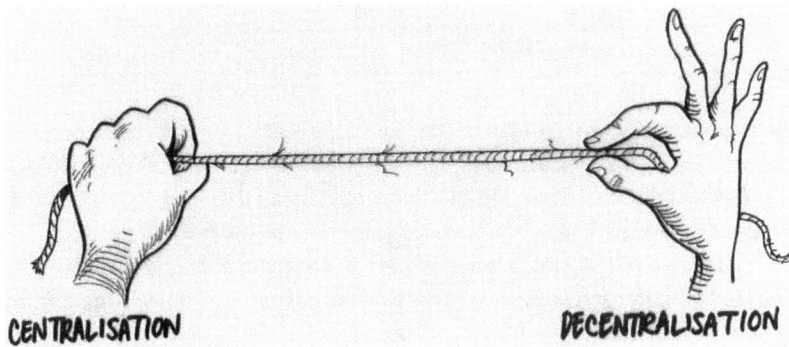

CENTRALISATION   DECENTRALISATION

Next, we force the single line into two axes and create a value continuum. This forms a 'culture space' where we can start the dialogue and explore new solutions. It means that one proposition does not necessarily occur at the expense of the other.

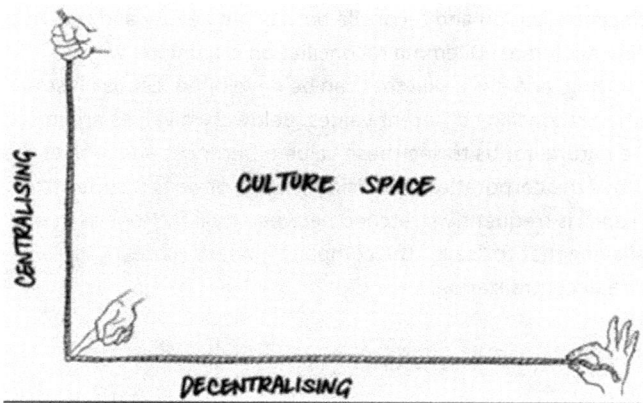

Finally, we look for ways to realize both values at the same time. In this example, we would be decentralizing activities, at the same time as centralizing knowledge about the activities. The reconciled solution would be an Inquiring System and Knowledge Generating Corporation, which gathers data and information from business units and transforms this into a body of knowledge. This knowledge can then be shared with each unit, so that each decentral part has the wisdom of the whole centralized system. As the saying goes you must "Act Local" but "Think Global". Local actions provide the information from which global conclusions are drawn.

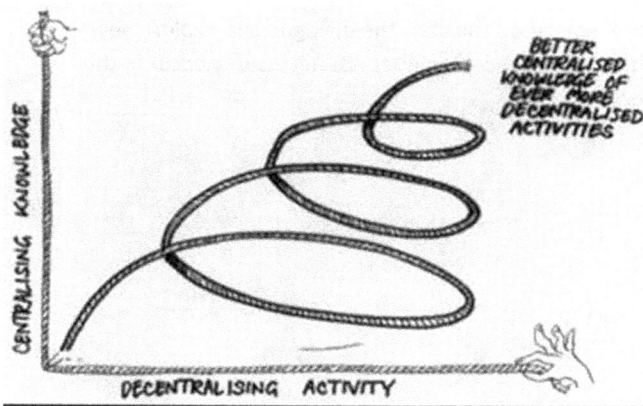

Research by Trompenaars and Hampden-Turner has found that leaders succeed not because they are good at choosing one side over the other, but because they are able to reconcile values. Integrating two desirable aims, which were in a creative tension creates a new more valuable reality.

Change management is all about this process of enrichment. In addition, integrating diverse value orientations is not a matter of one party trying to understand the other and trying to adapt, it is a matter of the joint effort in mutually understanding and reconciling the differences. Any change process should be dealt with in the context of realizing business objectives and by solving joint business issues instead of by discussing differences for the sake of difference.

Dilemma-reconciliation process in six steps

Step 1: Identify the dilemma

a) Make the dilemma you have chosen as specific as possible:
- Think of a concrete situation that directly concerns or affects you and structure it as follows: "On the one hand we want/must... (Proposition A) ...., whilst on the other hand we want/must...... (Proposition B) ......"
- Identify the dilemma holder. This is the person who equally values both propositions and is in the position to implement a reconciliation.

b) Enter the name of the dilemma holder and the two opposing propositions in the heading of the worksheet.

c) Give your dilemma a catching title and enter it in the top left corner.

Step 2: Chart the dilemma

a) Enter Proposition A and B into the appropriate space next to the vertical/horizontal axes. Rewrite the noun as a Present Participle (e.g. changing instead of change)

b) Enter the two sides of the Dimension of Culture that best explains the tension between propositions A and B.

c) With a cross (X) mark the current (preferred) position of the dilemma holder in the grid and add the (x,y)-coordinates

Step 3: Stretch the dilemma

a) List a maximum of five advantages and disadvantages of Proposition A.

b) Similarly do so for Proposition B.

Step 4: Create epithets for the undesirable positions

a) Emphasize the undesirability of the positions (1,10), (10,1) etc. by stigmatizing them with an epithet. This is a "sweet and sour" action or expression.

a) Start with position (1,10) and think of the consequences of taking Proposition A too far. Do the same with position (10,1) and enter the epithets in the clouds.

b) Create epithets for the (5,5)-compromise and (1,1)- denial position.

Step 5: Reconcile the dilemma

a) Use the following reasoning:

b) "How can we increase the benefits of Proposition A through the use of the positives of Proposition B, or vice versa?"

a) Describe your reasoning in the box in the bottom left hand corner.

b) With a clockwise or anti-clockwise spiral indicate if your reasoning started with using the positives of Proposition B or those of Proposition A.

c) Think of a short statement for the (10,10) position and enter it in the ellipse

Step 6: Make an implementation plan

a) What actions should be undertaken, by whom and when?

b) Who should sponsor this change?

c) What obstacles need to be overcome?

d) How would you monitor the progress?

1 Identify and describe the dilemma and dilemma holder
on the one hand _____
on the other hand _____
Dilemma holder _____

10

0,10

4. _____

10,10

5. _____

3 List positives of Y-axis
+ _____
+ _____
+ _____

List negatives of Y-axis
- _____
- _____
- _____

5,5

4. _____

10,0

4. _____

2 Y-axis label

0,0   2 X-axis label _____   10

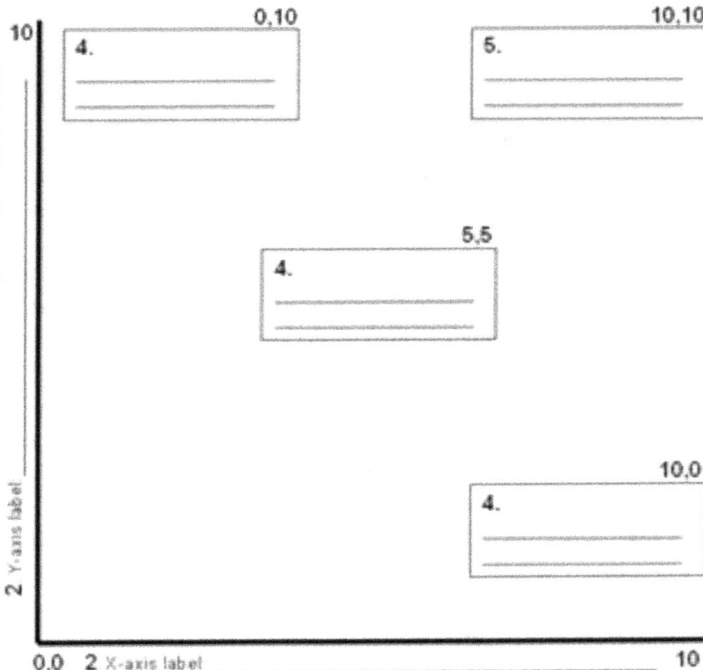

3 List positives of X-axis
+ _____
+ _____
+ _____

List negatives of X-axis
- _____
- _____

1. Identify the dilemma

2. Chart the dilemma

a   Specify the dilemma and identify the dilemma holder

b   Label the axes reflecting the opposing positions (positive or neutral)

3. Stretch the dilemma
List the positives and negatives of each side of the dilemma

4. Make epithets
Put epithets (labels, "sweet and sour" descriptions) in each of the boxes

5. Reconcile the dilemma
Ask how Value A can support Value B and vice versa

6. Develop action plan

6a Action plan
1 _____
2 _____
3 _____
4 _____
5 _____

6b What behavior(s) support this
1 _____
2 _____
3 _____
4 _____
5 _____

50.   Getting acquainted globally

Sander Schroevers, Ian Lewis

The way people are welcomed, can influence the atmosphere substantially, as is illustrated in the following example; Delegates from Bangalore, India and Shenzhen, China arrive at the airport, and are unpleasantly surprised by the fact that they weren't welcomed personally, but only received detailed (perfectly) written information. Such misunderstandings can influence the atmosphere negatively. Also first impressions are important. Research shows that during the first seconds of meeting individuals interpret the other person's character, mood, and even manner in how they are going to negotiate. We therefore need to give some thought as to how best present ourselves. This is also relevant when you have met the person or persons previously. The way you greet someone is a form of respect. Each culture has developed its own norms of greeting. Some are better than others at learning about another's greeting norms and being prepared for them. In most cultures of the world, seniority and hierarchy are important in whom to greet first.

Handshakes
Any face-to-face contact requires some handling. The English verb to handle is related to the word hand, and in most countries a handshake is the preferred way of greeting. In some countries a handshake is not acceptable, particularly between male and female, and in others, a bow is more appropriate. Handshakes with Iranian women aren't appreciated, whereas a lady from the Saudi delegation, for example, might shake your hand. Additionally, there are subtle differences in how long a hand-shake should last. These may be mere seconds, as between European countries, but can last much longer further afield. A short handshake in some cultures means you're not to be trusted.

Welcoming words

In addition to a handshake, some welcoming words need to be said. Please note that the question *'How do you do?'* is best answered with *'How do you do?'* or *'I'm fine, thank you. How are you?'* A commonly made mistake by non-English speakers is to take such phrases seriously and reply in detail. After having the greeting, and welcoming words in place, how do we best introduce ourselves?

Names and titles

The easiest approach throughout the world when introducing yourself in English is to use your first name (or the name you generally use as your first name) and surname: "I'm John Smith, pleased to meet you." Listen to how the other party introduces itself. For example, in Britain, Ireland, the US and Australia they may only give you their first name: "Hi, I'm John, glad you could join us today." Some professions may continue to prefer the more formal surname: "Good afternoon, I'm Mr. Smith, partner solicitor in this firm." Certain professions such as doctors or professors continue to use their title: "Hello, I'm Dr. Riana Van den Bergh, from the part-time department." If you have received correspondence in advance, letters or emails, they may give a clue as to how they would like to be addressed.

Job positions

Stating your job position in the company differs from country to country. For example, in the UK, people may be shy about indicating their job title. John's title is General Manager of Sales Department but he is more likely to introduce himself as: "I'm John from Hounslow Engineering." In the US, job titles are very important so they will usually specify: "I'm Joe, vice president of Sales, Houston Engineering." In China or Japan people may give you their company name, followed by department, job title and finally their name.

- I'm from Donghua Daxui, the International Department.
- I'm the vice Dean, and my name is Frances Liu.
- I'm the exclusive representative for....
- I'm one of the many local sales teams.

Business cards

A lot has been written on how to receive a business card. For example, that it is important to study them respectfully instead of simply sticking someone's card into your pocket, or that in Asian cultures, people give and receive cards with both hands. Very little, however, has been written on what information is written on cards and their actual appearance. In a country like South Korea someone's job description is considered very important, or in France people may add extra information. In many cultures a card is simply something practical, containing contact information, but there are also cultures where much more attention is given to the quality of the material or the printing technique. It is logical that when visiting such countries you want to pay some attention to such details. Finally, it is advisable to have your business card translated on the reverse of your card in cultures where English is less commonly spoken. For example, if travelling to South Korea, have a Korean translation on the reverse. It is advisable to have your business card translated into English on the reverse when travelling to English-speaking countries, unless it is clear. Being confronted with a business card in another language makes many English speakers uneasy. Take enough time to have the translations and proofs double-checked by native speakers from the target country itself. Too many companies have made silly bloopers without knowing it.

Addressing others

For many English-speaking cultures, first names have become the usual way of introduction. It feels very formal and pompous to give your full name such as Mr. Smith unless in a specific job such as Dr. Smith. Thus, when doing business with Americans, Australians, New Zealanders, Canadians, British, South Africans or Irish, it may surprise you, how quickly they can switch to using first names. Many East Asian countries (China, Japan, South Korea)
reverse the order so the surname comes first. This is a difficult hurdle for any cultural group to overcome, so we tend to find ourselves being called Mr Stefan instead of Mr Aust and we refer to them as Mr Jintao instead of Mr Hu. East Asians prefer to be more formal initially, particularly when older people are concerned. They are uncomfortable using first names and also nicknames.

'You can say you to me'

People from cultures that use family names in combination with Mr and Mrs, may feel a bit uneasy. Nevertheless, it is important to think about the social consequences of not being on first-name terms with people. It may seem too distant or even unfriendly. Therefore, simply follow the approach of your conversation partner. The cultures known to have larger scores on status orientation, have a preference of using a person's title also when addressing them. It may be better in such situations to say: "Thank you vice president Lee", instead of "Thank you Mr. Lee".

Nicknames

Many Americans or other English-speaking people commonly use nicknames in their business contacts. The English language often shortens first names. Examples of common nicknames are: *Harry* for *Harold, Tony* for *Anthony, Bob* for *Robert, Gene* for *Eugene, Jack* for *John, Bill* for *William, Frank* for *Francis* and *Ted* for *Edward*. To address business partners with their full first name could look somewhat strange. Some people will even mention their nickname on their business card (in quotation marks), for example: *Robert 'Chip' Loeffler*. Their first name will naturally appear in full on most judicial documents. It is not uncommon for people to be known by another name other than their first in the British Isles. For example, *Francis Gordon Lacey* is known to everyone as *Gordon* except on official documents.

Socialising and small talk

For the majority of cultures, socialising in the work environment plays an important, sometimes vital role. Getting to know the person you are doing business with is as important as the actual business itself. In most of the Arab cultures it is practically impossible to do business without knowing the person very well. Leaving room for getting to know people is an important element in any negotiation. Small talk is used both to get to know other people, as well as help put people at ease. Some cultures place more emphasis on this than others, but it's important at all times. Always begin with small talk even if late for a meeting. Never begin with business. If you arrive in the middle of a meeting, apologise even if it's not your fault for being late before you make your business points. If you start immediately with business, you are in danger of being thought of as anything between nervous to rude to downright dangerous.

Small-talk items
What is discussed during small talk is generally not business-related. This comes naturally to many people, but can be an issue for others. Items such as the weather, your journey to the meeting and sports are often the only topics mentioned, as they are usually non-controversial. Americans are happy to talk about their families in detail but other English-speaking cultures tend to keep family private. Talking about family is vital to cultures that need to build a relationship, such as certain Asian, Middle Eastern, African and South American countries as they need to have an overview of your family and your role in the family group. However, you do not have to go into great detail. Politics, cultural differences, sex and religion are best avoided unless you already know they can be discussed. If these come up at any time during negotiations then it's best to be curious and open, rather than state opinions. Health is a subject most English-speaking cultures talk freely about. It is important to show sympathy with any illnesses mentioned, even if you may think they're purely psychological. 'Let's get down to business' is a signal many use as the reference moment when enough small talk has taken place. It is best to try to feel the atmosphere before proceeding too quickly. You want to avoid making the other side feel uncomfortable.

How it works
Small talk is used in English speaking cultures to influence conversations in a positive way. Small talk is functional to introduce or end a conversation with a few phrases about friendly and risk-free topics. It helps to create a polite and friendly atmosphere. Try to use open questions (see section on Asking questions). It is also possible to answer a question with another question if you don't want to respond to the question asked.

Useful phrases
- How was the flight over?
- Is your hotel comfortable?

- Is this your first visit to Amsterdam?
- You must be jet-lagged after such a long flight.
- Would you like me to order some coffee?
- How's the weather in Dubai at the moment?
- How's business in your sector?

51.   Country specific negotiating

Sander Schroevers

In the previous chapter you became acquainted with useful theories on negotiating. The next part of this book is dedicated to specific communication habits and local value differences per country. And as the world seems to be getting smaller and smaller, the chances of negotiating with partners from less familiar cultures are greatly increased. Such negotiations often take place in English, but because language only counts for some twelve percent of communication, it is helpful to have some insight into the other elements that influence the way people communicate in particular countries.

National culture is one of the factors that influence behaviour at the negotiation table, just like personality, gender or organisational culture. But recent scientific research has shown that there are considerable differences in approach. Now trainers, consultants and Chambers of Commerce offer various seminars (just as we did indeed...) to help business people prepare for negotiating with foreign opponents. It seems there is a practical need, a need for which this CCBS Minor was developed at the Hogeschool of Amsterdam. And since these topics rely so strongly on communication, a fair amount of it will relate to cross-cultural awareness. In the next subchapters we describe such country-specific behaviour.

China

Despite the fact that the word 'foreigner' translates as *'yang guizi'* (foreign devil) in Mandarin, China is becoming an export market, and it is an important import partner. Looking at the economic forecasts, the export of goods will increase substantially in all likelihood. When dealing with Chinese take the following aspects into account;

Meeting
Preliminary meetings mainly serve to get to know each other better, business therefore isn't really discussed. The Chinese speak less, and use longer periods of total silence (in China silence is also eloquence). The Chinese language also knows many different wording possibilities depending on the status of someone. This calls for skilled interpreters or translators. Individual expression of thought is less common in China, as it may harm consensus. Creative brainstorming during a meeting will not produce many results; it will be better to adjourn, allowing your Chinese opponent room for thinking. There are usually (hard working) note takers present at meetings to produce detailed minutes. Chinese feel less ruled by their agenda.

Negotiations
It is interesting to see how Chinese make deals, as they tend to think much more about the consequences of a deal for their relationship networks. Preparation therefore usually includes collecting data on people and the involved relations (*'guanxi'*). Important business decisions tend to take a long time, due to the desire for consensus. Foreign parties negotiating mainly need *patience*, and that's something the Chinese have plenty of. Government approval is indispensable (national, local, as well as provincial) for any major project. This influences both planning as well as profits sometimes. Contracts are considered less binding than in western trade cultures.

Relevant values
- Confucian values still influence the Chinese society to a large extent. Protocol and hierarchy are omnipotent. Chinese schools, for instance, are used to very strict discipline. Corruption is not uncommon.
- It's not what you know, but who you know (*'guanxi'*),
- Seniority and connections cancel out achievements,
- Behave harmoniously and show respect to authority,
- It's impolite to say 'no' or openly criticise (loss of face),
- Only do so in private with close ones (*'naixin'*),
- Do not directly display negative emotions.

Czech Republic

The Czech Republic represents the westernmost presence of Slavic culture in Europe. It is a stable environment for foreign trade and business investment opportunities, given the fact that nowadays foreign-owned companies account for seventy percent of its exports. When dealing with Czech counterparts take the following aspects into account:

Meeting
As is the case in German business life, Czechs prefer to plan meetings in advance. Points on an agenda are to be followed; people are good listeners and do not really interrupt each other. During meetings, the Czech shows calmness and self-control. A display of emotions is less likely than in neighbouring countries such as Poland or Hungary. As a result the (measured) tone of voice is usually softer. Discussions proceed in an orderly fashion and decision-making is usually methodical.

Negotiations
Just like Northern cultures, the Czechs are task-oriented, meaning that very little time is spent on small talk at the beginning of negotiations. Besides, the Czechs are known for a very direct communication style. The only difference is that they can be less straightforward when saying 'No', and might feel less comfortable giving negative answers. Argumentation is best done with empirical evidence and facts supporting the proposals. Step-by-step consensus seeking techniques give better results than aggressive negotiation tactics. Czechs aren't very fond of arguing or haggling; therefore it is advisable to keep the difference between the starting price and the final price within a logical margin. Business meals play less of a role, as Czechs separate business and social circles.

Relevant values
The Czechs have a tradition of avoiding conflict and confrontation, as the Czech national history proves. Take, for instance, the 'Velvet Revolution' of 1989 which took place without violence as did the 'Velvet Divorce' of 1993, when Czechoslovakia peacefully split into the Czech and the Slovak Republic. The values scores aren't very different, except for the hierarchical acceptance, which is almost double that of the German score. Other significant differences are the amount of bureaucracy and the relatively higher corruption perception index.

Command of languages in the Czech Republic:
German: 28%, **English**: 24%, **Russian**: 20%.

France

France has been an important export partner for many years now, and those who have dealt professionally with *'la douce France'* know how different business communication can be. Some relevant differences are described below:

Meeting
The French are trained in both debating skills as well as analysis from an early age. It is generally considered important to prove a point by way of logical argumentation. The simple notion that the facts are different is not always accepted, if not backed up by lengthy rhetorical argumentation. Meetings are not always grounds for discussion, but are often used to inform about what has been decided. Business lunches may last two hours. Don't let business be a topic of conversation too early, and therefore prepare something else to talk about.

Negotiations
The French can be persistent at times when a strategy has been chosen. Compromise isn't considered a very positive thing by everyone. A direct 'No' is (unlike in Germany) generally avoided. The French prefer to say something like: *'Oui mais'* (yes, but), *'Oui-non, nous verrons'* (yes-no, we'll see) or even *'Si vous voulez'* (if you like). It is a mistake not to understand such remarks as a 'Non'. Whatever is being proposed or agreed upon during negotiations, will only be a sure thing when approved afterwards by the PDG (*Président Directeur Général*).

Relevant values
▪ In France some forty percent of higher functions are occupied by women,
▪ Using beautiful language combined with semi-philosophical logic seems to be a goal in itself,
▪ Etiquette is a French word, and knowledge thereof may give some self-assurance,
▪ Being refined or special is an important quality that is reflected in the choice of negotiation venue, restaurant, wines, as well as clothing.

Command of languages in France:
English: 36%, **Spanish**: 13%, **German:** 8%.

India

India is the second most populated country of the world, and it will play a more prominent role in global economics. First of all the population is growing faster than China's and the GDP is also increasing rapidly. Today India has about three hundred million middle class consumers, but the country adds an Australia or North Rhine-Westphalia every single year (…).

Meeting

Indians have a preference for eloquent respectful speakers. Too many dry facts don't work well. Meetings will contain a semi-euphoric atmosphere with sympathetic verbose talks in Victorian English. Despite the fact that certain Hindi words have become part of (financial) Indian English, it is advisable to study the most common of these beforehand. Many meetings will not follow an agenda, will have plenty of interruptions, and may possibly go over time. Therefore, don't make too many appointments on one day, and take the dense traffic into consideration as well.

Negotiations

Negotiations normally start in a sympathetic atmosphere, whilst the negotiation part can be serious with long haggling. Expect negotiations to be long, but usually changes will be proposed in a polite way to find agreement. The ease of doing business ranking, as well as legal contract enforcing possibilities are low compared to European standards. Insert mediation and arbitration clauses in all legal contracts. Be careful that Indians cannot directly say 'No', and will therefore normally revert to expressions like: 'maybe', 'we'll try' and so forth. Vice versa, Northerners should be careful with saying 'No' too directly. Decisions need to be ratified by the higher levels; therefore check already during negotiations which parts have been firmly agreed and which not. Socialising can be a pleasant part of business in India, and Indian hospitality has a lot to offer visitors. On the other hand, I know that Indians visiting North-West Europe can be surprised or disappointed with the treatment given.

Relevant values

- India is a *contact* instead of a *contract* culture, where relationships are more important than a deal at hand. Companies are strictly hierarchical and empowerment is hardly seen, although a younger generation is getting a taste of it at universities now.
- Getting frustrated will neither help, nor win friends,
- Value is placed on empathy and consensus,
- Dinners start late and last long.

Italy

Italian culture has had a demonstrable influence: the Roman Empire, the Renaissance or the weight of the Vatican. Most of the Italian businesses are SMEs *(MKB or KMU)*, almost three-quarters of the Italian economy in fact. Moreover, quite a few of these are family run. It is plausible that this might affect negotiations in some way.

Meeting
Initial meetings in Italy are usually intended to get people acquainted, not to do straight business. Meetings themselves often seem noisy and unstructured compared to Nothern standards. There is a considerably longer time frame reserved for small talk, and mobile phone calls are often acceptable during a meeting. Improvisation is valued, just as interruptions, and indeed many Italians think that following the agenda strictly could interfere with the quality of a discussion. Italians also prefer to present an argument in an articulate way, partly because 'feeling' is recognised in decisions making.

Command of languages in Italy: **English**: 29%, **French**: 14%.

Negotiations
Negotiating in Italy can sometimes be a lengthy process, where patience works much better than irritation, because business and social life can be so intermingled. Personal alliances are often influential in Italy. It's not 'what' you know, but 'who' you know, and people are also judged on their ability to cultivate relationships. Smaller companies tend to have a rather hierarchical structure, often with an autocratic style of management. In the Netherlands, facts are much more separated from the person; Italians tend to take direct rejections more personal. They also may feel that people like the Dutch or Germans are overly concerned with facts and procedures. Where they also likely to explore a contextual background, and perhaps feel that the over-pragmatic Northerners lack a sense of deeper thinking.

Relevant values
Jokes and private remarks are exchanged much more than in the North of Europe, and are judged as functional in a business environment. Italians have difficulty saying 'No' directly. Successful business relations invest in socialising, Pay attention to dress and style, as often someone is judged on that, 'La bella figura' refers to more than just fashion; charm, formal elegance, tact and confidence also play an important role in Italy, Italian contracts can be written in a labyrinthine way and contain complicated terminology,

Japan

Although its economy has stagnated recently, Japan is still one of the world's richest societies – with Greater Tokyo as the largest metropolitan area in the world, with over 30 million residents, and an economy which alone is larger than that of Russia.

Meeting

Initial meetings in Japan are intended to get people acquainted, and reinforce a consensus that may already have been established. They do not serve to do straight business. The atmosphere in Japanese meetings tends to be highly formal (in contrast to the business entertaining afterwards). Japanese negotiators generally like to be well informed about the focus of a meeting and who will be attending, so they can prepare a well-matched team. Be clear about the status of the members in the organisation (also on business cards). Some communication distinctions influence Japanese business meetings compared to elsewhere. This primarily has to do with: (1) Difficulties due to English language abilities, (2) The particular importance of inexplicit and polite conversational style, (never interrupt, apologize non-stop), and (3) The long silences in between phrases.

Negotiations

Negotiating in Japan can be a lengthy process, where patience is a necessary commodity. This is because teams never make decisions at the meeting. The main reason is that a consensus has to be reached within the own company departments, as well as with other existing relationships. Japanese negotiation teams give the least information compared to other cultures, whereas German negotiation teams score highest. On the other hand, the Japanese are willing to make the most concessions, while the Germans are the toughest negotiators. In Japan, the customer and supplier relationship shows a very different power balance than is customary in North-Western Europe, where the customer does not play as strong a role. The Japanese value long-term relationships.

Relevant values

- Japanese businesses prefer to first establish the right relationships before business can be conducted. After this, people work in a quite task-oriented manner and with self-effacing dedication. The Japanese expect people to show self-knowledge of their position and behave accordingly; therefore, what is not said can also be very important.
- The Japanese tend to be inconceivably conscious of detail,
- 'Saving face' is essential in interpersonal contact,
- The Japanese have one of the highest scores on status.

Netherlands

This small country has the highest density in Europe (in comparison: one fifth of the German population, living on one tenth of its area). And it may come as a surprise that the Netherlands have become Germany's number one trade partner.

Meeting
Dutch meetings are pragmatic and quickly focus on results and responsibilities with clear action plans. During meetings, everybody may contribute and voice an opinion, whether it is positive or negative. The goal of meetings is consensus-building and planning. The Dutch are used to freedom and assertiveness starting from a young age and they communicate accordingly. They are quicker on first-name terms and seem less driven by protocol. The Dutch value experiment, and don't mind making tentative suggestions during meetings.

Command of languages in the Netherlands:
English: 87%, **German**: 70%, **French**: 29%, **Spanish**: 11%.

Negotiations
Negotiators tend to get right down to business, with little time for small talk or getting acquainted. Dutch can be direct in asking what they are looking for. Despite well-defined divisions of tasks, the Dutch are used to speaking up openly in negotiations. And although time efficiency is usually a leitmotif, the decision-making process may take time because of the need for in-company consensus.

Relevant values
- The Dutch society is characterized by open-mindedness and tolerance. It is also remarkably egalitarian, with flat and transparent management structures. The biggest value differences between the Netherlands and Germany is the lower Dutch score on achievement orientation, and the stronger position of women in society.
- Dutch can be more pragmatic and as such, deviate from fixed procedures,
- To discuss business details during lunch or dinner is quite normal,
- Socialising mainly happens after a good working relationship has been established between parties,
- Too open displays of wealth are generally distrusted, partly due to their (mainly) Calvinistic background,
- Dutch are allowed to make jokes, while being serious.

Poland

Poland constitutes the largest market in Central Europe; from the Polish perspective Germany is the largest trade partner, the Netherlands are the second largest investor.

Meeting

Meetings in Poland start and finish relatively on time and few interruptions occur. Poles do not always prepare for meetings, since they also have a social function. Poles prefer a face-to-face meeting over an e-mail. This proves that despite the fact every culture uses the same means of communication, the difference often occurs in how and when the media are deployed. Initial meetings in Poland, for instance, are often just opportunities for establishing relationships, not making business decisions. Socialising after work is very common and a necessary aspect of gaining trust. Meetings can start earlier, as the Polish daily schedule starts and finishes earlier.

Command of languages in Poland: **English**: 29%, **Russian**: 26%, **German**: 19%.

Negotiations

The fact that the Poles use the word *'rozmowy'* (conversation) more than the word *'negocjacje'* (negotiation), indicates the importance of enough warming-up time in developing business relationships. In Dutch business life, people are used to strict planning, detailed discussions and a separation between their private and professional lives – three things that are quite different when doing business in Poland. Poles value improvising skills more; therefore general task descriptions or milestones have proven to be more acceptable. In addition, negotiations may take more time; therefore only the patient managers manage in Poland.

Relevant values

- Generally speaking, Polish business culture has been characterised as one with a hands-on mentality mixed with emotional decision-making. Foreign managers initially seem unaware of the patience and understanding required for the local differences.
- If we look at the style of communication, Poles tend to express themselves in a formal but more indirect way than Dutch or Germans, and prefer expressive capacity and anecdotes or metaphors over literal messages. On the other hand, people can ask explicitly for information or when making requests. But generally they don't like to say 'No' ('nie') directly, and likewise, they also don't like to be told 'No'.
- Leadership uses hierarchy to a large extent,
- The Catholic religion is a powerful value in Poland,

Russia

Russia is the world's largest country in size. The Russian economy will connect more and more with the European Union and hence the number of professional contacts is also increasing. Visiting negotiators find that the Russian business culture has its own characteristics, as described below:

Meeting
Russians tend to care less for punctuality, as meetings do not only start later, but also run longer than anticipated. Interruptions and conversations on the side are frequent, and the agenda is not always adhered to. Russians are generally very well educated and like ornamental metaphors or story-telling in business. Therefore an exposé full of facts will not challenge their minds. Meetings in Russia are not always result-focused, while much time may be devoted to discussing and understanding a problem. This may challenge the minds of Western managers. In Russia, meetings might end with the signing of a protocol, which is simply a report of what was said but has no serious legal implication.

Negotiations
As in many countries, a senior negotiation team will receive more respect, regardless of the decision-making authority. Russians in general negotiate to win, not to find a consensus. It is wise to slot in enough time for negotiations or trade-offs. Just as in chess games, negotiators will think several moves ahead. Vodka toasting is a symbolic element in Russian business entertainment, and may happen directly after an agreement. A contract is often considered less binding than it is Western countries, and in several companies unanimity is prescribed for essential choices.

Relevant values
- Russians have a strong sense of national pride for 'Motherland' (родина or *rodina*). Unlike in North Europe, planning is not seen as omnipotent, and work and private life will be quite mixed. Just as in Asia, the so-called 'loss of face' is an important value. It is important to use the word 'No' carefully, or give direct criticism or complaints. Some business can still be bureaucratic, and to obtain faster results in Russia, the use of personal networks (блат or *blat)* can be indispensable.
- Power is very centralised and often concentrated,
- Status is an important aspect of Russian society,
- A person who only concentrates on business, might come across as less trustful,
- Instead of dry facts, intellectual and philosophical debate is higher valued,
- The working day may start quite early.

Spain

The country Spain is one of the largest countries in Europe. Business in Spain is usually acquired through personal relationships; therefore business entertaining is an essential pro-cess of any professional contact. The substantial differences in conducting meetings and negotiations are explained below:

Meeting

Initial meetings in Spain are usually just meant for becoming acquainted, not to do straight business. Meetings are different compared to North European standards, as they often don't follow an agenda order, and people frequently interrupt each other (which isn't judged negatively). Agendas play a lesser role, because meetings serve more to exchange ideas and to invest in the personal relationships, than actually reaching decisions. Meetings also often run over time. On the other hand, a Spaniard doesn't say that 'time flies', but that 'time walks'. And indeed the word 'mañana' can refer to a moment in time, not necessarily being tomorrow. The siesta interruption was abolished by the Spanish government in 2005, although certain companies might have a separate morning or (late) afternoon staff.

Negotiations

Hierarchical acceptance in Spain is double that of what it is in Germany, and indeed Spanish leadership is characterised by both its charismatic and autocratic aspects. In order to successfully negotiate with Spaniards, it is also essential to realise that the need for facts and planning isn't supported in the same way in Spain.

Spanish negotiations often follow the win-lose concept. Therefore preparations should focus on negotiable points and parrying bargaining. Spaniards are also articulate and meandering speakers, connecting to the larger picture, perhaps even philosophical concepts. With a preference for relationship and no task-orientation, a fair amount of socialising will probably take place after negotiation rounds.

Relevant values

- Face-to-face contact is preferred over e-mail or phone,
- Wait long enough before talking business at business lunches, or let your Spanish counterpart lead,
- To openly damage someone's pride is a cardinal sin,
- There are very strong regional sentiments, with their own language and identity,
- Most people speak 'castellano' as the term 'español' denotes federal things,
- Spain has an enormous number of public holidays.

United Kingdom

The United Kingdom comprises Great Britain and Northern Ireland. And although described as incurably insular and different, Britons are nevertheless an important trading partner. Those who conduct meetings and negotiations with British people often describe them as different from those on the continent.

Meeting
Meetings in Britain typically begin and end with small talk. Meetings will be structured, but perhaps less so than one is used to at home. During the course of the meeting it is acceptable for people to take calls, or join later (or walk out earlier). In addition, people will not always have spent a lot of time preparing for a meeting. Discussion is an essential part of meetings, as is debating, but the British don't appreciate open verbal conflict. Their communication style uses politeness as a courtesy. Not only do British managers use their sense of humour in business meetings, they also have a great many varieties: irony, sarcasm, self-mockery etc., and these are generally called for with professional purposes in mind.

Negotiations
When preparing negotiations, it is useful to know that British managers prefer target-driven proposals that yield short-term benefits. A non-disclosure agreement is quite common, and shouldn't really be seen as distrust. Negotiators are often empowered to make decisions and get things done; most British firms nowadays have an increasingly flat hierarchical structure. After the initial meeting, first names are quickly used; academic credentials don't play much of role. After-work drinking is quite a common thing. British negotiators can be rather vague when declining an idea or proposal. This indirectness is referred to as *'coded speech'*. An example is when someone doesn't agree and she/he will say: *'hmm, that's an interesting idea'*. It might help to study facial expressions closely or the tone of voice for that matter. Command of foreign languages is limited in the populated south part of Britain.

Relevant values
- British managers look for a leadership style in which they will seem reasonable and righteous.
- Although British value scores hardly differ from Dutch ones, British culture has a higher degree of individualism. In fact, it is the only language which capitalises the word 'I'.
- One should never make a scene,
- The British typically have a sense of fair play,
- The class system is still evident in Britain.

United States

Knowing the United States through popular culture (for instance cinema), isn't the same as doing business with Americans. The following paragraphs inform you in brief about the cultural business norms of the United States of America, a country spanning six time zones.

Meeting

Meetings generally are seen as a platform to make decisions and drive action by the end of the meeting. Most Americans tend to have a preference for to-the-point empirical information, adhering to the KISS axiom (keep it short and simple). They are quick to use first names or even nicknames, and do not care for academic credentials. As most professionals are very busy, meetings can take place over business breakfasts or after work. The focus on time management is very strong in the United States.

Negotiations

Negotiating in the States is often characterised by so-called 'hard sell'. American negotiators prefer to secure a favourable deal or short-term commercial results. They do so in an informal way, using a direct assertive communication style and logical reasoning for the most part. Self-promotion is judged positively, because a confident strong pitch creates trust. Americans negotiators expect decisions to be taken during a negotiation, and are usually empowered to agree, without approval of senior leadership. In wanting to secure an agreement, some negotiators may 'take no for an answer'. Americans generally prefer target-driven proposals that yield short-term benefits. Convincing arguments will focus primarily on speed, cost and efficiency. Although information is shared openly between partners, information may be released in negotiations only after signing a non-disclosure agreement. Contracts and legal documents tend to be very lengthy in the US.

Relevant values
- The cultural value scores aren't that different from ours, expect that Americans are highly individualistic, in fact English is the only language which capitalises the word 'I'.
- America is a can-do, achievement-focused culture,
- Americans might prepare less in advance than Japanese, Dutch or Germans,
- There is a high tolerance for failure in the US,
- Not so many US citizens have travelled abroad,
- Time is money!

52.   What is Culture Shock?

Leonel Brug

Introduction

Culture, as we have seen, comes in layers. It hits you first on the explicit level, where culture elicits itself through its products and artefacts. Once you hit this level a variety of reactions might be evolved in you. These reactions might be referred to as culture-shock. And culture shock comes in layers too. Research by Leonel Brug and Clyde Sargeant have elicited that the disruption of emotional and psychological stability is only partly due to the most superficial, explicit layer of culture. The fact that one is irritated by the lack of sugar lumps in New York or the mixing of salt and washing powder in Nigeria. The irritation is just so much larger than at home because it raises general feelings of anxiety so normal in less predictable environments. This anxiety is very much more the result of the fact that one experiences different rules of behaviour (norms) and different values attached to those. And finally the most severe and profound hits caused by culture shock are produced by the challenge of your own basic assumptions about relationships, time and nature. Culture shock comes in stages: Clyde Sargeant distinguishes different patterns in the psychological stability of a person over a certain period of time.

The "Honeymoon phase"

First of all there is the honey moon-phase. It is the psychological feeling of excitement - a high feeling or kick - once one prepares for and enters into a new cultural environment. However, it is like with most of our honey moons, it is exciting but short. The newness of the environment is in most cases stimulating. It is like being on vacation. You feel the sun burning like in Spain or Mexico. The food is appealing because it departs from gravy, potatoes and the famous other national dishes like hamburger, the split-pie soup and the fish and chips. What a delight to have the real chicken curry and the genuine Chinese chopsticks, rather than our Western version of it. And what about the architecture, isn't it beautiful over here? Yes, but it's nothing compared with the airconditioning over here. At home we rather melt in the few days of summer we have than to spend some dollars on keeping the temperature down a little. And the kids love the beach. We will have an enjoyable time over here. Indeed, most of the expatriate families are very excited and enthusiastic in the first three months. It's like vacation. And the people are ok and much more hospitable than at home. Again, it is honey moon time, so be prepared for the dip.

The "Sauerkraut stage"

After some 3 to 6 months (average) the first signs of irritaton show. The manager, like in any new job, gets the first serious problems at work, which couldn't be blamed on the fact that he or she was new in the job. So you blame it on the locals and their culture. And at home things are not exactly as they should go. Cissy, we already had such problems in finding good schooling for her, is not doing well in class. Obviously, because the teachers there don't speak proper English. And my spouse is having great trouble in fixing the elevator of our condominium. And the locals are blamed for it, regardless of why and what happened.

Leonel Brug told us a wonderful story when he was taking a tour in Brazil, finding some German expatriates. They were clearly in their dip-period. When he saw the deserted Amazon jungles the German said : "Jee, you see these Brazilians don't know to earn their own money. If they would build a resort with a swimming pool here they would attract a lot of foreign currency". Not more than half an hour later we passed by an amusement park, in the middle of the jungle. The same German commented directly about the lack of taste of the Brazilian mind : "How can they build such an awful park here. For some foreign money they destroy beautiful nature." He was clearly in culture-shock. You are not logical and rational if you're in shock. Regardless of what your host does, it's not good. And it is confirmed by the family.

How to recognize culture shock

Recognition of the symptoms of psychological disequilibrium in culture shock is not easy. You're living in your own logic and the people around you confirm your feeling. However, in this second stage there are some clues of recognition.

The behaviour of your family

Since the expatriate manager is often coming into a familiar company and business, those who suffer earliest of culture shock is spouse and children. If we analyse the traditional role of the spouse we see that she (and sometimes he) has most genuine contacts with the locals. Irritations are most likely occurring with daily activities of the spouse such as shopping, repair management, etc. A first sign you should be aware of that in case your partner or children behave oddly it might be the result of the second stage of culture shock. In the extreme case the partner asks frequently to go home for whatever reason you can imagine. Moreover, spouses need to take more responsibility over the care of children; one of the most painstaking tasks when you are abroad. Their educational, health and language problems first hit the spouse. And reaction of these shock stimuli are getting on the back of the home-coming expatriate manager. The latter has enough problems in the new job, so very frequently little understanding is given to these mundane problems of the large family; in a period where they need it most. Another symptom is the expatriate partner's urge for closing him or herself off from local activities. The joining of other expatriate spouses is ok as long as it is not overdone in frequency as a sign of complete ignorance of the local environment. Second the reason for joining need not be negative, such as a great opportunity to discuss the latest sick jokes about the local over a deep glass of alcohol.

Physical signs within the expatriate family

Culture shock reveals itself in the most serious cases by physical reactions. Some of these reactions look very much like the symptoms of stress : eruptions of the skin, a faraway stare, lack of appetite, severe depressive moods, and finally an ache at both lungs and liver to obvious reasons. Talking is about home rather than about their actual life at present.

Reactions within the expatriate manager

The expatriate manager clearly recognizes culture shock by some of his or her own behaviour. Fast irritations about little things at work, which are blamed on the locals. They will be seen as undereducated, stupid and obviously in need of your expertise and excellent management competences. You will frequently think of your former jobs which went so well and where the sky was always blue. Now, it has all been polluted by these damned locals. And you will tell yourself that a good move of their part (if recognized at all) was just good luck.

Once home at night and in the week-ends the genuine symptoms of the second stage of culture shock hits you when you start to frequently (i.e. every day) join the local country-club where expatriates join. That's ok as long as it doesn't become your haven of joining with three most intimate friends, Johnny, Al and Benny. Johnny Walker keeps you from reality, Al Cohol keeps you sharp for the sick jokes about the locals by Benny Hill. These three partners take your hand to lead you through your experiences in culture-shock and they are the only ones who really understand your feelings.

A second symptom of culture-shock is the idealization of everything at home. That's one of the reasons why Brug calls the second stage of culture shock the "sauerkraut stage". Sauerkraut is one of the national dishes of the Germans and the Alsace in France. You eat it during winter-time and infrequently. Compare it with Fish and Chips for the British, "Dropjes" (licorice) and raw herring for the Dutch and Cheese cake for the Americans. These dishes you really start missing when you're gone. And once you get these postcard pictures in your mind of food an climate at home, start to be careful. The amount of food cannot be eaten without stomach ache (and you ate it less than you might have thought). The snow in the Centre of Amsterdam was not as white as you might have thought, and rain gets boring after two days. In the last chapter on reversed culture shock we will come back to this phenomenon. This sauerkraut stage, however, is a very normal one to go through as an expatriate manager. It is just an introduction to the third stage of culture shock "the recovery stage".

The recovery stage of culture shock

Severe highs and lows in the first six months of your stay abroad are very normal for any expatriate family. The crucial moment, where different types of personalities do take different journeys is at the end of the "Sauerkraut" stage. Here the alternatives are wide open. Empirical research shows that just 5% of all expatriates follow the D-route. This is one of the worst of all cases where the locals are despised, your work is getting impossible, your family is ready to leave. And you join them. The D-route is indicating the route where you psychologically die and return home. It is the most expensive route because it happens after generally 6 months. Never forget the extreme cases. It is known that some people take as the honey-moon the glass of whiskey on the plane, followed by the sauerkraut stage when landing, and returning home on the same plane once the initial impressions of the airport are so shocking that nobody who wasn't insane could stay there. Other people take 3 years before they realize they die psychologically. Returning home is the expensive but only way out. The alternative is to close off from the world completely turning expatriate managers into loners, especially once the family has chosen to quit.

A more common road to take is the C-route. About 15% of all expatriates take this journey. This is the most painstaking route for the expatriate manager and his or her family. Financing this route seems less expensive for the company. True, but if you add all non-financial costs up the C-route is the most painstaking. First of all the expatriate manager doesn't perform well in this continuous state of alienation of local society. Relationships within the organization and in larger society are ill. The locals are blamed. They need to develop and being educated. In other words, the locals are so far from the expatriate set of basic assumptions about life that it results in irreversible alienation. The expatriate manager and family look for people in similar positions and with similar attitudes. You share bad views about the situation with them and Al, Nico and Benny. It all becomes a self-fulfilling prophecy. The job, obviously, is performed poorly in most cases. Fortunately 40% get into the B-route. They perform their job adequately and think frequently at the end of their foreign assignment.

They do survive but great fun is at home. They, however, only hit the home-sickness syndrome (so continuous as a feeling for the C-expatriates) at the special moments at home, such as Christmas, birthday parties, etc.

The final 40% is reserved for those who really learn from their expatriate experience. They grow into the effective manager-they are used to be elsewhere. They perform even better, because they have integrated their feeling of respect for the variety expatriate life is offering in. The expatriate family, very often is very happy in their situation and feel sorry when their next assignment is forthcoming. They have grown as personalities and the local environment frequently appreciates the family as much as the manager.

How to cope with culture shock
Half of the coping with culture shock is in its preparation for it. In our workshops we have seen that half an hour introduction into what is culture shock, how to recognize it and to deal with it makes the difference. People recognize themselves as being in a certain situation which could be described as culture-shock. Especially in the Sauerkraut stage the steep descent into a depressive and homesick feeling can be somewhat smoothened. Furthermore, it seems that if you recognize the emotions half of the possible damage can be psychologically shared. And you know better times are coming. Everybody goes through it, anyway. A second way of dealing with culture shock is to take it by the roots and prepare you in more detail about the society you are going to. Very important it is to involve the larger family with the preparation. It need not be limited by the technical details of the society like governmental issues, health and education systems within that society. Obviously, the technical details are of importance, but the context in which these technical details of the political, social, economic, health, and financial environment need to be discussed too in the preparation. Culture, as the contextual environment, enclosing the transactional environment need to be discussed otherwise it all makes little sense. We frequently get postcards from people after half a year of their stay thanking us for the details we have given them about the society they were going to in general and culture shock in particular.

Prepare at the top what you need at the bottom

The preparation for the negative aspects of culture shock need to be done in the early stages i.e. in the "honeymoon-phase" or before. This is quite obvious because once one is hit by the "Sauerkraut" phase or beyond preparing for it is difficult if not impossible. The environment is taken in such a negative way that the courage and stimulus lacks for taking countermeasures. If, however, one is in the middle of the "honeymoon phase" the looking around for your favourite tennis- or golf-club, to discover your natural surroundings or to make an appointment with your music teacher is much more effective. Even in case you do not use these facilities immediately, they are of use once you feel down in the second stage of culture shock. You need to prepare yourself and your family when you don't really need it in order to be prepared once you do.

Take your "teddy bear" with you

Another piece of advice for preparing for culture shock is to not forget to take your materials with you which are most probably not very available in the society you're going to. So in case you have scuba-diving as a hobby, take it with you once you're going to a society with lakes or sees. Or don't forget to take your violin if you're fond of playing it. In the beginning this might not seem reasonable, but once you're sliding into the "Sauerkraut" phase you will need it.

Ask the hosts

A very frequently asked question deals with how to find out in detail about the peculiarities of a society. You cannot prepare for all details, regardless of how important they are. And how to recognize if you're dealing with a personality trait or with a genuine cultural characteristic. The best way of getting inside information is to ask local hosts. Preferably you need to ask local people you have known for some time and that you might trust as a friend. They will be delighted to give you information about the local society, if you don't ask things in a too judgmental way: "Can you tell me how this stupid behaviour in your society can be explained?" How would you feel if people ask about your society? Great, isn't it? However, be aware of the fact that very many aspects of cultural society are things taken for granted. People might not know the answer because it is so normal.

53. Cross-Cultural Bites

Sander Schroevers

Entrée

Imagine a dinner party with invitees from the countries: Argentina, Costa Rica, India, Israel, Italy, Mexico, Peru, South Korea, Spain, Turkey, United Arab Emirates and the United States. It would certainly face the cook with a difficult task. Especially if the guests from the Emirates, Israel and India would be faithful in their religion. As the former two (e.g.: Muslim, Jew) cannot eat pork meat and the latter (e.g.: Hindu) no beef.

Another uncertainty is what beverage to toast with? And even when a majority decision for wine has been made, people from certain countries may have strong feelings about the oenological options at hand. Still in the end, all cultures will probably have to 'water the wine' to some extent.

As for example: strict Muslim Emirati might be seated next to women, and the Koreans might have to eat without chopsticks. Also the starting time might be somewhat later, examining the background of the invitees, making the American stomach unquestionably rumbling with hunger. Our example already shows how much one's cultural background can influence dinner. But in the end, food is important for all people, not just to nourish oneself, but most of all to enjoy! Despite the fact that in the international business world, deals often are prepared at restaurant tables, very little has been written on this topic. From that perspective this chapter might give a refreshing bite.

Codes for behaviour

The way cultures value eating can differ substantially. We often hear it said that the Dutch eat to live, and that the French live to eat. This may be an over-simplification, but there is no denying that the amount of plastic sandwich bags or lunch boxes around computers in the Netherlands, is incomparable to the luncheon Diaspora in any Parisian office quarter. Recent German research has shown that the average time office workers spent on lunch is 30 minutes flat.

Besides eating, this includes going to the company cafeteria, standing in line at the counter and paying. The Scandinavians show a comparable behaviour. How different this is from the social importance French, Spaniards, Portuguese or Greeks attach to the midday meal, which generally lasts from one to two hours, and may include some wine, a dessert and small coffee.

From a more general perspective: as children we are taught a code for behaviour. We more or less know what is right and wrong, respectable and disreputable, in short: we are aware of the taboos our own culture imposes. As with so many other localisms, also dining etiquette differs from country to country. Who didn't feel uneasy in a Belgian, French or Japanese setting for the first time? I certainly did when I was younger. New 'rules' applied, that I wasn't aware of: the order of dishes, the knowledge of wines or a certain formality needed. It all can make someone feel uneasy, and that's a feeling that doesn't help of course, when concluding business. The main problem is that international etiquette as such, is lacking. What is considered good manners in one country can be an absolute faux-pas elsewhere. An example from my own experience which I simply cannot forget: I was on a panel in a conference in Teheran, where a most charming old gentleman professor from Vienna was giving a lecture. In his elegant three-piece suit and his well-chosen anecdotes, he would have been an absolute hit anywhere in Europe, and the Persian audience seemed to enjoy his discourse. That was, until Herr Professor took out his handkerchief and blew his nose, comparable to a short Miles Davis' trumpet solo. After this clamorous act, he then took a moment to swiftly observe the result in his handkerchief, all of which was projected on the screen of a good twenty meters wide or so...
Sitting in the panel, I then saw how quite a few participants stood up and walked away shaking their head in discontent. A lesson learned.

Varying dining practices
What is a useful behaviour pattern for international businesspeople? Probably to try to be sincere and show you are making an effort. Besides that it can be very helpful to prepare beforehand, and study the important social norms and know which behaviour is strictly taboo. In Fiji and some other countries it is polite (even mandatory) to belch or burp after completing your meal, to show

appreciation. In Bolivia, you are expected to clean your plate; Egyptians and Filipinos, however, consider it impolite to eat everything on your plate. In China, avoid taking the last item of food from the serving platter unless you want to convey to the host that you are still hungry (Turkington, 1999; Axtell, 1993). Anyone who has travelled in South-East Asian countries not only knows about chopsticks, but also about the noisy slurping, that are nevertheless perfectly good manners. People in Japan are used to raising their cups or glasses when someone at the table is (supposed) to pour their drinks. In Europe I have seen some nice crystal wineglasses end their existence that way, as both the person filling the glass with a bottle, and the guest holding up the glass apparently were following their own cultural pouring habit, resulting in shatters. The same goes for ordering salads or soups, as for instance salads in Anglo-Saxon countries are often served *before* the main course rather than after. Soups are considered a starter in many cultures, but in Asia also can be part of the last courses. Soups that are by the way, consumed with chopsticks. Even close to home there can be differences in the way fork and knife are used. Ever noticed that North-Americans use the so-called zigzag technique? Where the meat is being cut with a knife in the right hand and the fork in the left, after which the knife is put on the plate, and the fork is shifted to the right hand to eat. In Europe the knife stays where it is, and is used to push food onto the fork. Where British even use the fork upside down when eating vegetables (even peas...). British also aren't supposed to put their elbows on the dining table and ought to sit with their hands in their lap when finished. Hiding ones hands under the table is considered taboo in many other cultures. Another point of local cultural variation exist in the number of courses typically served. Latin cultures generally serve luncheons that consist of several courses, even factory workers can really sit down in a more formal way. During dinners in Italy or even stronger in China, North-Western Europeans may feel intimidated by the amount of courses served. or at least their stomachs might be... When entertaining visitors from other countries, it might be considerate to ask them whether they prefer the main meal at noon or in the evening and take them to restaurants where they have a choice of a light or heavy meal (Devine & Braganti, 2000).

When to eat?

Cultural dining practices vary widely. I remember how I have been kept waiting *l-o-n-g* hours in hotel lobbies in my first job as a young European civil servant. After some waiting most available sugar bags of the lobby had found their way into my stomach, as my Dutch biological clock simply wasn't used to the local dining custom. And when the dinner finally had started it also lasted much longer than I ever had envisaged, forcing me to practice my PowerPoint for the next day, way into the nightly hours. Had I only known the table below, it would have made that first year on the job easier. It is good to know that in many parts of the world, the main meal is around lunchtime, and that in countries like for instance Spain, the actual dishes may be served as late as 10 p.m. The moral: bring sugar bags.

		Luncheon	Dinner	Remarks
Argentina		12:00-13:00	21:00-22:30*	17:00 merienda (cake)
Costa Rica		12:00-13:00	19:00-20:30*	casado or gallo pinto, can be also (heavy) breakfast
India		13:00-14:00	20:30-22:30*	the left hand is considered unclean
Israel		13:00-14:00	20:00-22:00*	Business dinners are less common
Italy		13:30-15:00*	20:30-23:00*	breakfast is quite small 17:00 merenda (cookie)
Mexico		14:00-16:00*	21:00-23:00	
Peru		13:30-15:00	20:00-22:30*	extensive socialising beforehand.
Korea		12:00-13:00	19:00-20:30*	Koreans eat similar meals
Spain		13:30-15:30	21:00-23:00*	16:30 la merienda, roll or cake and coffee
Turkey		13:00-14:30	19:30-21:00*	
UAE		14:00-15:00*	20:00-21:00	lunch (Ghu|daa) is main meal. Dinner is light.
USA		13:00-14:00	18:00-19:00*	

© Sander Schroevers, 2010

Table: eating times per country: main meal is with an asterisk.

Of course the above mentioned times are just average times, all depends on individual people and circumstances, which are however difficult to list in a table. Another point is perhaps that cultures tend to change habits, due to techno- logical or economic factors. Who studies history will notice that traditionally dinner was served around noon, and only for those who had to work it was served later. With the invention of gas light and afterwards electricity the times shifted gradually. Nowadays we can even see that the factor time is losing influence on what is eaten when. In just a few decades customs that persisted for centuries seem to have disappeared. Like many rituals, once followed with iron-clad discipline, our meal times are now as fluid and changeable as the rest of our lives.

Timing differs

The right moment to start business talks differs culturally. Do all cultures follow the same timing pattern as in, for instance the Netherlands? The answer must be: absolutely not. Even people in neighbouring countries such as Belgium and Germany have different ideas on this. When, for example, would be the right moment to make an offer during a business lunch (dînatoire) in France? The answer here is: probably close to the time dessert is being served. It is often felt that starting business any earlier could be too blunt. The overview on the next page shows which (selected) trade cultures open their talks immediately and which cultures indulge in more small talk, when starting straight away would be considered less well-mannered;

Country	Early	Half	Late
Argentina		☑	
Costa Rica		☑	
Emirates			☑
India			☑
Israel	☑		
Italy		☑	
Korea			☑
Mexico		☑	
Netherlands	☑		
Peru		☑	
Turkey			☑
United Kingdom		☑	
United States	☑		

© Schroevers, 2010

Table: starting moment of business talks, by country.

Freakiest foods

One of the joys of travelling is being confronted with new experiences, especially those culinary. Although often enriching every once in a while the limits of your own adaptiveness may be challenged. In Slovenia I simply enjoyed a succulent steak of bear. Also in Central Africa I became habituated to seeing crocodile or porky pine on the menu of speciality restaurants. I even savoured deep fried tarantula in Cambodia (well just its oily, hairy legs). Strange though such foods may seem, most dishes are edible and even tasty once you have familiarised yourself with them. But ordering steamed dog or snake-soup is something I have never given myself up to. Also in the countries described in this book some particular dishes can be seen. For instance in Peru stomach of guinea pig or cow (menudo) is being enjoyed, in Korea live (baby) octopus tentacles can be ordered in many a restaurant. Mind you that the pieces of tentacle continue to move after swallowing. And especially in Mexico there are some rather peculiar dietary possibilities, like for instance chewing cactus leaves, eating black fermented corncobs, ordering spaghetti topped with mealworms, or roasted grasshopper (…).

Cartograms

The following page contains three maps (known as density-equalising maps), made by researchers at the Geography Department at the University of Sheffield (Gastner, Newman, 2004). Each map re-sizes countries according to the variable being mapped. For this book I chose some food-export related maps, of which the results may look perhaps somewhat shocking. For example almost two thirds (64%) of total worldwide net vegetable exports are realised just by four countries: Spain, the Netherlands, China and Mexico. Also with exports in dairy products or exports in meat products, more than half of world trade is realised again by just four countries, which indeed looks shocking.

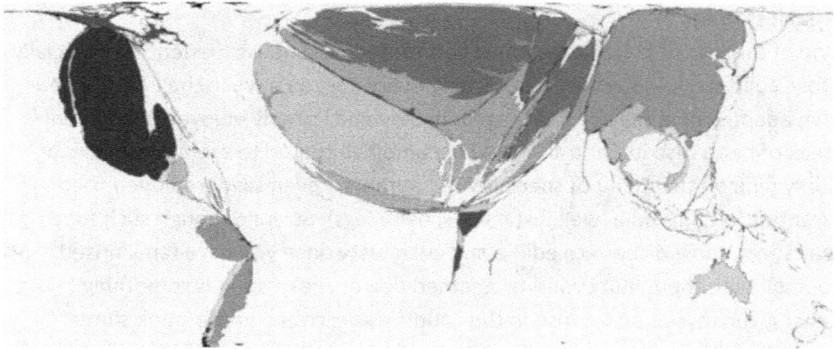

Map: exports of vegetable products.

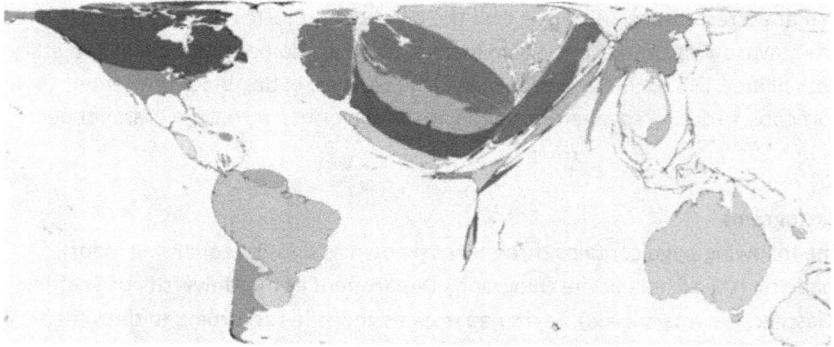

Map: exports of dairy products.

54.   Intercultural PR differences

Sander Schroevers

More and more Public Relations consultants are facing client demands for cross border support. The framework for such international Public Relations is developing, although compared to other fields in PR, international PR doesn't seem to have much theory. And despite the fact that former deputy of corporate communications from Johnson & Johnson, *Bill Nielsen* believes that: *"There is a need for a more global approach of PR"*, after crossing the border many (small) differences in the local PR context, have an impact on the campaign results. A study of European PR (Van Ruler, Vercic, 2005) shows that Public Relations are the same in their outlines. It is under the surface however that local differences and practical implications appear. In this chapter is tried to introduce some of the practical or operational apparent differences, when dealing with cross boarder PR. It focuses on Public Relations between European countries where the languages English, French, Spanish, German, Italian and Dutch are used.

Intercultural unities in PR

Whereas the importance of knowledge in internationalisation has always been well documented (Liesch & Knight 1999; Vernon 1966), the differences in PR related fields are less studied. Historical and cultural developments in Germany, France, Spain, Italy, United Kingdom, Belgium and the Netherlands have led to different journalistic conventions. For instance the influence of letter conventions as formulated by the different national standardization-institutes like the German DIN or the French AFNOR, have been projected on the making of press releases. Since this medium is mainly used within the own culture certain norms have been established over the years, and have been propagated by business literature or schooling. Comparable regional differences can also be seen in the printing standards which developed. This resulted in different column sizes for each country, or the amount of characters per line. In Germany for instance it is customary for (printed) press releases to make mention of the amount of characters per line, in a separate header. Where North American press releases tend to use capitals in their headlines, Europeans prefer to romanise their headlines. Although French family names usually are spelled in capitals as well.

Particular journalistic conventions may differ from country to country as well. Like for instance the heading *'editor's note'* or graphic indications like the string of slashes in Dutch press releases, or the string of pound signs in Anglophone releases. Looking at press packs also different aspects come into sight (Burton, Drake, 2004). When preparing press packs for a trade show in France for example it is important to know about the different approach which a French *'dossier de presse'* takes. They are generally carefully made colourful documents. Whereas press packs in Eastern-European countries are more textually focused. In German press documentation generally speaking more detailed documentation is given, where Latin press packs can also inform on the history or management of the company. They are all press packs, but certainly different 'flavours' exist: some sweet, some spicy.

Intercultural unities: timing
Timing is of the utmost importance in the field of Public Relations. But anyone working in cross boarder PR will soon be aware of the actual differences. People involved in PR follow the daily schedule of a culture, and cultures happen to use quite different shifts of the day. In countries like Switzerland or the Czech Republic people start to work very early in the day and go home relatively early. Polish people tend to take no lunch during office hours, and go to lunch after 16:00 or 17:00 hours in the afternoon. Spanish lunch on the contrary is between 14:00 until 17:00, after which people can work until 20:00. People working in Brussels or Paris will have a longer lunch than someone in Stockholm, Frankfurt or Rotterdam. It gives an indication of the difficulties of planning a simple (press) conference call. Certain days are also influenced by religious aspects. On a Friday Muslim believers will prefer not to work, other religions take the Saturday off, or the Sunday as do the Christians. Although daylight-saving is a simple fact, it influences those working in areas where it doesn't apply. Like Thailand, Iran or the state of Arizona, which have abolished daylight-saving.

The same goes for time-zones, it seems a simple thing, but when dealing with public relations campaigns between the European continent and Britain or Portugal, it limits the work force by one hour. Countries like Spain have parts of their territory which lies in another time-zone. One last element of timing concerning international PR is the vast amount of national and official holidays. Only within Europe a large variety of days exist, where larger countries like Italy or Germany know local varieties and multiform states like Belgium or Spain have official days for the cultural groups. For planners of events or others making direct contact, knowledge of such dates seem to be an inescapable necessity.

Linguistic unities

Differences from a linguistic background may influence the actual presentation of a message. This has to deal with several reasons. First of all many different alphabets exist in Europe. A selection of deviating letters is made for the languages which this paper discusses: Spanish (CH, LL, Ñ), French (Æ, Œ), German: Ä, CH, Ö, SCH, ß, Ü, Dutch: 'IJ' and the Italian alphabet uses 21 letters instead of 26. Dealing with any of these letters in an international context doesn't have the same problems as some years ago, but nevertheless still can cause mistakes. The keyboards in the different countries are hardly comparable. German keyboards as many in Central Europe make use of the QWERTZ arrangement. French keyboards differ from French-Belgian or French-Swiss ones. Besides this change, many separate keys exist for so-called diacritical marks (i.e.: é, ö, à etc). For all those different letter signs specific codes exist. Now the main problem for communication professionals going international is that not all technologies use the same character codes. In this way PDF-files may look strange without the proper plug-ins. When sending an e-mail or SMS from one country to another, because of the same reason messages may undergo a considerable change. Looking at the following example accentuates this;

- **Avez-vous oubliÃ© vos codes d'accÃ¨s - tÃ©lÃ©chargez ici.**
- *(Avez-vous oublié vos codes d'accès - téléchargez ici)*

The linguistic influences mentioned above are of a more technical nature. But other influences can unexpectedly change a message as well. For instance the use of abbreviations. For reasons of efficiency texts often refer to organisations or affairs by using it's abbreviation. Most international organisations as we know them make use of language dependant acronyms. For instance the European Investment Bank (EIB) can be referred to in German as Europäische Investitionsbank (EIB), in Italian as Banca Europea d'Investimento (BEI), in Finnish as Euroopan investointipankki (EIP) and as Europejski Bank Inwestycyjny (EBI) in Polish. What to use: EIB, EBI or BEI?

When dealing with cross boarder PR a commonly made mistake is that the responsible PR-manager demands a literary translation. But culture is such a complex phenomenon that a 'good' translation is capable of transcoding the typical cultural elements in the message to another setting. It is often said that a good translator needs somewhat of an intercultural mind, in order to be able to truly translate the meaning, not just the words. Besides to this intercultural aspect, also a knowledge of the particular target group is essential for successful communication. Since there is very much variation within cultural categories, sometimes more than between other cultures (Trompenaars, 1994).

In Europe alone already more than thirty-five official languages are being spoken. The European Union employs more than one and a half thousand full time translators. They produce about 1,5 million pages per year. The cost of these translations amount to approximately half of the total administrative budget. For this reason perhaps pan-national organisations like the Council of Europe in Strasbourg, only use French and English as working languages (unless paid for by local governments). On the other hand it seems that the dominance of the English language on internet seems to be decreasing. In a report of *Technorati*, which is globally monitoring blogs, states that Japanese and Chinese are both gaining ground. Also these days the brand world becomes less dominated by North-American companies. The *Interbrand* ranking of the top-100 global brands, shows that the number is decreasing on a yearly basis. With Indian companies buying up European brands at high speed, such listings are shifting even faster.

Education in the field of communication, public relations and journalism tend to pay little attention to intercultural differences or an international scope. And although marketing theories in recent years have been 'injected' with the writings of Hofstede, it is still often that international marketing bloopers happen. Especially the American and Japanese automotive industry is known for its wrongly chosen names. With brand names like 'Laputa' (Mazda), or 'Nova' (General-Motors). And although Europeans generally have a better understanding of cultural differences, still things can go wrong. For instance the localized websites of a large German electronics retailer (*MediaMarkt*) use for instance the 'thumb-sign' on their web communication. This sign originally comes from pilots (and not the Roman empire as is commonly mistaken). The marketing department probably didn't realize that there are countries where using this sign has a very negative meaning, like Iran, Greece or Nigeria. Indeed non-verbal communication can have a strong influence on its success. The same applies to the circle made by thumb and the index finger; as this signs will be used to express quality or refinement. Nevertheless one should be careful using it in France, where it represents the value zero or in other words worthless. In Brazil it can be even more painful, whereas in Japan it used to indicate pocket change. In short: all non-verbal elements which we feel familiar with may mean quite different things. This includes images, colours, but also the correct reading order (left to right, or vice versa).

Inside India
Comparing the visual culture in ads or billboards in India with that of Europe, it must be said that the graphic and photographic quality is fairly high. Nevertheless the differences mentioned in last paragraph also apply here. For instance both the gestures referred to above, play a supporting role in Indian everyday visual street culture. As brands like (I want my thunder) 'Thumbs Up Cola' or 'Bharat Petroleum' make intensive use of both gestures. And although India is a huge market in itself, the world seems to be getting smaller and smaller. Globalisation and the rapid internal growth of the Indian economy have, and will lead to regional or global Indian brands. On that scale things cannot be taken for granted. Just like mentioned above, also in India different keyboards exist, as a Bengali one is slightly different from other keyboards, it is to be expected that the result of someone's work will look different from country to country. And it is an interesting (and often painful) experiment, to simply ask a

few international contacts, to scan or print and fax a document which has been produced in India, and compare the local varieties.

Another point of interest is the existence of pluricentric languages. That refers to the fact that some languages can be official language in different countries, often leading to variations. Especially the English language has a lot of local varieties, due to a lack of an overall controlling body, like the French *Académie française* (www.academie-francaise.fr) already founded in 1635, or the Spanish *Real Academia Española* (www.rae.es) founded in 1713. These institutions have guarded the unity of both languages fiercely. Not the English where the American-English and British-English differ substantially. Not even mentioning certain aspects of Indian English. Expressions like: 'neck to neck' or 'I have *hazaar* things on my mind right now' (i.e.: a thousand things) will not always be understood. The second aspect might be more of cultural thing; as people in India probably tend to be much more polite than in Western countries, this reflects in correspondence techniques that may appear somewhat cloudy to the less cultivated Westerners. Who on the other hand are always willing to criticize telephone habits like: 'Hello, What do you want?' or 'Tell me.': used by some when answering a phone call. Comfort is in the fact that the telephone etiquette of most cultures in the world (including the French, Spanish, Italian and Japanese), make use of similar expressions (respectively: 'allôh', 'diga', 'pronto' or 'moshi moshi'). Are such details important? They probably are, as the call centres constitute an substantial element of the economy of certain areas.

Besides differences based on language or timing, quite a few intercultural aspects simply have to do with chosen conventions. One of the basic tools of PR are probably contact addresses. Looking at the products of some of the larger publishers of PR databases show that despite being a supplier of international contact information, the intercultural element has not been taken into account concerning the database. Worldwide many different forms of addresses exist, post codes can have quite specific forms, as is the case in Sweden, Greece or the Netherlands. The mentioned guide books all write addresses in the British format. Due the automated envelop recognition a wrongly printed address can cause up to four days of delay.

Four days seems to be a lot in the world public relations. A second important mistake in the databases is the fact that for certain countries the wrong telephone prefixes are entered. Nowadays many countries are changing their national numbering plans. This often results in giving up the initial zero or replacing it by another figure. In Italy this transition is half way, therefore fix telephone numbers will need to be dialled with the initial zero, also with an international call. Mobile telephone numbers however can be reached without the initial zero. When mistaking in this a telephone line will seem to be busy all the time. It is therefore recommended to also pay attention to the quality of the data. But then again internet allows a quick double check.

What legal aspects need attention when crossing the border in communication? In fact in National laws very little is regulated concerning PR. With one exception perhaps: the German and also Swiss 'UWG' law (*Gesetz gegen den unlauteren Wettbewerb*) which forbids exaggerating in for instance press releases. One other legal aspect plays a role, however this after complaints or incidents with the press. Some countries like France have the so-called '*droit-de-réponse*' (the right to answer) which specifies that a comparable space in a medium will be dedicated for replying. Other countries know institutions for *auto regulation*, often called press-councils. Such a council can judge the journalistic ethics, and is often referred to as 'deontology'. Parallel to this all countries allow civil court cases.

55.   Gestures, the world-at-hand

Sander Schroevers

According to psychologists and anthropologists non-verbal communication plays an ever bigger role in situations where we are emotional, up to ninety percent even. This is probably one of the reasons why experienced business people may find it hard to communicate effectively, even though both parties possess a fair amount of knowledge of a common language, say English.

Implicit communication apparently influences our thinking patterns to a larger extend than we seem to realise. Gestures or symbols are closely linked to cultural practices, as products of tradition, not biology. Gestures may seem like rituals within a certain culture, symbols of which only a shared knowledge allows sense-making, thus reducing the risk of misinterpretation. Because *how* people understand a gesture, largely depends on *where* they are in the world. May I introduce this with a simple anecdote? As a speaker at a conference on international communication in Tehran, I was crossing a road. And honesty makes me admit that the pedestrian traffic light might have already changed its green colour, but being late as I was, conscience can be very forgiving at such moments. That road however seemed a lot less small by the time the traffic actually started to move. I quickly established eye contact with the drivers in order to let me pass safely. Their true gentlemen reactions gave me a feeling of passing through the Red Sea, and out of gratitude I gave them the thumbs-up, indicating my positive evaluation. The very moment I did, I realised my faux-pas. The thumbs-up gesture in Iran, traditionally an obscene gesture, is the equivalent to the use of the middle finger. Within seconds the gentlemen drivers in that Red Sea turned into pursuing Egyptians with their chariot-wheels, making me run for my life and my lecture (which I certainly made on time now). Conclusion: gestures matter.

It was the French phenomenological philosopher Maurice Merleau-Ponty, who once wrote that the hand was a 'vehicle for being in the world'. But *how* Merleau-Ponty's vehicle will be understood in the world, very much depends on culture. Speakers can make use of a whole repertoire of schematic actions of the hand, representing conceptual metaphors or simpler said: meaning. And in the same way different cultures developed their own language, so did the hand-forms, say gestures.

What is a gesture?
Gestures are in fact elusive phenomena; they leave no traces and last for a fraction of a second. The *Concise Oxford Dictionary* defines a gesture as: "A significant movement of limb or body' or 'use of such movements as expression of feeling or rhetorical device'.". This definition includes any facial expression or bodily movement that transmits messages, also referring to symptomatically expressed feelings like blushes or pain grimaces. In the broad sense, 'gesture' can refer to any wilful bodily movement, and although the focus in this volume mainly is on hands gestures, also proactive displays like body posture, head-gestures or eye-contact will be described where relevant in this publication. We studied gestures as a set of culture specific non-spoken practices that produce socio-cultural situated understandings (Erickson 2004). Simply because nuance can play a substantial role in understanding the meaning of a movement. An example: nodding your head to indicate 'yes' isn't as simple as it may seem, the table below lists some varieties of 'yes';

Variety	Meaning of 'YES'
Acknowledgement	'Yes, I am listening.'
Agreement	'Yes, I will.'
Confirmation	'Yes, that is right.'
Encouragement	'Yes, how wonderful.'
Understanding	'Yes, I see what you mean.'

Finger-talk

After having stated what 'a gesture is' earlier in this publication, let me also say that (except for in this chapter) mere erotic and obscene gestures have been excluded. Not so much out of shame but simply because their relevant use in business communications can be seen as naturally limited.

Nevertheless: do allow me to share two more faux-pas, besides the mentioned obscene and erotic vertically extended thumb with curled fingers. The picture in the middle has caused former US President, George Bush Sr., some 'V' sign confusion, when he visited Australia in 1992. Meaning to signify 'Victory' to a group of protesting farmers in Canberra who showed their discontent with US farm subsidies, he instead told them to f*** off. Pictures of his gesture made it to most of the front pages down-under. The third drawing was used on the packaging by a Dutch producer of round croquettes, showing a classic culinary chef forming a ring or circle with the thumb and forefinger. The only problem with this particular gesture is that it is understood as 'nulle' or 'zéro' in France, the companies wished for export market. But still the French market would be a lot less disastrous than for instance the Brazilian market, where the sign refers to the posterior opening of the alimentary canal... Now situations like above offer us funny anecdotes, but they also are a warning of the ambiguity that so-called multi-message gestures constitute. Although disaster signs like the three above are comparatively rare, still large numbers of signs have more than one basic message, because cultures have developed their own repertoire of visual signals.

YES and NO signals

Those of us with international experience know only too well that simple words like 'YES' and 'NO' aren't expressed universally at all. Certain cultures have no hesitation to disagree whereas others will avoid a direct 'NO' at all cost, as in the wonderful reply I once got when I asked if the sold certain fruits: "Yes, we don't sell bananas". Or the fact that Japanese colleagues claim that their language doesn't have a suitable word for 'NO' (despite the existence of the word 'IE', which I remember from my own Japanese vocabulary drills), and that Bahasa Indonesia is supposed to have seven different shades of 'NO'. Examples like these explain all too well how complicated (dis)agreeing across cultures may be. Let alone to do so with a gesture, since the South-East Asian experiential frames in terms of which communicative gestures are made meaningful, simply differ too much with the Western European ones. Exploring websites like YouTube with sample country names and gesture keywords will prove this within minutes.

But let us shortly move back to Tehran, where (just like in parts of Turkey, Greece, Bulgaria or even the Balkan) more contra posing differences also appear. For instance the movement of the head which I normally would understand as a 'YES' nodding, in Iran actually means the exact opposite: 'NO'. Often with a small tongue sound accompanying an upwards nod. In fact many people from Turkish decent, brought up in North-Western Europe might use this gesture to disagree. And to make things even more complicated: to indicate 'YES' in the aforementioned areas, people often tilt their heads rhythmically from side to side. A movement that probably would be understood as 'Maybe yes, maybe no' in North-Western Europe, but here is meant as an affirmative 'YES'. And indeed the Bulgarian language shows some prove of that, in proverbs such as: "I offer you my ear". And you may remember the remarks made on that during the Bulgaria Ooopen lecture.

Gestures differ in the degree of conventionality of their forms and functions. The table below reveals us that gesture nuance can be geographically influenced, and its relative meaning subjective;

YES/NO signals					
YES tilting head from side to side	☑	☑	☑	☑	☒
NO nodding head upwardly	☑	☑	☑	☑	☒
YES nodding head downwardly	☒	☒	☒	☒	☑
NO shaking head from side to side	☒	☒	☒	☒	☑

Table: research on yes-no signals in Turkey, Iran, Bulgaria, Greece and the Netherlands.

Looking in the rear-view mirror

There is nothing new about the study of gesture. Already Roman writer Quintilian described gestures and since the Renaissance attempts have been made by physiognomists to codify facial expressions, sometimes also including descriptions of 'national character'. It was Charles Darwin, who believed to have discovered that physical expressions was biologically inherited (…).And it is true that certain very basic emotions like laughing or crying cross linguistic and national boundaries. But reading some paragraphs of Erasmus's 'De civilitate morum puerilium' (*Groot ceremonie-boeck der beschaafde zeeden*) can make me wonder how it was ever possible that his name became connected to the movement of over two million European students with the Erasmus programme. As Erasmus condemned the Italians as uncivil because they 'speak with their head, arms, feet and the whole body'. Today, *gesture studies* is carried out by numerous scholars across many disciplines. The Amsterdam based publishing house John Benjamins, offers a journal called *Gesture*, which was founded by a.o.

gesture-icon Adam Kendon and now there even is the Berlin founded
International Society for Gesture Studies.

Gestures primarily take place during face-to-face conversations and therefore
will be co-occurring with spoken language. Streeck mentions that research in a
large variety of areas, from child development, to neuropsychology, to linguistics
and anthropology, has shown the intimate link between oral production, gestural
production, and thought. Finding after finding has shown, that gestures are often
produced in astonishing synchronicity with speech, that they develop in close
relation with speech, and that brain injuries affecting speech production also
affect gesture production. But this linguistic context still doesn't solve the
communication puzzle, as it does not explain *how we see - what we see. Because*
like all other languages, the language of gesture can separate as
well as unite.

56. Meeting styles

Sander Schroevers

European meeting styles are interesting if we take into account the unprecedented political collaboration that 28 European nations have undertaken, with each one of them gradually relinquishing more and more of its autonomy in the process. That 'process'– based in Brussels – translates into some 20,000 meetings on an annual basis. Considering the fact that a good 40,000 European civil servants and about 15,000 lobbyists are involved in those meetings, I was amazed that I could hardly find a single good book on this topic. Even more when you take into account that the recent ELUCIDATE study, commissioned by the European Commission, indicated that about 40% of all European projects fail due to cross-cultural misunderstandings. How many of those misunderstandings will have originated at the meeting table?

The problem is that most people who need to meet with international discussion partners haven't been schooled in this area. Usually only governments or large multinational corporations have specialists in this field. On the other hand, with the increasing impact of globalisation – not to mention the European single market – on the way we work, we find ourselves having to meet more and more often with professionals from other countries. Subtle cultural differences complicate such international meetings. Many reports from Dutch and Flemish business people reveal how difficult both groups find those to be in practice, for example. While the Dutch seem not to understand why the Flemish fail to speak up, the Flemish appear uncomfortable with the risk of making mistakes or feel that speaking confidently might come across as arrogance. And those two groups share the same language! So if speaking a common language is not even a key to successful meetings, why do our educational programmes put so much emphasis on learning languages?

But then again, the 'meeting culture' also has its own *kabbalah* or secret language for the initiated. For example, I was familiar with the abbreviation AOB ('any other business') in English and with its Dutch equivalent WVTTK (*'Wat verder ter tafel komt')*. But it took me quite a while before I could decipher the meaning of 'TOP 1' and 'TOP 2' on the agenda, written in English, for a meeting in Germany. Eventually I learned that 'TOP' stands for *Tagesordnungspunkte* or 'agenda items'.

Sociolinguistic influences

Interpreters at the European institutions in Brussels only know it too well: translating also is cultural enciphering. A word by word translation hardly represents the original intention of a text, because of the interlaced sociolinguistic influences. Is there any consequence for people attending a meeting? That is plausible, when we look at the British-English examples. The British are taught from childhood, to use polite and indirect signals in their communication. And despite the different images that may exist about British, Americans or say Australians, linguistic research has shown that all Anglo-Saxon cultures share a strong emphasize on verbal politeness. Dutch people don't interweave their phrases with the same amount of 'thank you' and 'please', but for native English speakers, this is imperative. Therefore just being able to translate Dutch vocabulary into English, simply isn't enough. English can be a rather formal language, which reflects its subtle sense of hierarchy. An easy memory aid for trying to be more polite, is to simply use longer sentences. There are various ways to express differences. Many of these are unspoken codes, or subtle distinctions. Differences that can be hard to distinguish for foreigners. The point is that in our upbringing we are often taught certain values. Cultural groups like, for instance, the Germans, Swiss, Scandinavians or Dutch tend to be quite direct in their communication, and usually express exactly what is being meant. Scientific research has shown that the way Germans express their thoughts can be quite to-the-point. However, other cultures sometimes may perceive this to-the-point as just 'blunt'. Native English speakers tend to opt for highly scripted, requesting behaviour.

One funny anecdote, I would like to share with you is from a qualified diplomat who was dispatched to an Italian Ministry. Here his colleagues of Italian descent wanted to make him really feel at home, and therefore organised regular meeting sessions, because that's how 'Northerners' work best (focalised from their perception of course). Nevertheless some 'Southern' new colleagues clearly stated that there was no apparent need for such use of (their) time... A sort of reverse experience happened to me. After having finished my studies, I soon went to Brussels to work for the Directorate General for Trade of the European Commission. Accompanied by plenty of spoken audio cassette tapes and a 'walkman'(the grandparents of iTunes) I was studying meeting styles, negotiating and of course the French language, on the 'long' trips to Brussels. I still remember my discomfort about all the unexpected behaviour within each meeting room. Why were there so many chairmen interrupting each other, and where was the agenda, or why did all these people come in that late, or worse: left during my carefully pronounced French stuttering words? Who wrote the scripts of my expensive audio tapes? Because the gap between Dutch or translated American management books and what went on in those meeting rooms seemed irreconcilable. Honesty obliges me to admit it took me quite a while to assimilate with this environment, but like with almost all things: it can be done, and can be done with style. I finish this chapter with uttering a wish that you will have gained a clearer insight into how fine style is best used in a country specific way, after a semester full of case studies and storytelling.

Figure: You've now mastered cross-cultural intelligence, a soft-skill with a hard result.

www.ingramcontent.com/pod-product-compliance
Lightning Source LLC
Chambersburg PA
CBHW061136220326
41599CB00025B/4261